# MANAGING QUALITY IN THE CATERING INDUSTRY

## Janet P. East

CRAVEN COLLEGE
Skipton

Croner Publications Ltd
Croner House
London Road
Kingston upon Thames
Surrey KT2 6SR
Telephone: 0181-547 3333

Copyright © 1993 Janet P. East
First published 1993
Reprinted 1996

Published by
Croner Publications Ltd
Croner House
London Road
Kingston upon Thames
Surrey KT2 6SR
Telephone: 0181-547 3333

The right of Janet East to be identified as author of this
work has been asserted by her in accordance with the
Copyright, Designs and Patents Act 1988.

All rights reserved.
No part of this publication may be reproduced,
stored in a retrieval system, or transmitted in any form or by
any means, electronic, mechanical, photocopying, recording
or otherwise, without the prior permission of
Croner Publications Ltd.

While every care has been taken
in the writing and editing of this book,
readers should be aware that only Acts of Parliament
and Statutory Instruments have the force of law,
and that only the courts can authoritatively
interpret the law.

British Library Cataloguing in Publication Data
A CIP Catalogue Record for this book
is available from the British Library.

ISBN 1-85524-089-0

Printed and bound by Whitstable Litho Printers Ltd., Whitstable, Kent
Typeset by Concept Communications Ltd, Crayford, Kent

# Contents

# Acknowledgements

I wish to thank the following people for their invaluable help in assisting me with my research and the production of the book. Firstly, my colleague Tina Richards for producing the chapter on BS 5750, Janet Nicholls from the St. Helier NHS Trust, Morag Robertson, Gary Barnes and Michael Allen from Enfield Borough Catering Service, Sheila Makings and Steve Stubley from Crown Point Foods, John Barnes, Brian Curtis, B.M. Smith, S.M. Roberts and Paul Taylor from the Department of Health, Ken Dale from MAFF, Laurie Floyd, Roger Peters (Solicitor), Paul Davies from TQM International, Rosemarie Pearson and Lesley Bojko from Food Dialog, Cathy Lees from HCTC Ltd, Gary Katzler from Berkeley Scott Group and Mark Watson.

A very special thank you to my family for their support, particularly Lauren for endless hours of work.

I would like to dedicate this book to
Jo and Miles

# Introduction

The catering industry has undergone considerable change in size and structure over the last decade and is poised to face one of the greatest challenges of all times — managing successfully the quality of its products and services to meet the needs of the ever demanding customer.

UK industry in general has been tackling the issue of quality for many years and we have seen the emergence of a real growth in quality management systems such as BS 5750, Total Quality Management (TQM) and internally designed quality systems.

The catering industry is having to cope with new powerful food safety legislation, increased competition and a customer base that is demanding quality products and services, in particular value for money.

There is no doubt that developing and implementing quality management systems will provide the benefits to the catering industry already being achieved in manufacturing and other service-based industries.

This book endeavours to provide an overview of the catering industry and to look at the various systems available to assist in the management of quality.

It is fair to say that the impact of the 1990 Food Safety Act, whilst not specifically related to quality *per se*, has activated a surge in the quest for quality. The impact of the European Community is also bringing about participative change and forcing Member States to look internally at existing practices and procedures.

For many caterers, the idea of introducing quality systems is daunting and far from the reality of serving the customer. It is hoped that this book will remove the mystique attached to quality assurance systems and assist caterers in understanding why the issue of quality is fundamental to managing a successful business.

# Chapter 1

# The Size and Scope of the Catering Industry

Catering today is a vast, diverse and exciting industry which has undergone a dramatic change in size and scope over the past 20 years. The global term "Hotel, Catering and Leisure Industry" encompasses a large number of differing businesses, but they all have a single element in common — they provide a service.

The industry is particularly difficult to define and this is accentuated by the continuing development and widening of the scope of its activities. Several attempts have been made to organise the industry into acceptable "groups". The Standard Industrial Classification (SIC) is probably the main form of classification used to identify the various sectors of the hotel and catering industry. The SIC was updated in 1980 and identifies nine divisions, each of which is subdivided into classes, then groups and finally activities. This classification is used by the Central Statistical Office for the production of employment figures for the industry. For the purposes of qualifying the term "catering", a popular definition is

> all establishments whose main business comes from the sale of meals and refreshments, the sale of alcoholic drinks, or the provision of accommodation.

This book concentrates on discussing and applying the principles of quality assurance to a major part of most catering operations, namely the production and service of food, be it for a leisure centre, hotel or café. However, these same principles can equally be applied to the sale of beverages and to the provision of accommodation.

1

The industry is now regarded as a major contributor to the well being of the economy, as a strong source of invisible exports and as a significant employer of staff. However this has not always been the case. Before the Second World War, it was not even considered to be an industry by the Government, let alone an important one.

# THE CHANGING NATURE OF THE CATERING INDUSTRY

Today, catering is a very high profile industry and demand for catering services is mainly influenced by the prevailing economic and social climate. A number of important factors have affected the demand for catering services and have consequently brought about a change in the nature of the industry.

Of significant importance has been the changing lifestyle of the public in general. Households today want and have more leisure time, and expect to spend minimum amounts of time in their own kitchens preparing meals, other than for special occasions such as lunch and dinner parties. Households are much smaller — the average household size fell from 3.09 persons per household in 1961 to 2.51 in 1989. In addition there has been a rise in the number of one person households, both single young people and pensioners. The rise in consumer affluence has brought about an increase in the expenditure by households on meals eaten outside the home; indeed it has become the norm to eat out for pleasure, and sometimes even a necessity. Between 1986 and 1989 expenditure on eating out rose by 27% to £8.68 per week per household, according to the Household Food Consumption Survey. However the rise in disposable income which had been apparent throughout the 1980s has taken a reverse turn and during the first quarter of 1991 there was a real decline in disposable income of 2%. This trend is also indicated in a slow down in the demand for hotel and catering services.

Another factor which has influenced the nature of the catering industry has been the change in the workforce. More women are now at work in all age groups. The pressure on women to return to work after starting a family has increased considerably over the last 10 years, partly as a result of the increase in home ownership: the rapid rise in UK interest rates experienced in 1990 and 1991 and the impact of the recession have often made it essential to have two incomes to finance the running costs of the home. More women are raising a family and continuing to work than ever before. In addition, older women who have raised their family are embarking on a career or working on a part-time basis. Where all the members of a household are working, it is now considered less acceptable for women to spend their precious leisure time shopping and then preparing meals. This factor has also led to the greater acceptance of convenience foods which require limited "finishing" in the home.

Both the retail sector and the commercial sector have responded well to these demands and changing trends. The food industry has made a tremendous impact by providing the retail sector with an extensive range of convenience products, not just complete meals which require reheating, but also meal components, both raw and cooked, such as raw prepared vegetables and ready to use salads. The challenge facing the food industry has been to remove the stigma attached to the original convenience foods, which were often seen as low quality bulky meals, to providing products which resemble home produced foods of high quality. It is fair to say that organisations such as Marks and Spencer have been very pro-active in making this change happen. They, and many other large retail organisations, now produce high quality products, which in many instances are of a higher quality than most households and many restaurants can produce.

The change in the nature of the workforce has also led to the development of more eating out at lunchtimes. The increase in the female element of their clientele has influenced the industry by requiring it to provide lighter products in smaller quantities. Whilst there is still a requirement to provide the traditional meal (often involving a minimum of three courses), the trend has definitely been towards a more simplistic approach to the provision of catering services. This has brought about the emergence of themed restaurants, sandwich bars and a greater variety of fast food operations.

The demographic situation in the UK is also changing and in recent years there has been a reduction in the numbers of children aged 16 and under and a larger increase in the young adult and pensioner numbers. In general the population has been ageing, and over the next decade the catering industry will need to take this into account. The teenage market is particularly important to the industry and it may be that more effort will be required to attract and meet the needs of the older section of the population.

The development of international tourism has created a growing awareness of the role of catering services in meeting the needs of tourists to this country. Furthermore, the growth and changing pattern of industrial and commercial activity and the development of the EC has generated an increasing volume of travel and demand for both accommodation and catering facilities away from home. The inflow of immigrants into the UK from all over the world has meant that both the retail and commercial sectors of the food industry have widened their range of products to suit their differing food tastes and requirements. The industry has responded and there are now an increasing number of both Eastern and European restaurants to meet the demands of this sector of the market.

Finally, the catering industry has had to respond to pressures from the public and the media concerning food safety. Growing media attention and often inaccurate reporting on food safety issues has raised public awareness to an all time high. Food poisoning incidences have increased sharply since the beginning of the 1980s and almost 54,000 cases were reported in 1991. Approximately eight million working days are lost in the UK each year due to food poisoning, with an estimated cost to the country of £350 million per year. Consumer attitudes to food safety were radically altered by the Edwina Currie affair concerning salmonella in eggs, which marked a watershed in public awareness of food safety and can be singled out as the start of food safety as a national issue. Other scares in the late 1980s included listeria in frozen chicken and soft cheeses. Product tampering has also grown over the last five years — it is estimated that 1,000 threats are received by UK companies each year, of which only a handful are made public. The number of actual cases of tampering is probably small, in the tens rather than the hundreds.

In July 1990 the Government issued a White Paper entitled *Food Safety — Protecting the Consumer*. This document described the Government's arrangements at that time for protecting the consumer, highlighted action which had been recently taken and set out the proposals for the future. It was in this White Paper that reference was first made to the proposed Bill "to adapt the law to tomorrow's needs". The subsequent 1990 Food Safety Act came into force on 1 January 1991. The Act now governs the safety of food from the farm to the consumer and places the responsibility for food safety on each link in the chain. Whilst the catering industry has been governed by legislation previously, the new Act will increase the caterer's responsibilities. The full impact of the Food Safety Act has yet to be realised, but as a long term strategy it has certainly been welcomed as a positive step towards greater protection for the consumer.

There is no doubt that the industry has shown tremendous growth over the last 20 years but the current economic climate has certainly had an impact and many catering businesses have suffered. The recession, the Gulf war and rising unemployment have all had an impact on consumer spending in the hotel and restaurant sectors of the industry, resulting in a downturn in demand. Demand for catering services is projected to recover but it has been encouraging to see how the industry has acted quickly, and successfully, by modifying their products to suit the less buoyant economic climate by offering "bargain breaks", "two for the price of one", "children free", and other imaginative marketing campaigns and offers. This effort will have to continue if the catering industry is to remain one of the UK's major employers and contributors to the economy.

# THE STRUCTURE AND SIZE OF THE CATERING INDUSTRY

There are a variety of different sectors within the industry which are continually changing and developing to meet the needs of the consumers. The structure of the industry is therefore extremely complex. Distinctions are often made which attempt to provide some structured form to the industry, such as public or private, commercial or institutional, contracted or in-house, profit making or non-profit making, and each have a particular set of definitions and methods of measurement. There have been several significant changes in recent years which have challenged some of these definitions used in the industry, particularly in the public and private arena. One such change was the introduction of the competitive tendering concept into the National Health Service and local authorities. It is fair to say that in both schools and hospitals, the catering service has taken a more commercial approach (albeit maybe not directly as a result of tendering) to the services it offers; one reason being the need to compete with local competition and, second, to remove the stigma that has so long been associated, perhaps unfairly, with these types of operation.

The structure of the industry is also further confused by the large variety of terms used to describe it. The use of the term "industrial catering" has often been associated with the services provided to employees within an organisation, these services being provided on a free or subsidised basis. However this term now overlaps with "contract catering" since many non-catering businesses contract out their catering requirements. The term "commercial" is normally associated with profit making and this overlaps with "contract catering" too.

For clarity, the different industry sectors referred to in this chapter are taken from Marketpower's *Catering Industry Population File* (Fifth Edition). The sectors are quite clearly identified and the terminology used is very familiar. An interesting factor about the structure of the industry is that over 76% of catering businesses comprise sole proprietorships and partnerships, with companies and corporations accounting for a further 13% and general Government and non-profit making bodies about 11%. In 1990, 90% of all catering businesses had a turnover of £250,000 or less and 60% of those averaged less than £100,000 per business.

The size of the catering industry can be measured in a variety of ways, but probably the most useful indicators are the number of outlets, turnover, numbers of meals served and employment statistics — these are used to provide an overview of the size of the industry in this chapter.

In 1990 Marketpower's *Catering Industry Population File* estimated that there were 320,688 catering outlets in the UK. Table 1.1 shows a breakdown of the UK catering market and the segments of the industry in two main sectors, namely profit and cost.

All sectors of the catering industry have been growing over the last decade, with unprecedented growth in 1989. Between 1985 and 1990 Government statistics showed that consumer spending on "meals and other catering" more than doubled to approximately £29 billion at current prices. However 1990 and 1991 have seen the industry hit by the Gulf war and the recession. Total turnover in the UK catering industry amounted to about £37 billion in 1990 and it has been projected by Marketpower that total turnover in the industry will fall in 1991 to about £36 billion. Table 1.2 illustrates the breakdown of the 1990 turnover figures.

Reluctance by consumers to spend in the current economic climate has inevitably led to a projected depressed picture.

By far the hardest hit has been the hotel sector with turnover estimated to be down by 10%. Almost all of the major organisations have commented in their company reports (1990/1991) that they have faced major difficulties,

## Table 1.1: UK Catering Market — Number of Outlets, 1990

| Market Sector | Number of Outlets | % of All Outlets | % of Profit Outlets |
|---|---|---|---|
| **Profit Sector** | | | |
| Large Hotels | 11,590 | 3.6 | 4.9 |
| Small Hotels | 47,110 | 14.7 | 19.8 |
| Restaurants | 16,110 | 5.0 | 6.8 |
| Public Houses | 73,100 | 22.8 | 30.7 |
| Fast Food | 1,072 | 0.3 | 0.5 |
| Travel | 1,164 | 0.4 | 0.5 |
| Cafés | 16,010 | 5.0 | 6.7 |
| Takeaways | 18,925 | 5.9 | 8.0 |
| Clubs | 33,750 | 10.5 | 14.2 |
| Leisure and Entertainment | 19,190 | 6.0 | 8.0 |
| Subtotal | 238,021 | 74.2 | 100.0 |
| **Cost Sector** | | | |
| Staff Catering | 23,990 | 7.5 | |
| National Health | 7,385 | 2.3 | |
| Private Health | 14,560 | 4.5 | |
| State Education | 31,110 | 9.7 | |
| Private Education | 2,570 | 0.8 | |
| Public Services | 1,523 | 0.5 | |
| Welfare Feeding | 1,529 | 0.5 | |
| Subtotal | 82,667 | 25.8 | |
| Total | 320,688 | 100.0 | |

Source: Marketpower's *Catering Industry Population File*, Fifth Edition

| Table 1.2: Summary of Turnover in the UK Hotel, Catering and Leisure Industry 1990 | | |
|---|---|---|
| | £ Million | % of Total |
| Food | 16,473 | 44 |
| Alcoholic Drinks | 12,300 | 33 |
| Soft Drinks, Confectionery, Tobacco, etc | 1,700 | 5 |
| Accommodation | 6,400 | 17 |
| Admission Charges | 500 | 1 |
| Total | 37,373 | 100 |
| Source: Marketpower estimates | | |

particularly in terms of declining world travel and its effect on hotel occupancy rates. Small businesses with a turnover of less than £50,000 have also been declining by a rate of about 7% in 1990 and it is primarily the larger companies that have maintained their *status quo* or continued to grow.

The worsening unemployment situation has had an overall impact on the amount of disposable income that consumers will spend, but sectors of the industry which are dependent on the number of people at work, such as staff catering, are facing a difficult period.

Another key measurement used when evaluating the size of the catering industry is the number of meals served by the various market sectors. Table 1.3 clearly shows that public houses served more meals than any other segment of the profit sector — 1.34 billion in 1990. Another measure of the relative importance of different categories of catering outlets is the average number of meals served per outlet in a year. In this respect, fast food outlets serve by far the biggest volume of meals, some 391,000 per outlet per annum.

Marketpower have projected that the number of meals served will drop in 1991 by about 3%, but that a small increase is expected in 1992.

## Table 1.3: Number of Meals Served 1990

|  | Million Meals Served | % of All Outlets |
|---|---|---|
| Market Sector |  |  |
| **Profit Sector** |  |  |
| Large Hotels | 375 | 4.2 |
| Small Hotels | 190 | 2.1 |
| Restaurants | 372 | 4.1 |
| Public Houses | 1,340 | 14.8 |
| Fast Food | 419 | 4.6 |
| Travel | 363 | 4.0 |
| Cafés | 573 | 6.3 |
| Takeaways | 978 | 10.8 |
| Clubs | 58 | 0.7 |
| Leisure and Entertainment | 890 | 9.8 |
| Subtotal | 5,558 | 61.4 |
| **Cost Sector** |  |  |
| Staff Catering | 1,610 | 17.8 |
| National Health | 480 | 5.3 |
| Private Health | 308 | 3.4 |
| State Education | 824 | 9.1 |
| Private Education | 130 | 1.4 |
| Public Services | 98 | 1.1 |
| Welfare Feeding | 42 | 0.5 |
| Subtotal | 3,492 | 38.6 |
| Total | 9,050 | 100.0 |

Source: Marketpower's *Catering Industry Population File*, Fifth Edition

With the UK poised to climb out of the recession, the catering industry is expected to resume growth in most sectors. However the extent of this growth will not only be dependent on outside forces but also on the ability of operators to be innovative and to really understand the needs of the consumers, and to be able to match products to requirements.

# EMPLOYMENT IN THE CATERING INDUSTRY

The Department of Employment estimates that there are approximately 1.25 million people employed currently in the catering industry; this represents a growth of 22% since 1985. This figure is slightly misleading in so far as the numbers only include businesses whose mainstream activity is catering. Therefore those people who work in hospitals, schools and other organisations where catering is a support service are not included in this figure. It is estimated that the real total number of employees working in the catering industry is probably nearer to 2.4 million (Source: Hotel and Catering Training Company). Figures supplied by the Department of Employment suggest that the largest increase has been in the restaurant, café and snack bar sectors (30%) with the next largest in public houses and bars (29%).

However the employment market has been hit very hard by the effects of the recession and the Gulf war. The hardest hit sector has been the hotels, particularly in the South East of the country.

Whilst the industry employs a significant number of people there is a continuing problem relating to the recruitment of skilled personnel at all levels. The *Hotel Catering and Business Review* published jointly by Berkeley Scott Group and Marketpower (First Edition — September 1991) states that

> once again, the question of the availability of skilled candidates will present itself when the economy improves; the effects of poor or reduced training programmes could make filling the available vacancies either difficult or a matter of unsatisfactory compromise.

A number of factors have affected the recruitment situation and probably one of the most significant is the issue of pay. The catering industry has always been considered one of the more badly paid industries in which to work but this situation has been improving steadily. According to Department of Employment statistics, earnings of employees in the catering industry rose by 18.4% between 1988 and 1990; this was marginally below earnings within the whole economy which rose by 19.7%. A salary survey undertaken by Berkeley Scott in 1991 indicates that people do not automatically expect a salary increase when moving jobs — in fact many appear to be prepared to accept a real reduction in pay in order to secure a job. This could have important knock-on effects with operators taking full advantage of the current situation which enables them to attract a far higher calibre of staff than would previously have been possible.

The issue of pay has often been linked with the issue of service charge. There has always been a great debate on the subject of the service charge and invariably the arguments revolved around the fact that the industry was seen to pay relatively low wages. No doubt this debate will continue but it is becoming less common for operators to state that a service charge will be included.

A further issue affecting the ability of some operators to attract high calibre staff has been the reluctance of people to move from London and the South of England. This is now changing and, according to Berkeley Scott the South has lost popularity and approximately 68% of the company's job seekers state that they are now prepared to move "anywhere". This trend in greater mobility should aid the recruitment process and provide employers with more opportunities to attract the calibre of person they require.

There is an extraordinary imbalance on the subject of age, between what the operators require and what is actually available. Employers are seeking to recruit people who are very young, ie below 25, but the problem is that those who are available for work are predominantly over 25 and a fair percentage are over 40 years of age. With the population getting "older" this situation is not going to improve. It is unfortunate that operators are looking for the younger element of the workforce when many very skilled and experienced older people are leaving the industry through redundancy, early retirement or general dissatisfaction. It will be for the operators to give serious consideration to the alternatives and think carefully about the merits of retaining the skills they have already and building on them, rather than repeatedly experiencing the high costs involved with recurring recruitment.

# TRAINING AND EDUCATION

Training in the catering industry has received a great deal of attention and publicity in recent years. With the difficulty experienced in attracting and retaining employees in the industry, training and education has been high on the agenda.

However when times are good, training budgets get total backing but during more difficult times, as are being experienced at the moment, training is one of the support functions which invariably gets axed. The Hotel and Catering Training Company estimate that the catering industry, taken as a whole, spends £200 million a year on training its employees.

According to a report published by the Employers Association on *Training in Britain: Employers' Activities*, approximately 45% of employers in the catering, recreational and personal services industry trained their employees — the national average is about 48%. The survey indicates that employees in the catering industry do receive below average formal training "off-the-job" and are expected to learn as they go along. The survey also states that for more than half their time in employment those in catering receive no training at all.

The industry is now supplied by diverse and flexible education and training programmes. Catering organisations themselves are providing a wide range of internal training programmes for their own employees, and where necessary employees are also given the opportunity to attend off-the-job training courses.

Large operators, such as contract caterers, have established extremely comprehensive training and management development programmes. One of the major catering contractors now offers programmes which range from operating a youth training scheme to sponsoring employees for an MBA.

In terms of formal education there is a wide range of well structured courses at all levels, both full-time and part-time, for particular skilled occupations. Other less specific courses are available for management and supervisory careers. In the UK there are in excess of 330 colleges, polytechnics and universities offering catering related courses, ranging from craft-based courses such as City and Guilds 706/1 for basic cookery, to a BSc (Hons) in Hotel and Catering Administration. Apart from formal educational establishments, there are many professional associations who offer a variety of courses for their members. The Hotel Catering and

Institutional Management Association (HCIMA) is one of the main professional bodies for managers in the food and accommodation services industry. One of the objectives of the HCIMA is "the advancement of education and training and the promotion of research", and to this end it offers two new programmes of study: the Professional Certificate and the Professional Diploma. (These courses have replaced the HCIMA Part A and Part B courses.) With the single European market now a reality, the HCIMA have been seeking active involvement with European policy matters, education providers and companies with a base in other EC Member States. The impact of the single European market has considerable implications for educational establishments and, consequently, the training and education of the future catering workforce.

Acceptance for the majority of formal courses is still very much linked to school achievements and academic qualifications. Formal qualifications, whether gained whilst working or on a full-time educational basis, have been one of the major yardsticks used during the selection and recruitment of personnel. What is now transpiring is that even with the substantial sums of money invested in training and education, there still appears to be a gap between the standards wanted by the employers and the standards of the workforce.

The Government recognised this problem across all industries a decade ago and have continually urged companies to raise standards and improve quality as a means to improving profitability. The Government addressed this issue by initiating the National Standards Programme which aims to set standards of competence across all industries ranging from operational to management activities. These standards would then form the basis for future training and would aim to produce clear, nationally recognised vocational qualifications. The National Council for Vocational Qualifications (NCVQ) was formed, together with the Scottish Vocational Education Council (SCOTVEC) to develop a framework of qualifications based on relevant industry standards. The Government has set up 150 industry-led bodies whose responsibility will be to develop the framework for their own industry sector. This approach enables both employers and employees to input into the framework and standards, thus ensuring that the real needs of the industry are reflected. National Vocational Qualifications (NVQs) will ensure that employees who take part in the programme will have the right qualifications to do the job and employers can be satisfied that their workforce is trained to nationally recognised standards. There is often criticism of the lack of practical experience gained during full-time college courses, and indeed previous vocational qualifications were often viewed as poor relations to academic qualifications. Rightly or wrongly these criticisms are made and it is to be hoped that the launch of the NVQs will, in part, help to provide relevant training and education, which is developed and provided within the industry and which will therefore mean acceptance by the industry. Improving the quality of the catering industry workforce can only bode well for improving the overall quality of the products and services the industry provides. Training and education will help employers to retain valuable employees, attract more people to the industry and encourage those who have left to return. In this way the industry will start to overcome some of the current problems it faces with the shortage of the right type of people for the right jobs.

# THE IMPACT OF TECHNOLOGY ON THE CATERING INDUSTRY

In the past decade, the catering industry has seen a tremendous upsurge in the development and introduction of new technology both in terms of methods, procedures and equipment.

Conventional catering is still probably the most widely used system in the UK, but increasing pressure on both capital and revenue costs is forcing companies to evaluate their current systems with a view to maximising efficiency.

In the first instance, catering "systems" such as cook-freeze and cook-chill were seen as opportunities to increase efficiency and improve levels of food safety by divorcing production from service. Pioneers of these systems proclaimed them to offer greater utilisation of labour, equipment, energy and space.

In the 1980s, the cook-chill system became very popular, particularly in the NHS and other organisations which were multi-site operations. However, cook-chill came in for a great deal of criticism in the latter half of the 1980s and many operators were forced to evaluate the safety of their systems, particularly concerning food safety. The *Big Chill Report*, published by the London Food Commission in 1987, put doubt and apprehension into the minds of caterers who had or were considering implementing cook-chill.

Neither the cook-freeze nor the cook-chill system was governed by separate legislation, but both were subject to a set of separate guidelines produced by the Department of Health. Of major concern was the lack of adherence to the guidelines by operators and the weakness of the guidelines themselves. Since the publication of the *Guidelines on Pre-Cooked Frozen Foods* (1970) and the *Guidelines on Pre-Cooked Chilled Foods* (1980), technological advances and the growing interest in cook-chill systems forced the Department of Health to set up a working group to review the two publications. Consequently a new combined set of guidelines was published in 1989 which took account of users' experience and considerations of scientific data from both established and new cook-chill systems. Whilst no changes to operating temperatures were made, the new guidelines clarified aspects of the systems, such as pre-planning, management, distribution of food products and service.

Of major importance was the recognition by the Department that a quality assurance system should be developed to ensure that the strictest control is applied to the system at all times. The guidelines recommend the adoption of the Hazard Analysis Critical Control Point (HACCP) approach — this approach to quality assurance is just one approach and is discussed in much greater detail in Chapter 4.

It would appear that confidence in the system has been regained, and this has been assisted by the continuing expansion of the chilled foods market in the retail sector. There are now over 300 cook-chill installations in the UK and whilst the growth rate has slowed, new installations are still being commissioned.

Other "systems" which have found a place in the catering industry include Sous-vide and Capkold. As with cook-chill both these systems depend on the separation of production and service and the storage of food in a chilled state — the difference being that both systems use a plastic pouch as the storage and transportation medium, and they both offer quite substantially extended shelf-life over cook-chill products. It is fair to say that both Sous-vide and Capkold have not been as successful as cook-chill. It may be that these systems are so different from conventional catering that their place in the UK catering industry will take some time to become established and accepted. Furthermore, whilst these techniques are not new, the Department of Health has neither condemned nor fully supported either system, even though both are operating successfully in this country.

With the rise in the systems approach to catering and the requirement to manage quality effectively, caterers have looked to the food manufacturing industry for direction and guidance. Whilst catering and food manufacturing are different in many ways there is no doubt that certain catering operators are verging on being classified as food manufacturers, due to their size and the sophistication of their operations.

The impact of new technology on the catering industry has been significant, but with the ever-increasing number of food poisoning incidents being reported each year, the pressure is on the industry to develop and implement systems which can be controlled and which can guarantee consistently high quality products.

# THE FUTURE FOR THE CATERING INDUSTRY

The future for the catering industry looks good, and economic forecasts suggest that the industry in general is set to resume its pattern of long-term growth. However as the industry becomes more and more competitive, organisations will have to be looking to improve the quality of the products and services they offer as a means of staying in business. A better educated and trained workforce will assist in this process, but it will be the total commitment of the whole business to quality which will be necessary for success.

Different standards of catering services are required in the industry to reflect the needs of customers and the amount of money they are willing to spend on a particular product or service. This differentiation in standards is acceptable and needed, but it is the unacceptable variation in the standards of quality for each particular market sector which will need to be addressed by the industry.

The introduction of formal quality assurance systems in the catering industry is in its infancy, but it is becoming widely acknowledged that the benefits they bring to the individual catering business and the industry in general are far reaching. This book introduces the basic concepts of *quality assurance* and looks at the implications for the catering industry. A number of alternative quality assurance systems are discussed and guidance given to enable catering managers to decide the most appropriate route to pursue in the implementation of a quality assurance system to meet the needs of their operation, no matter how big or small.

# Chapter 2

# What is Quality?

There is no doubt that the issue of quality is now uppermost in the minds of many caterers today and the reason is very simple — the provision of a quality product or service will be a major contributing factor between staying in business or failing to survive. These words may seem harsh, but the hard facts of business in the 1990s and beyond are that everyone is operating in a very competitive market and only those companies who can give their customers what they want will continue to succeed.

Traditionally many organisations have managed their business with limited emphasis on long-term profitability and little or no attention paid to the customer. Many companies have survived with no clear strategic plan, fire-fighting on a day-to-day basis and treating the customer with a "take it or leave it" attitude. This style of management is now becoming rare. To move from being such a traditionally managed organisation to being one which is pro-active and quality driven often involves a change in organisational structure, management style and attitude, and the elimination of management and operational weaknesses. Typical weaknesses may include:

–   doing things the way they have always been done: changing management and working methods may not always be appropriate, but increased competition is forcing companies to look at more effective means of achieving the same quality of product or service demanded. An example of where a real change in practice has been of benefit to the catering industry is the wide use of prepared foods to substitute for the labour intensive preparation of such items as vegetables

–   excessive departmentalisation: departments which work to meet their own goals and do not consider the impact of their actions on others cause "internal" problems which may affect the quality of the service offered to the customer

–   excessive control and a dictatorial attitude to staff: the staff are a valuable resource and should be given opportunities to generate ideas on how the business should operate — greater commitment to quality is gained in this way

–   accepting a certain degree of error: this is very common in the catering industry. Every effort should be made to find ways of eliminating mistakes and planning to do a job "right first time". The waitress who takes an order incorrectly will incur the probable waste of a meal, the subsequent preparation of an alternative and even a reduction on the bill — a costly error

–   fire-fighting: many managers think that a full day sorting other people's problems is a good day's work. Managers should spend time preventing mistakes happening and helping others to do likewise — a pro-active not reactive management style. A major UK service organisation discovered that more than a third of every employee's daily work was spent doing extra work to sort out problems — a very costly waste of time which ultimately gets passed on to the customer.

Businesses are now operating in an environment where competition is very strong, customers', shareholders' and employees' expectations are much higher and where technology changes almost daily.

In many organisations, traditional styles of management are being replaced by methods based clearly on effective leadership and a total commitment to quality. In this way these organisations stand a much better chance of survival in a very competitive world.

# THE GROWTH OF QUALITY SYSTEMS

Interest in the concept of quality in the catering industry has only really come to the forefront in the last decade. Traditionally, quality systems have been associated with products from manufacturing, not service-based industries. Such products are tangible, they can be inspected and, of course, rejected if they do not come up to standard. It is not surprising, therefore, that early quality systems were developed in the manufacturing sector. However, managing quality in a service industry is just as important as managing quality in a manufacturing environment — failure and reject costs still exist and affect net profits and the ultimate customer.

## The Evolution of Quality Systems

One of the pioneers of quality systems was Dr. W. Edwards Deming, an American management scientist, who created the road map that positioned the Japanese as front runners in today's international business and industrial development race. Few would deny that the Japanese success in the second half of the 20th century is based on Deming's work on the statistical control of quality and the understanding that the customer is the most important part of the production line.

In the manufacturing industries in the UK it was (and still is) common to plan to produce 10,000 items in order to have 8,000 to sell. The Japanese proved that it was possible to make 10,000 items and be able to sell 10,000. Deming's work is now reflected across America and Europe and quality systems are now being adopted by very many large manufacturing and service-based organisations in the UK, including British Airways, National Westminster Bank and Mercury Communications.

The catering industry is currently very concerned with quality, although many interpret this as the "safety" of food rather than the total quality of the service provided. Introducing and developing quality systems in the catering industry is a very new concept which, for many operators, the real benefits have yet to be explored and enjoyed.

## What Does "Quality" Mean?

Whilst many caterers talk about providing a quality service, it is probably fair to say that the term "quality" is misunderstood. What exactly constitutes a quality service has long been the subject of debate. The quality of a service can only be determined by the customer — if the customer is not satisfied, the service, in their view, was not good. Quality is not about being the best or the most expensive restaurant or hotel, but simply about meeting the customer's needs.

19

There are many definitions of quality which are used, including the ever popular "fitness for purpose". The British Standards Institute (BSI) use a more technical definition: "the totality of the features and characteristics of a product or service that bear on it's ability to satisfy a given need". Whatever interpretation is used of the meaning of quality, in essence it is about providing the customer with the desired product and level of service expected every time.

While there is often confusion as to the exact meaning of the word quality, many people similarly confuse the term "quality assurance" with "quality control". In very simple terms quality assurance is about preventing quality mistakes and providing an error free service; quality control involves checking the various parts of the product system.

Quality has many dimensions and in order to meet the needs of the customer, each organisation must define quality for themselves, by understanding what factors are most influential in satisfying their customers' needs. Research carried out by a team of quality experts (Berry, Zeithaml and Parasuraman) determined that customers use five main categories when evaluating service quality:

– tangibles: physical facilities, equipment, personnel, etc
– reliability: the ability to produce the service required accurately
– responsiveness: the willingness to provide customers with a prompt, helpful service
– assurance: knowledge and courtesy of employees, their trust and confidence
– empathy: the caring, individual attention provided to customers.

It is clear how applicable these categories are to the customers requiring catering services. It is these factors (and others) against which the level of quality service provided to customers can be assessed and measured.

People often refer to the expensive restaurant they visited and yet did not believe they received a high quality service for the money paid while, in contrast, were extremely pleased with the quality of service and product provided by the local branded roadside restaurant at a lesser cost — this is a good example of "fitness for purpose". It is therefore plain that high quality does not always mean high cost, and that different people have different quality desires, dependent on a need at a particular time. (However, there will always be those people who believe that the higher the price the better the quality — this is true for *some* but not all catering products and services!)

It is interesting to note that the catering industry is often put into categories relating to quality standards by various bodies such as the Automobile Association (AA) and the Royal Automobile Club (RAC). In addition, a wide variety of guides are produced annually, such as the Michelin guide, the Good Food guide, the Good Pub guide, etc and these attempt to rate catering establishments based on a set of criteria against which standards of quality are measured. What many of these grading systems concentrate on, particularly those relating to the hotel sector, are the tangible aspects such as the size of rooms and the availability of services, and not on the less tangible aspects such as comfort, speed of service and choice.

There is no doubt that grading systems are useful in identifying tangible standards, but what is also important is the measurement of customers' other requirements associated with a stay in a hotel or the experience of dining out, such as the five quality categories referred to earlier. It is in these intangible aspects of the catering service that many caterers are lacking sound, unbiased knowledge of their customers' needs. Understanding customer needs and requirements is one of the major starting points when embarking on the quality route.

## QUALITY SYSTEMS

A quality system has been defined by the British Standards Institute as "The organisational structure, responsibilities, procedures, processes and resources for implementing quality management". In essence, the quality system encompasses all parts of a business which will affect the quality of the service provided to satisfy the customer.

The most widely recognised formal quality system now being implemented by organisations in the UK is the British Standard BS 5750. This British Standard sets out how an organisation can establish, document and maintain an effective quality system which demonstrates to customers both a commitment to quality and the ability to supply their quality needs.

BS 5750 has, up until recently, been used primarily by manufacturing industries, but it is now starting to be used by service-based industries and, indeed, a small handful of catering organisations have achieved certification to BS 5750.

There is a school of thought which believes that the use of a quality system such as BS 5750 is conceptually too narrow and that quality is a discipline to be implemented right through an organisation, not just those parts which need controlling and checking. Taking this approach, the concept of Total Quality Management (TQM) is now being introduced in a wide range of organisations. TQM is about recognising that everyone has a role in the effort to satisfy the customer, and ensuring that everyone's contribution is valued at all times. Very simply, the TQM philosophy is about completely satisfying and delighting customers now, and continuously improving the organisation's ability to satisfy customers in the future.

There is much discussion about whether TQM or BS 5750 is the right route to take or whether both systems are needed or, indeed, whether organisations should develop and implement their own, tailor-made quality system. Many organisations have not adopted a formal system such as BS 5750 or the TQM approach, for a variety of reasons, but have developed their own tailor-made systems based on sound quality principles.

The catering industry is not a world leader in quality systems, but what has become apparent is the growing awareness in the industry that the adoption of some form of quality system is crucial to survival. The tailor-made approach, however formal or informal, is the approach that most catering organisations have tended to adopt, whether due to the absence of knowledge or information on other alternative systems, or a conscious decision not to adopt a recognised quality system.

In many cases the catering industry focuses on quality control issues forced on them by food safety legislation and not on the wider aspects associated with adopting a full quality system. For many caterers this focus on control will continue. However, caterers must now be aware that quality control, whilst important, is only a part of a full quality programme. As such, it should be seen as the preliminary step towards introducing a more comprehensive quality system.

The Government has played a part in this drive towards recognising the importance of quality by the implementation of the Food Safety Act (1990), which focuses clearly on the responsibility of individuals to provide "safe" food products to customers. In addition, the Government is recommending that caterers follow a disciplined and carefully structured approach to the identification of hazards and control points by adopting the Hazard Analysis Critical Control Point (HACCP) system. So whilst many caterers are perhaps being "forced" to introduce a form of quality control, it must be seen as a very positive step for the future of the industry.

Chapter 1 stated that over 76% of catering businesses comprise sole proprietorships and partnerships and that in 1990 60% of all catering businesses averaged a turnover of less than £100,000. With this in mind, it is extremely unlikely that many catering businesses will be able to afford the initial set-up costs associated with striving for certification to BS 5750 or introducing a full TQM system. What many caterers *are* able to do, in an attempt to move their organisation towards a quality-based operation, is to develop and implement a simple, effective, quality system themselves. BS 5750, TQM and the tailor-made approach are all discussed in more detail in subsequent chapters.

# THE PRINCIPLES AND BENEFITS OF INTRODUCING A QUALITY SYSTEM

No matter which type of system or which approach a caterer takes to develop and implement a quality system, the principles are similar, although there may be some differences of emphasis.

## THE ELEMENTS OF QUALITY

An organisation wishing to pursue quality needs to understand the key elements and principles which will apply. These include the following:

(a)  customers are the priority
(b)  a clear mission statement and objectives are vital
(c)  quality is everyone's business
(d)  appropriate systems and processes are essential — "the job must be done right first time"
(e)  communicate and co-operate
(f)  measure performance.

## Customers are the Priority

The whole issue of quality is based on understanding the customers' needs and requirements and delivering them every time. It is therefore essential to get close to the customers and to find out exactly what delights them and what irritates them. Only then can the organisation begin to understand the quality of the service or product which needs to be delivered. This task is not easy and involves understanding both the tangible and intangible aspects of service delivery. In the catering industry the criteria against which the customer measures quality may include speed of service, temperature of food, ambience of environment, staff attitude, value for money and many others.

The catering industry has certainly made extensive efforts to segment the catering market in order to provide services to different groups of customers. Successful examples include the roadside restaurant chains which provide quick service and good value for money to the traveller. More recently the "Travelodge" concept was launched to provide businessmen and families with cheap, overnight, value for money accommodation.

## Mission Statement and Objectives

Senior management need to have a very clear vision of how the service demanded will be delivered and whether, indeed, the organisation is capable of delivering that service within its current structure, systems and procedures.

It is often necessary to review radically the organisation's *raison d'etre*. In the catering industry it is essential to determine what the organisation's mission statement is. The provider of school meals will have a different mission statement to the roadside restaurant chain, as will the provider of hospital catering services and a caterer to a major sporting event. Yet all these organisations are providing a food and beverage service.

A mission statement supported by clear objectives will provide the organisation with a clear focus and vision for pursuing the quality route. The objectives should address:

– the commitment to quality
– target sectors of the catering market and the organisation's customers
– internal and external relationships
– the measurement of performance.

## Quality is Everyone's Business

Senior management commitment to the quality programme must be evident from the outset. It should begin at the top of the organisation with commitment to the mission statement, which management must really believe. This commitment must be real, as staff lower down in the organisation will soon detect if only lip service is being paid to quality initiatives.

The driving force behind this commitment is leadership. Top, middle and junior managers have to lead the way in quality management. This means directing, controlling, understanding, listening, recognising problems and difficulties and adjusting the system to overcome them.

From management commitment comes employee commitment and it is essential that this is gained. Without it the quality programme may fail. Gaining employee commitment takes considerable time, but as long as managers maintain their commitment and accept their responsibilities in the pursuit of quality, the necessary changes in attitude required throughout the organisation will eventually happen. All staff must be involved in the quality programme from the outset, and be involved with problem solving in their own areas of work. If they do not understand fully what the quality system is concerned with, there is a danger that the quality programme will be seen as yet another "management initiative" which will fade away.

Quality is everyone's business and the delivery of a catering service to a customer is made up of a series of interlinking activities. The production of a meal and its subsequent service is all part of one process, and achieving the right standard at every link in the process, from the delivery of the raw materials to the serving of the meal, is vital if total customer satisfaction is to be achieved. Everyone from the storeman to the waiter is and must be involved in the quality system. Any break in the chain of events from production to service may cause a product of unsuitable quality to be served, resulting in a dissatisfied customer.

## Do it Right First Time

The old saying of prevention is better than cure is very much at the forefront of implementing a quality system. How many times have hotels and restaurants had to give a discount to a customer because the room was not cleaned properly or the meal was unacceptable? Much time, effort and money is spent in the catering industry putting right jobs which have gone wrong. If jobs were done "right first time", time and money would be saved and expensive resources could be channelled into worthwhile activities. The ability to do a job "right first time" will depend upon there being clearly identified systems, procedures and standards in place for each job, that there are the right tools to do the job and by ensuring that all the staff have received the right level of training. In other words, the quality system in place must enable the organisation to produce the right level of service demanded every time.

The relationship between staff, ie the "internal" supplier and customer relationship, is also very important in enabling the job to be done "right first time". In any catering organisation there are a number of internal suppliers and customers, as well as external suppliers and customers. The porter is a supplier to the chef, the chef is a supplier to the head waiter, the secretary is a supplier to the manager, and so on. These relationships are commonly referred to as *internal quality chains* and are often the most difficult to manage.

Before the actual external customer receives the service required, there are a complex series of transactions between departments to supply this service. Unfortunately, the transfer of information between internal suppliers and customers relating to requirements and performance standards is often lacking. It should be recognised that to improve the quality of service to external customers, the level of the internal service offered within an organisation must also be of the highest standards achievable. It is important that all staff and departments understand who their internal customers and suppliers are and what their needs are. A good internal service will assist in ensuring the efficient working of the organisation's systems and procedures, increasing job satisfaction and individual commitment to quality, improving communication and generally making everyone's working life easier and more pleasant. This in turn will assist in maintaining the required level of service to the ultimate external customer.

## Communicate and Co-operate

Effective communication and co-operation are essential to ensure that everyone knows what they should be doing, where they fit in and with whom they interact.

There are many ways of communicating information, but to be effective it must be up, down and across all levels and departments within the organisation.

## Measurement

It is vital to measure performance and to know how well the customer's needs and expectations are being fulfilled. All employees must know how well they are doing and should be encouraged to measure their own performance.

An important aspect of the measurement process is to ensure that performance results are communicated in a way which is understood by the department or staff to whom it applies. Graphs and diagrams are often a more effective means of presenting information than pages of words.

If performance standards are not up to the level required it is essential that action is taken and that the staff are involved in determining the way forward. Quality mistakes cost money and must be rectified if the organisation is really committed to quality.

# THE BENEFITS OF QUALITY

These quality principles are relatively simple in theory, but their effective implementation is not straightforward and involves a great deal of commitment, energy and patience. Developing and implementing a quality system cannot be done in a short space of time; rather, if the philosophy of TQM is adopted, an organisation commits itself to a never-ending process of continuous improvement.

The benefits to be gained from introducing a quality system are both operational and financial. An effective quality system places the emphasis on preventing mistakes and failures occurring and, therefore, satisfying the customer's needs. The potential benefits to the catering industry include:

(a) increased ability to meet customer demands
(b) improved efficiency
(c) enhanced food safety performance
(d) minimised risk of failures
(e) reduced wastage

(f)  improved working conditions
(g)  increased staff morale and lower staff turnover
(h)  increased business opportunities
(i)  development of image and reputation.

If an organisation is to reap the benefits outlined above it will require investment, both in terms of time, manpower and finance.

The question of how much it will cost will depend upon how far down the quality route the caterer decides to go and, therefore, which system to adopt. In general terms, implementing a quality system involves initial increased expenditure, with later payback realised through a reduction in the costs of quality mistakes.

It is probably fair to say that most catering businesses are unable to identify the extent of the costs of mistakes or of poor quality, and many caterers have probably never even looked at their business in this way. There are quality mistake costs which are immediately obvious and which can be identified readily, such as food waste, rejected food and unpaid bills due to dissatisfaction, but there are others which cannot be costed easily. The costs of quality can be likened to an iceberg (see Figure 2.1). On the surface, obvious for all to see, are the costs that everyone lives with and accepts as part of everyday life. However, the worst costs are hidden below the surface, like the bulk of an iceberg, and include elements such as bad publicity and lost trade, duplication of effort and poor productivity.

Quality related problems will often be shown to be far greater and more expensive than most companies imagine — few managers realise that waste and putting things right can account for anything between 15% – 40% of turnover in a typical company. Prior to embarking on the implementation of a quality system, it is important to evaluate the human resource costs and other associated costs which will be incurred. In this way it will be easier to determine the financial benefits which may arise. The evaluation of costs should address:

–  the development costs: personnel, external consultants, equipment, etc
–  the operating costs: the cost of getting it right, finding out what is wrong and the cost of getting it wrong.

Over the last decade many organisations have started off down the

# Figure 2.1: The Quality Iceberg — Hidden Costs of Poor Quality

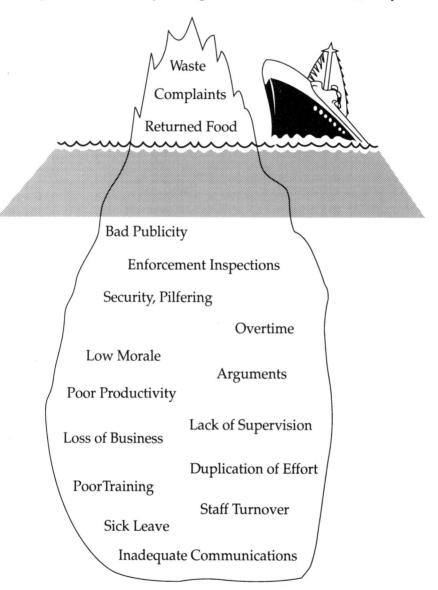

Adapted from "The Wyvern Quality Iceberg" Published by Wyvern Business Training.

quality route and have failed to achieve the potential benefits. Many of the reasons for this failure are because many people do not understand properly what quality is all about. Many think that quality is another division, an add-on to the real work. To be successful quality systems must be an integral part of every employees' daily work. Again, some people are under the illusion that quality means having all the best equipment, the best decor and most expensive china and glass. Rather it is the commitment of management and staff to understanding the customer's needs and meeting them every time that really makes quality work. Finally, because of the great interest in quality and the extensive work that has been carried out in this field, many organisations lose sight of the fact that quality systems are mainly based on common sense, not science.

Whichever quality route an organisation selects to pursue, understanding and implementing the main elements and principles of quality must be at the forefront of planning the future of the business.

# THE OPTION APPRAISAL

There are a number of quality routes an organisation can choose to pursue. Before embarking on the introduction of a quality system, these options need to be fully appraised. Undertaking this option appraisal is crucial to ensuring that the right way forward is chosen.

Currently the main options available to a caterer include BS 5750, TQM, the King's Fund scheme for the NHS and the self-design system. HACCP, in its truest sense, focuses on food safety, but it can be considered as part of a full quality system which would encompass the whole business. It is worth noting that with BS 5750, organisations have the choice as to which part or parts of the operation will be included in the quality system — it need not necessarily cover the entire organisation.

The appraisal itself may take a number of forms, but the primary issues which need to be discussed include:

– why is a quality system required?
– what benefits will accrue?
– what resources will be required, both in terms of finance and man-power?
– what are the time-scale implications?

- will external help be required?
- where is the organisation in terms of standards, procedures and other quality aspects?
- what is known about the customer's requirements?
- if a quality system is not introduced, what are the business implications?
- what are the competition doing?
- are there legal issues?

The importance of the decision to select the right way forward cannot be underestimated. Much has been written about those organisations who have failed to achieve the successful implementation of a quality system. Many cite the reasons for failure as inadequate preliminary thought and discussion coupled with lack of *real* commitment from all levels within the organisation. It is a costly exercise to get wrong, not only in terms of finance. Organisations which have gone down the quality route and have had limited success will find it very difficult to reinstate any further quality initiatives. The workforce will certainly be sceptical and mistrusting of the management's efforts relating to quality, and the failure will be tagged as another management fad that eventually went away.

Help to make the decision on the right way forward is available from many sources. Local Trading Standards Officers, the Department of Trade and Industry and external consultancy experts in quality are examples of people who may be able to offer assistance in this important decision-making process.

There is no common right way forward — each organisation has varying objectives relating to quality. The right route is the one which enables these objectives to be achieved and the customer's needs to be met.

# Chapter 3

# Food Safety and the Food Safety Act 1990

Food safety is very high on the public agenda and this awareness has been brought about by increasing problems relating to food safety and recent food scares. Salmonella and listeria have attracted much public discussion and concern and serious problems have occurred with foreign matter intentionally being put into foods, such as glass and mercury.

Higher standards are being demanded by the retail food industry and the food manufacturing industry as well as the consumers themselves. The food industry as a whole now employs in excess of three million people and contributes nearly 10% of Gross Domestic Product. The industry is growing and becoming more sophisticated as it strives to meet the increasing demands of consumers, scientists, nutritionists and the shareholders.

Techniques of food manufacturing are becoming more complex, farming is becoming much more sophisticated and genetically engineered products are entering the food chain. All these radical changes raise new food safety concerns and it is critical for the public to feel confident that the current food safety legislation, its maintenance and regulation, are sufficient to protect their health.

The food chain has many links and at each link there is a real responsibility to the critical issue of food safety. Ensuring food safety becomes an enormous responsibility for all individuals involved in the food chain to bear. A misunderstanding of this powerful position that farmers, retailers and caterers are in, can lead to the potential to cause serious harm to individuals and, in extreme cases, the loss of life. It could be said that until recently, many operators in the food chain were not aware of their own responsibility for food safety.

The Government has had to respond urgently to the problems of food safety, demonstrated in the alarming food poisoning statistics which continue to rise each year, and by the increasing demands from consumers for their own personal safety.

# THE GOVERNMENT AND FOOD SAFETY

In July 1989, the Government produced a White Paper entitled *Food Safety — Protecting the Consumer*. This paper described the (then) current situation relating to legislation governing the food industry, highlighted major improvements made at that time and set out the Government's proposals for the future.

The White Paper stated clearly the Government's overriding concern to protect the consumer and provided an overview of its Food Safety Strategy; namely, that the Government:

–   insists on stringent hygiene standards throughout the food chain
–   controls the use of additives, such as colourings and preservatives
–   monitors chemical contaminants and lays down stringent limits, often with very wide margins of safety
–   aims to ensure that danger to human health from microbiological contamination is kept to an absolute minimum
–   assesses novel foods and processes to ensure their safety.

The White Paper recognised that regulations made under the Food Act 1984 left significant gaps. For example, new food businesses could be established without any system of vetting or prior approval, either of the premises or people involved. (Some exercise of control was available over premises where planning applications and building regulations were required, for example there was prior vetting of such establishments as abbatoirs, dairies and poultry slaughterhouses before granting a licence to operate.) Of real importance was the inability of the enforcement officers to close businesses which were an imminent health risk as quickly as possible. Closure powers existed, but were not effective because of the time delays involved.

In 1990, a national Food Premises Condition Survey was organised by the Audit Commission in co-operation with the Institute of Environmental Health Officers. The survey (which was not part of the White Paper exercise) covered in excess of 5,000 premises in 300 local authorities in England and Wales. The results were astonishing in that more than 12% of the premises inspected were judged to present a high health risk. Figure 3.1 illustrates the level of risk by category of establishment visited.

### Figure 3.1: High Risk Food Premises

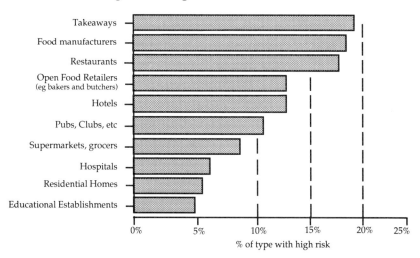

% of type with high risk

Source: Audit Commission survey 1990

It became clear that food safety was a real area of concern and that new legislation would be required to stem the rising problems in the food industry.

To tackle these problems, the Government's proposals in the White Paper for the new legislation included:

- tighter controls on unfit food and food which is not of the nature, substance or quality demanded, so that enforcement powers can be exercised even before food is put on sale and so that suspect unfit food can be detained while investigations take place

–   new enforcement measures to strengthen the existing system, so that, for example, action can be taken to condemn whole batches of food
–   provision for registration of commercial food premises, to enable local authorities to identify them more readily. There should also be provisions which will enable deficiencies to be put right, and to have premises closed down in emergency situations that present an immediate risk to health
–   extended powers to adapt the law to technological developments such as food irradiation
–   enhanced powers to control contaminants and residues, such as veterinary drug residues in meat, including those due to bad practices on farms or in manufacture
–   powers to make emergency control orders to deal with potentially serious problems, such as accidental contamination
–   provisions for the training of those who handle food commercially, to build on existing good practice and increase the numbers of people trained by the food industry, local authorities and others.

To meet the challenge of the evolving food industry and the associated potential problems relating to food safety, the Food Safety Act 1990 received Royal Assent on 29 June 1990 and came into force on 1 January 1991. The Government stated that the Food Safety Act "will set firm and clear ground rules, providing even greater security for the future".

The aims of this new legislation are to:

–   ensure that modern food technology and distribution methods are safe
–   ensure that food is not misleadingly labelled or presented
–   reinforce present powers and penalties against law breakers
–   ensure that new European Community directives on food can be implemented
–   streamline the current legislation, by combining the Acts which apply in England and Wales and in Scotland.

Consumers, at whatever stage of the food chain (see Figure 3.2) are entitled to expect that the food which they buy should be of the quality demanded, particularly in terms of food safety.

The Food Safety Act 1990 applies to all sectors of the food industry

## Figure 3.2: The UK Food Supply Chain

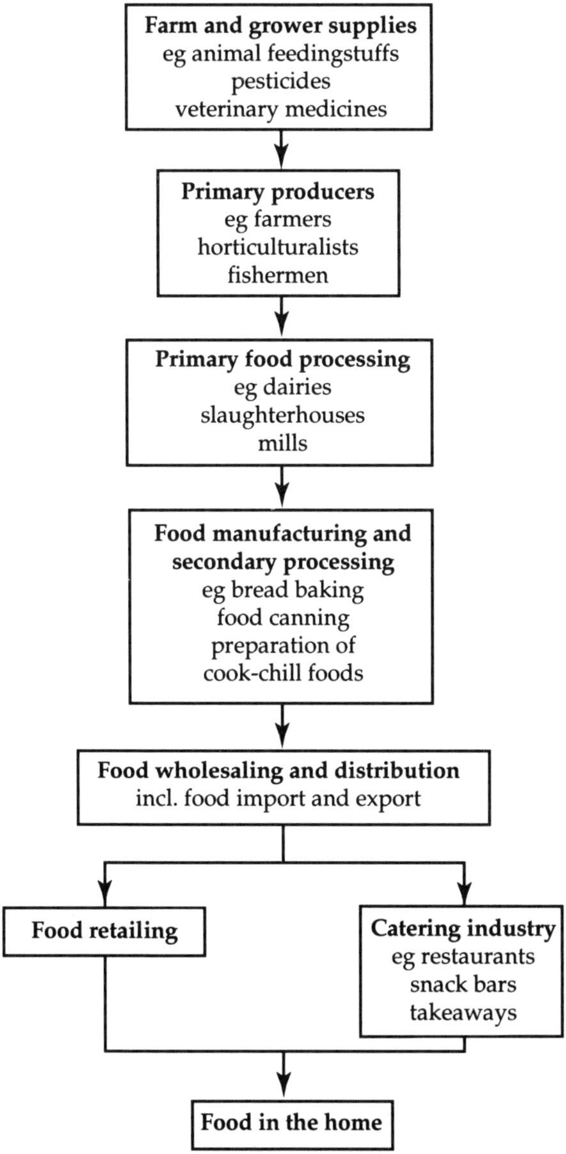

```
┌─────────────────────────────┐
│   Farm and grower supplies  │
│     eg animal feedingstuffs │
│           pesticides        │
│       veterinary medicines  │
└─────────────────────────────┘
              │
              ▼
    ┌─────────────────────────┐
    │    Primary producers    │
    │       eg farmers        │
    │     horticulturalists   │
    │        fishermen        │
    └─────────────────────────┘
              │
              ▼
    ┌─────────────────────────┐
    │ Primary food processing │
    │       eg dairies        │
    │     slaughterhouses     │
    │          mills          │
    └─────────────────────────┘
              │
              ▼
    ┌─────────────────────────┐
    │  Food manufacturing and │
    │    secondary processing │
    │     eg bread baking     │
    │       food canning      │
    │      preparation of     │
    │      cook-chill foods   │
    └─────────────────────────┘
              │
              ▼
┌─────────────────────────────────┐
│ Food wholesaling and distribution│
│   incl. food import and export   │
└─────────────────────────────────┘
        │                 │
        ▼                 ▼
┌───────────────┐  ┌──────────────────┐
│ Food retailing│  │ Catering industry│
│               │  │   eg restaurants │
│               │  │    snack bars    │
│               │  │     takeaways    │
└───────────────┘  └──────────────────┘
        │                 │
        └────────┬────────┘
                 ▼
        ┌──────────────────┐
        │ Food in the home │
        └──────────────────┘
```

Source: *Food Safety — Protecting the Consumer*, HMSO

from growers and producers to retailers and caterers. It covers all operations involved in the selling, possessing for sale, delivering, preparing, labelling, storing, importing and exporting food. The Act provides a flexible framework to meet the needs of consumers now and in the future because it contains wide enabling powers. Detailed matters are left for secondary legislation (regulations), allowing effective control for future problems.

# THE REGULATION AND MAINTENANCE OF FOOD SAFETY

Food safety is maintained and regulated in the UK by a number of measures such as legislation and enforcement, research and advice, and quality assurance and control systems.

Prompted by the rising concern about food safety, the Government commissioned a number of extensive studies to be undertaken, including the Acheson Report, *Public Health in England*, and the Richmond Report Parts 1 and 2 — *The Microbiologicai Safety of Food*. These reports have had an important impact on the current food safety legislation and on how food safety is maintained.

The new and existing legislation, which is based on extensive research and the best scientific advice, is designed with the consumer's safety as a priority.

# GOVERNMENT DEPARTMENTS

Within central government, responsibility for food safety lies with the Ministry of Agriculture, Fisheries and Food (MAFF) and the Department of Health (DoH). Their responsibilities are complementary and both aim to protect the consumer.

Both these departments maintain close, continuous contact at all levels to ensure that their efforts are fully co-ordinated. Proposals and any consultations concerning food safety and associated legislation are initiated and agreed jointly by the Minister of Agriculture, Fisheries and Food, the Secretary of State for Health, the Secretary of State for Wales and the Secretary of State for Scotland. Before making any regulations or issuing codes of practice, the 1990 Act requires that all interested parties are consulted, including the industry, the enforcers and the consumers.

Beyond the professional advice available within Government departments, expertise is also provided by several committees. Most of these committees are continuous and on-going, and their members include leading scientists and other experts who provide objective advice on a wide range of issues, such as:

− the approval or rejection of food additives
− the approval or rejection of pesticides and veterinary medicines
− the monitoring and surveillance of contaminants in food
− the development of novel foods and processes
− the microbiological safety of food.

Figure 3.3 shows the current committees which provide advice to the Government and also which bodies formally report to or seek advice from each other. These committees are the means by which the Government obtains independent expert technical, scientific and medical advice, on which ministers base their decisions.

Some committees have statutory roles under specific legislation, for example, the Veterinary Products Committee, but others may be formed when new developments or problems create the need for additional expertise. In 1989, the Government set up the Richmond Committee, chaired by Sir Mark Richmond, to report on the microbiological safety of food.

The Richmond Committee was set up in an attempt to understand why the incidence of food poisoning in this country was rising. The terms of reference for the Committee were to:

advise the Secretary of State for Health, the Minister of Agriculture, Fisheries and Food and the Secretaries of State for Wales, Scotland and Northern Ireland, on matters remitted to it by Ministers relating to the microbiological safety of food and such matters as it considers need investigation.

The Richmond Committee was a "limited life" committee which ceased to exist once it had reported.

The Richmond Report, Parts 1 and 2 (published in 1990 and 1991 respectively), has had, and will continue to have a far reaching impact on

## Figure 3.3: Government Advisory Bodies

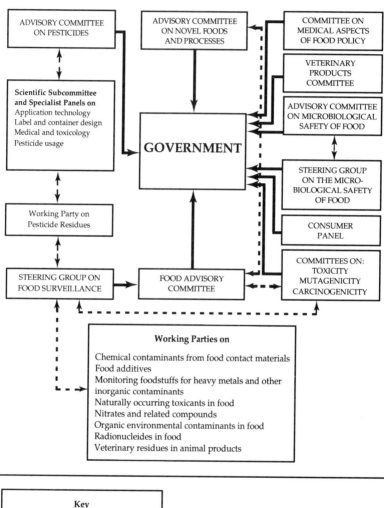

Key

Advice to Government

Formal links (ie. bodies formally report to or seek advice from each other)

NB: In addition to the formal links all these bodies routinely exchange data, maintain liaison, and seek advice from each other as circumstances dictate.

Adapted from *Food Safety — Protecting the Consumer*, HMSO

the food industry, since many of its recommendations tackle some very fundamental problems relating to food safety.

In particular the Committee looked at specific questions relating to the increasing number of food poisoning cases being reported, especially from salmonella, listeria and campylobacter. The main aim was to establish whether this increase was linked to changes in agriculture and food production, food technology and distribution, retailing, catering and food handling in the home, and to recommend action where appropriate.

The first part of the Richmond Report covered a wide range of topics including:

- epidemiological data on foodborne illness in humans
- the systems for epidemiological surveillance, collation and review of data and action
- arrangements for handling outbreaks of foodborne illness and the roles of the bodies involved, both centrally and locally
- the way in which food is surveyed
- the production of raw poultry meat
- manufacturing processes, particularly for meat and dairy products
- food processing by smaller enterprises
- suggested changes to legislation in the light of the Committee's recommendations.

The first part of the Report made many recommendations to the Government, enforcement agencies, professional bodies and the food industry. One important recommendation was that the Government should set up a national microbiological food surveillance and assessment system based on two new committees to safeguard microbiological food safety. The Government accepted this recommendation and in 1990 established the Steering Group on the Microbiological Safety of Food (to identify through surveillance the need for action to ensure the microbiological safety of food) and the Advisory Committee on the Microbiological Safety of Food, to advise on the public health implications of food microbiological safety.

The second part of the Report was published in 1991 and covered:

- general conclusions and themes emerging from the Committee's work

- arrangements in Scotland and Northern Ireland for gathering epidemiological data, managing outbreaks of food poisoning and food surveillance
- production of red-meat, milk and milk products, fish and shellfish
- the transport of food, retailing and wholesaling, catering and the consumer and the home
- education and training
- research into the microbiological safety of food.

Many of the recommendations from the Richmond Report are still being addressed. It is evident from the Report that there are considerable improvements to be made to all aspects of the food chain.

If the consumer is to be adequately protected from the risks associated with inadequate food safety systems, major changes will be required within many sectors of the food industry. Formal quality assurance systems based on sound basic food safety principles are currently uppermost in the minds of those in the food industry as means of achieving the highest quality of food which is now being demanded by the consumer and the Government.

## The Ministry of Agriculture, Fisheries and Food (MAFF)

MAFF's responsibility for food is aimed primarily at

> ensuring that a safe, nutritious, varied, high quality and appropriately labelled food supply is available so that consumers may choose a satisfactory diet.

Furthermore, it aims to encourage innovation and competitiveness in the production and processing of food through science and technology initiatives.

In 1989, some of MAFF's functions were reorganised and the Food Safety Directorate was formed. The Directorate's main responsibility is to ensure the safety and quality of food produced and sold in the UK.

In 1992 MAFF employed in excess of 340 scientists in the Food Safety Directorate to provide advice to ministers on food issues, to operate an extensive surveillance system and to direct its comprehensive Research and Development (R&D) programme.

Table 3.1 illustrates how the Food Safety Directorate is organised and details briefly the main focus of each of the four main groups.

The R&D programme is extensive and a major part of the Food Safety Directorate's work in developing and improving scientific knowledge in support of the Ministry's policy initiatives. The objectives of the R&D programme are to:

– promote the production and supply of foodstuffs which meet the demands of UK consumers and export markets
– encourage the development of efficient and competitive food and drink manufacturing and distribution industries
– promote high standards of food quality, hygiene and safety and to ensure that consumers are given adequate nutritional information.

MAFF is committed to a programme of food research which will assist in maintaining and improving the safety, quality and nutritional value of the UK's food. One particular research programme of special interest to the catering industry is the development of Hazard Analysis and Critical Control Point (HACCP) systems for the hygienic control of foods and processes.

Important links between countries within the European Community working on R&D programmes have already been established. FLAIR (Food Linked Agro-Industrial Research) has been set up within the EC framework for R&D which concentrates on the processing, distribution and consumer aspects of food.

Research and development is important to the food industry if it is to survive in a very competitive market, and to provide continually a safe, nutritious, varied and high quality food supply.

## Department of Health

The Department of Health is responsible for the protection of public health and takes lead responsibility for food hygiene and safety matters. Currently, one of the Department's main functions is to formulate

## Table 3.1: Food Safety Directorate

**FOOD SAFETY GROUP**

1. Consumer Protection
   (Food legislation and enforcement, food labelling and composition, food quality, diet and nutrition, Consumer Panel, Codex Alimentarius Commission, public enquiry point for FSD).

2. Chemical Safety of Food
   (Food contaminants, food contact materials, novel foods, irradiation, fertilisers and feedingstuffs, food additives).

3. Microbiological Safety of Food
   (Food hygiene policy).

**FOOD SCIENCE GROUP**

1. Food Science I,
   (Additives and chemical contaminants including radionucleides).

2. Food Science II
   (Microbiology, composition, nutrition and technology).

3. Chief Scientists' Group
   (Food science research and development; policy formation and appraisal).

4. Food Science Laboratory, Norwich
   (Research and development in food science).

5. Torry Research Station
   (Research and development in food science).

**ANIMAL HEALTH AND VETERINARY GROUP**

1. Animal Health (Disease Control)
   (Notifiable and other diseases).

2. Animal Health (International Trade)
   (Import/export of live animals and genetic material; control on artificial insemination and embryo transfer).

3. Animal Health Resource Management
   (Management services division).

4. Animal Health (Zoonoses)
   (Salmonella and other zoonotic diseases).

5. Animal Health and Welfare, Veterinary Section
   (Control and eradication of notifiable and other diseases, welfare of animals).

6. Animal Welfare,
   (Welfare of animals on farms, in transit and at markets; secretariat of Farm Animal Welfare Council).

7. Meat Hygiene
   (Public health matters relating to meat; import/export of meat and meat products; welfare at slaughter).

8. Meat Hygiene Veterinary Section
   (Public health matters relating to meat).

9. Veterinary Field and Investigation Services.

**PESTICIDES, VETERINARY MEDICINES, EMERGENCIES GROUP**

1. Pesticides Safety
   (Pesticide approvals and controls).

2. Veterinary Medicines Directorate Executive Agency
   (Approval and licensing of veterinary medicines, National Surveillance Scheme for Residues in Meat, Secretariat to the Veterinary Products Committee).
   * The head of the group is responsible for policy advice to Ministers on veterinary medicines. The Director and Chief Executive of the VMD report to Ministers on operational matters.

3. Emergencies and Food Protection
   (Planning to deal with emergencies affecting safety or security of national food supplies; and statutory joint authorisation of routine radioactive discharges).

4. Biotechnology Unit
   (Co-ordination and representation of the Ministry's interest in biotechnology with particular regard to genetic modification).

**Source: Food Safety Directorate Information Bulletin**

Regulations under the Food Safety Act 1990 and produce Codes of Practice under section 40 of the Act. Codes of Practice are prepared with MAFF and the Welsh and Scottish Offices.

The Department works very closely with MAFF, and each provides the necessary support to the other in terms of food safety, quality and hygiene.

The DoH has been reorganised and a separate division dealing with environmental health and food safety has been set up alongside the existing medical and scientific divisions dealing with microbiological and non-microbiological food safety hazards.

The Department of Health and other Government departments (in particular MAFF, the Department of Environment and the Welsh, Scottish and Northern Ireland Offices), health authorities and Environmental Health departments work jointly to ensure that action on food safety, particularly outbreaks of food poisoning, is properly co-ordinated.

The Secretary for State has overall responsibility for the work of the DoH, but specific responsiblity for food safety matters falls to the Parliamentary Under Secretary of State.

The DoH's overall objective in relation to food safety is to protect the health of the public. It is the Department's responsiblity to ensure that Government policy on food and water quality takes proper account of health, particularly where there is concern relating to hazards caused by microbiological, chemical and radioactive contamination.

Together with MAFF, the DoH undertakes the central co-ordination of the management of outbreaks of food poisoning and provides advice to the public, Environmental Health Officers, doctors and industry to assist in containing any outbreaks as quickly as possible to protect public health. The DoH also monitors data provided by the Public Health Laboratory Service (PHLS) and the Communicable Disease Surveillance Centre (CDSC) on the incidence of foodborne illness and offers advice to a wide range of bodies on the interpretation of the data.

In relation to the catering industry, the DoH aims to encourage the development of policy and good hygiene practice as a means of ensuring the safety of food produced in both the public and private sector.

## Local Authorities — The Enforcement Structure

Food law is enforced by local authorities, although ministers do have some powers, relating in the main to emergency situations.

The responsibility for enforcing the Food Safety Act in England and Wales lies with two main bodies of professionals—Environmental Health Officers (EHOs) and Trading Standards Officers (TSOs).

There is a third body of expertise, the Public Analyst, who is not an enforcement officer but who provides a service to the other two bodies. The organisation of these three bodies and their responsibilities vary across the country and in some instances overlap. This is illustrated in Figure 3.4. For example, in the unitary or "single tier" authorities (London boroughs and metropolitan districts), a single authority discharges all responsibilities under the Food Safety Act. In Shire areas, where both county and district councils co-exist, the responsibilities are divided between the two tiers. Matters relating to public health, for example the fitness of food and food hygiene, are normally dealt with by district councils through EHOs. Matters relating to consumer protection, for example compositional and labelling regulations, are the responsibility of the county council through the TSOs. (However, this is not the case in all areas, as some counties have delegated some or all of their powers to district councils under agency agreements.)

**Figure 3.4: Professional Groups in Consumer Protection**

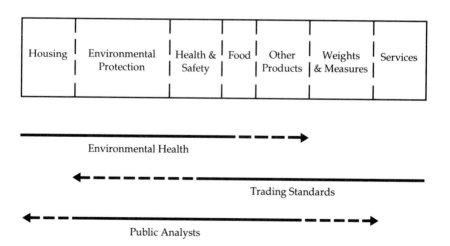

Source: Audit Commission Occasional Paper No. 15

The Food Safety (Enforcement Authority) Order prescribes which parts of the Food Safety Act can be enforced by either county councils, district councils or single tier authorities. In these circumstances the relevant section of the legislation refers to them as "food authorities" and to the officer carrying out those duties as an "authorised officer". A Code of Practice has been issued giving advice. However, the following parts of the Food Safety Act can *only* be carried out by *either* a district council *or* a county council:

- inspection and seizure of food can be carried out by any of the local authorities
- the issue of emergency prohibition notices can only be carried out by district councils (usually by an EHO)
- proceedings for falsely describing food can only be carried out by county councils (usually by a TSO).

Single tier authorities must enforce all parts of the legislation.

There are differing standards of enforcement between local authorities which affects both industry and the consumer; this should not cause serious difficulties as long as national standards and guidelines are not compromised. It is pleasing to see that many neighbouring authorities do liaise and share experiences and standards, and this co-ordination is essential. A number of Environmental Health departments are linked to the Institute of Environmental Health Officers' information service whereby there is a rapid exchange of information, problems and emergencies. Trading Standards departments also operate a similar system.

In 1978, a national Local Authority Co-ordinating Body on Trading Standards (LACOTS), was set up to co-ordinate guidance on trading standards. One particular area of development by LACOTS, which has been welcomed by manufacturers and retailers, is the "home authority" principle. This is operated by TSOs all over the country and involves companies dealing with the officers in their own area to establish standards for their products which may be distributed and sold nationally. Whilst the system is voluntary, standards agreed in the home authority are normally accepted by other authorities, although there are some exceptions to this.

This year has seen the extension of the remit of LACOTS to include food safety. Members of LACOTS have worked towards encouraging and supporting greater uniformity of standards in food work throughout the UK and in Europe through the forum of FLEP, Food Law Enforcement Practitioners.

Under the new Food Safety Act, Codes of Practice are now in operation and these are serving to set standards on a national scale for EHOs.

The enforcement structure does cause some confusion to the public, and to the food industry. The major issue seems to centre around unclear responsibilities — this also causes confusion amongst the enforcers. One of the biggest problems is the different interpretation of the law between and within local authorities. This can cause real difficulties for operators in the industry who work on a national scale.

The food industry structure has changed significantly away from the local producer and supplier to multi-national operators. However, the interpretation and enforcement of the law is mainly at local level. The benefits of local enforcement are still in evidence, and the new Codes of Practice will hopefully assist in bringing about a national standard of interpretation.

The Audit Commission has reported on this in *Safer Food: Local Authorities and the Food Safety Act 1990*. This report, published in December 1990, was the second in a series of four reports which focused on the work of Environmental Health Departments. It discusses in some detail the current enforcement structure and some of the major problems relating to responsibilities and interpretation of the law. The Commission concludes that changes to the enforcement structure are needed and that the recruitment of specialist staff at local level, for example food technologists, should be encouraged.

There is widespread concern that the enforcement structure is struggling to keep abreast of technological advances in the food industry, particularly in processing and manufacturing. The increase in the complex nature of many food processes is creating problems for enforcement authorities in terms of expertise, organisation and enforcement power, ie the ability to accept and pursue major offences which may involve extensive legal costs. Food safety is becoming more scientific and the Audit Commission comments that enforcement authorities will require expertise which goes beyond the standard training of Environmental Health and Trading Standards Officers.

Perhaps one of the areas which has not changed significantly in terms of technical processes and procedures, is the catering industry. Whilst the industry has changed in size and structure, very few new systems, other than cook-freeze and cook-chill, have occurred which require enforcement officers to have different expertise and qualifications. For the catering industry the existing local enforcement structure is relevant and in most cases appropriate. The problem of different local interpretations of the law is, however, a continuing problem.

The question of whether there are enough resources both in terms of numbers and expertise to adequately enforce the law is an important issue facing the enforcement authorities. The Richmond Report Part 1 stated that there were a significant number of EHO posts vacant because of limited financial resources within local authorities. In December 1988 a survey by the Society of Environmental Health Officers estimated an overall shortfall of about 8% in the existing numbers of EHOs. To a certain extent, the situation regarding insufficient resources to enforce the law has been counteracted by the food industry itself employing its own specialists to implement the necessary quality assurance systems to ensure that all aspects of the current legislation are being adhered to. The Richmond Report also referred to the lack of appropriately trained people available to fill the vacant EHO posts — part of this problem could also be related to the food industry employing suitably qualified people at salary rates above those achievable within local government.

The resource issue will be further compounded by the influence of European Community directives. For example, the Directive on the Control of Foodstuffs (89/397/EEC) will have far reaching effects. It calls for the regular inspection of the complete food chain, including additives, packaging and labelling. Additionally, the EC will be collecting statistics from Member States which will be an added burden for many local and national bodies.

Self-regulation is becoming increasingly important and many operators within the food industry are seeking certification to BS 5750 or other similar quality assurance systems. This trend of self-regulation is to be encouraged as it shows a real commitment from the industry to food safety. What should be developing in the industry is a working partnership with the enforcement bodies to ensure that every attempt is made to meet the current legislative requirements. This is starting to happen, but there are still many parts of both the food industry and the enforcement structure which still have to change their attitudes to food safety. For food safety to really become an integral part of the industry it can no longer be a one-way process of enforcement. The will to succeed must start with the operators.

# THE EUROPEAN COMMUNITY AND UK FOOD LAW

The Treaty of Rome (1957) set up the European Economic Community. One of its principal objectives was to remove barriers to trade between the Member States of the EC. As far as food law is concerned, Articles 30 and 36 of the Treaty address this issue.

In 1985, the EC Commission produced a White Paper in which it set out a plan to achieve a single market free of all barriers to trade by the end of 1992.

Following the 1985 White Paper on completing the internal market, the Commission published a further Communication on Community Legislation (COM (603) Final) on foodstuffs in relation to the internal market. This set out the Commission's position on foods. In summary, it stated that in view of the difficulties in reaching agreement on the very specific measures proposed in the 1969–73 programme for the harmonisation of food legislation, a new approach would be adopted. In essence, a clear division would be made between subjects still needing legislation and those which could be regulated by individual case law. The document COM (603) Final set out the future shape of Community food law and the policy surrounding it that would be followed by the Commission in making proposals for Community food law.

The aim of Community food legislation is to ensure a high standard of public health protection, adequate consumer information and fair trade. The 1985 Communication specifies that the following measures must be covered by legislation:

– those designed to protect the life and health of humans, as referred to in Article 36 of the Rome Treaty: ie those which concern food additives, materials and articles in contact with foodstuffs, contaminants, manufacturing and treatment processes and dietary foodstuffs
– those needed to satisfy mandatory requirements for fair trading and the protection of consumers: ie labelling, presentation and advertising of products, and those which provide for official checks.

# DEVELOPMENT OF EC FOOD LAW

The main bodies involved in the development of basic food law in the EC are the Commission, the Council and the European Parliament. The Commission has the sole right of making proposals.

In very simple terms, for a proposal to become Community framework legislation in the food sector, there needs to be agreement wthin the Council of Ministers on a Commission proposal for legislation. Such an agreement needs to take proper account of the views of the European Parliament, and there exists a structured, formal procedure to ensure this happens.

There are a number of ways in which the development and consideration of proposals for Community law may be influenced. First, before a proposal is made, the relevant Commission officials may be lobbied either by Government or by industry. In addition, the Commission occasionally convenes informal working groups to inform development of proposals they are considering. Second, when the Commission has made a proposal to the Council, the UK Government's negotiating position is informed by seeking views from interested parties in the UK. This is the opportunity for industry and others to feed in views and opinions. Third, changes may be achieved during negotiations in the Council and either via the UK delegation or via input from the European Parliament. Euro MPs from the UK can be briefed by UK interested parties either in Government or outside.

# DIRECTIVES AND REGULATIONS

These are the two main types of Community legislative instruments:

- Directives are directed to the Member States and have to be implemented into their own legislative frameworks
- Regulations, once adopted in Brussels, are directly applicable in the laws of the Member States.

Therefore, where the instrument is a directive, then relevant regulations have to be made under UK legislation in order that the directive has effect in the UK. The UK Food Safety Act 1990 provides powers for ministers to make regulations and put them before Parliament in order to implement Community obligations. Where the instrument is a regulation, with direct force of law in the UK, implementing action is not normally required, but often is required to introduce penalties.

# FRAMEWORK DIRECTIVES FOR FOOD LAW

The European Commission is carrying out a major programme to harmonise food safety law throughout the Community and the work is now well advanced.

In the context of food, the harmonisation process has taken two directions. First, *horizontal* measures which apply across a range of different foods or a widely defined group of foods, eg labelling, materials in contact with food, etc, and second, *vertical* measures which apply only to an individual specific food category, eg jams or meat products.

Progress as far as horizontal measures are concerned has been much faster and more effective than discussions relating to foods subject to vertical controls, perhaps because they deal with broad issues and also because of "comitology" changes. Old vertical directives required unanimous agreement, "new" horizontal measures are agreed by qualified majority voting. (Vertical measures are not part of the "new approach" set out in 1988.)

The need for well-balanced and convincing horizontal EC legislation has been recognised and, with few exceptions, industry does not support vertical, recipe standards. The difficulty of ever drafting legislation which would define a European standard for jams or meat products where national products vary enormously, defeated the legislators. The previous route of harmonising recipe laws has been abandoned in favour of mutual recognition of national standards, with informative labelling being the mechanism by which consumers can make their choice and distinguish between products. It would appear that the issue of "Eurojam" will not concern the present generation and may never come to fruition!

Five framework Directives have been agreed and passed by Council, which provide for subordinate legislation to be passed to implement the detail. These are framework Directives on:

(a) food additives, which sets out a positive list of authorised additives and gives a list of the foodstuffs in which the additives may be used with conditions of use

(b) food contact materials, which sets general criteria for the approval for use in contact with food of only those substances which are not transferred to foodstuffs in quantities likely to endanger health under normal conditions

(c) foods for special dietary uses, which provides a framework for future measures on foodstuffs which are clearly distinguishable from those for normal consumption. The nutritional use must suit either those people with disturbed digestive or other metabolic processes, or those who benefit from reduced consumption of certain substances, or infants and children

(d) food labelling, which sets general rules for label information to be provided for all foodstuffs sold to the ultimate consumer. It prohibits misleading information and removes national regulations which would restrict the free movement of goods. The latest amendment, Directive 89/395/EEC, replaced the "best before date" with the date of last consumption for perishable foodstuffs

(e) official control of foodstuffs, which sets general principles for the official inspection of foodstuffs from the farm to the point of sale, and materials and articles which come into contact with foodstuffs. All these issues must be encompassed within the Member State's inspection system.

It is likely that the Directive for the official control of foodstuffs will be followed by other directives in this area. The proposal for an EC Directive on the Hygiene of Foodstuffs (COM (91) 525) was published in the Official Journal (OJ) of the European Communities on 31 January 1992. The proposal has been circulated for consultation to interested parties in the UK and is concerned with a general, horizontal approach to establishing common food hygiene provisions in the European Community.

In particular this proposal would:

– establish broad principles and certain conditions for the hygienic production, distribution and sale of food to the final consumer
– introduce essential of legislative provisions, consistent with ensuring food safety, supported by voluntary documents of good hygiene practice to deal with the detailed application
– require Member States to encourage industry to develop such documents, based on the UN Codex Alimentarious Commission's *General Principles of Food Hygiene*.

Negotiations on the proposed Directive on the Hygiene of Foodstuffs are well underway and it is expected that the Directive will be adopted in the spring of 1993. The UK delegation is led by the Department of Health, supported by the Microbiological Safety of Food Division of the MAFF Food Safety Directorate.

The influence of Europe on food law has been considerable and will certainly continue to influence any future changes to UK law. The Single Market is here and if the proposed Commission timetable is to be met, the proposed legislation will need to be finalised in a very short space of time. While there was pressure to agree outstanding food legislation prior to 1 January 1993, this has not been possible, due to:

- some measures not having been tabled, and
- realistic implementation dates being built into the measures to give Member States time to bring in the necessary legislation and industry time to adapt to changes (eg two years is usual for labelling changes).

The main aim was to have the framework in place by the end of 1992, with negotiations well advanced on important subsidiary measures.

There is concern in the UK food industry that resources at national and Community levels are being stretched to meet the timescale being imposed. Consequently, the resulting legislation may not benefit from proper or sufficient discussion and consultation. However, the EC are not committed to meeting deadlines at the expense of properly thought through measures and realistic implementation dates.

Community legislation relating to the food industry will continue to be enacted and it is vital that the UK Government is a leader in the discussions formulating the detailed proposals within this legislation. Whilst the UK food industry has its problems, the Food Safety Act 1990 will assist in overcoming many of these difficulties. It is imperative that the future under this recent legislation is not compromised by EC legislation.

# THE FOOD SAFETY ACT 1990

The Food Safety Act 1990 which came into force on 1 January 1991, strengthens and updates previous legislation and widens the range of measures available to local authorities to enforce the law. By widening the legislation to cover "food sources", the Act applies to all sectors of the food industry from farmers to retailers and caterers and covers all operations involved in selling, processing for sale, delivering, preparing, labelling, storing, importing and exporting food.

UK food law is based on many historical precedents and the Government now also has the wider influence of the EC to consider in formulating new legislation. Table 3.2 summarises the history of food legislation.

The new Act replaces the existing primary food legislation in England, Wales and Scotland with a single statute covering the UK. In Northern Ireland, the Food Safety Act came into force on 27 May 1991. The Food Safety Act 1990 is now the primary legislation under which numerous Regulations govern such issues as compositional standards, the use of additives, food hygiene and labelling, as well as many others.

Any offences under the Act and Regulations are *criminal offences* and are prosecuted in the courts by local authorities. The Act has certainly given the enforcement authorities greater and more appropriate powers to assist in the maintenance of the food law. One of the main features of the Act is the wide enabling powers it gives ministers to issue regulations, under section 16, in response to developments in technology and science and the increasing number of directives being issued by the EC Commission. In

---

### Table 3.2: History of Food Legislation in England and Wales

| | |
|---|---|
| 1266 | Bread and Beer Act |
| 1872 | Adulteration of Food and Drugs Act |
| 1875 | Sale of Food and Drugs Act |
| 1875 | Public Health Act |
| 1928 | Food and Drugs (Adulteration) Act |
| 1938 | Food and Drugs Act |
| 1955 | Food and Drugs Act |
| 1984 | Food Act |
| 1990 | Food Safety Act |

this way, it will ensure that the public are protected properly now and in the future and that every effort is made to ensure that the highest standards of food safety are maintained.

To make sure that food authorities execute and enforce the Act to a common standard, section 40 gives ministers the ability to issue Codes of Practice, which serve as operating guidelines. In addition the Act introduces new offences, defences and penalties.

The philosophy behind the Act is to place the responsibility for food safety clearly where it belongs, ie with the relevant people in the food chain be it farmer, manufacturer, retailer or caterer.

The impact on the catering industry has been varied. Many organisations operate to a very high standard and will have few problems in complying with the new requirements. However, as the Audit Commission/EHO *Premises Condition Survey* (June 1990) illustrated, many catering organisations will find complying with the legislation an expensive and time consuming process.

The new legislation is an ideal opportunity for operators who have not given food safety the priority it deserves, to plan for the future and to ensure that they succeed as a reputable catering organisation providing a safe quality product to all customers.

# THE MAIN PROVISIONS OF THE ACT

The main provisions of the Act, which are contained in Part II, are summarised in this chapter, the detail can be found in the Food Safety Act itself.

*Sections 1 to 6 — Definitions*

Explains the definitions used in the Act.

## Food Safety

*Section 7 — Food Injurious to Health*

Offences under the Food Safety Act are divided broadly into two groups: food safety offences and consumer protection offences.

Under section 7, it is an offence to render any food injurious to health by adding to it, subtracting from it, processing or treating it.

This section not only covers the person who purposely tampers with food but also includes such actions as undercooking which may make a food unsafe to eat.

In deciding whether any food is harmful to health, the short and long term effects of eating the food will be taken into consideration. The definition of harmful to health will include any impairment, whether temporary or permanent.

## *Section 8 — Selling Food not Complying with Food Safety Requirements*

The second food safety offence is selling food which does not comply with the food safety requirements. This provision is particularly relevant to catering establishments. There is no definition of what the food safety requirements are in the Act; instead the Act specifies when food fails to comply with those requirements.

This is a wide ranging provision which defines failure to comply as follows:

–   food which has been rendered injurious to health by means of any of the operations in section 7
–   food unfit for human consumption
–   food so contaminated that it would not be reasonable to expect it to be used for human consumption.

When any food which fails to comply with the food safety requirements is part of a batch or consignment of the same type, it shall be presumed that all of it fails to comply.

It is an offence to sell, offer, display, advertise, have in possession or send or deliver, for the purposes of preparation or sale, any food which does not comply with the food safety requirements.

The Act defines a sale in very broad terms and any food will be assumed to be for human consumption until the opposite is proved.

## *Section 9 — Inspection and Seizure of Unfit Food*

Powers are provided to authorised officers to inspect any food which they believe may not satisfy the food safety requirements. If the food fails to comply the enforcement officer can either:

- issue a detention notice to the person in charge of the food, requiring it not to be used for human consumption and to be kept in a safe place, or
- seize the food and remove it in order to have it dealt with by a magistrate.

If it appears that the food fails to comply with the food safety requirements, an authorised officer need not necessarily inspect the food before seizing it or issuing a detention notice. The officer can act solely on the information received.

If a notice is served, the officer must decide within 21 days whether the food complies with the food safety requirements or not. If the food does comply, the notice must be withdrawn. If the food does not comply, then it will be seized and dealt with by a magistrate. Any person who contravenes a detention notice is guilty of an offence.

If the magistrates' court decides that the food fails to meet the food safety requirements, then the food must be destroyed.

If a detention notice is withdrawn under section 9 or a magistrates' court does not condemn the food, the food authority must compensate the owner of the food for any depreciation in the food. Code of Practice No. 4 gives a series of guidelines to food authorities on the inspection, detention and seizure of suspect food. Figure 3.5 summarises the procedures under section 9.

*Section 10 — Improvement Notices*

Section 10 of the Act is a new, powerful tool for enforcement officers, since failure to comply with an improvement notice is itself a criminal offence.

Power to serve improvement notices exists where there are reasonable grounds for believing that the proprietor of a food business is failing to comply with one of the relevant food hygiene or processing regulations.

There are initially two forms of action that enforcement officers can take if they suspect that the aforementioned regulations are not being adhered to and that the contravention does not pose an imminent risk to health:

- issue an informal notice in the form of a letter requesting certain measures to be undertaken, or
- issue an improvement notice.

## Figure 3.5: Summary of Procedures under Section 9 of the Food Safety Act 1990

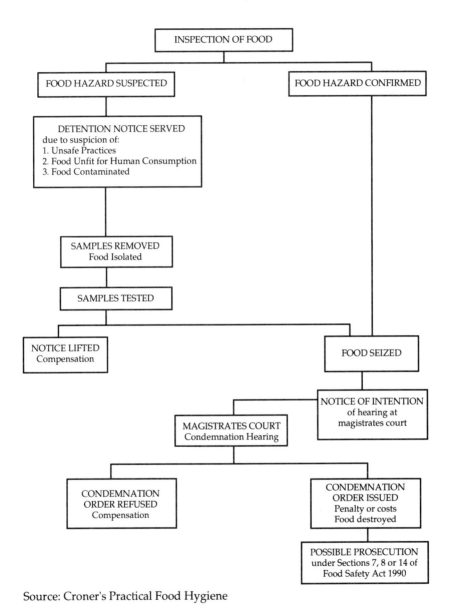

Source: Croner's Practical Food Hygiene

This notice must specify:

- the reasons for believing that the proprietor is not complying with hygiene or processing regulations
- the ways in which the regulations are being breached
- the measures to be taken to put things right
- the time allowed (not less than 14 days).

Any person who fails to comply with an improvement notice shall be guilty of an offence.

Section 37 provides an appeal to the magistrates' court against the service of an improvement notice. The time limit for an appeal against an improvement notice is either one month from the date the improvement notice was served, or the period specified in the notice if this is shorter.

Code of Practice No. 5 provides guidance on the use of improvement notices.

*Section 11 — Prohibition Orders*

This section enables a magistrates' court to make a prohibition order on public health grounds.

The section deals with the health risk conditions in respect of the operation of a food business. A health risk condition is one which involves the risk of injury to health in respect of:

- a process or treatment
- the construction of the premises or the use of equipment
- the state or condition of any premises or equipment.

Prohibition orders may only be made after the conviction of a proprietor for violating any of the hygiene or processing regulations; and they can only be made against the proprietor or manager of a food business. Circumstances that may lead to a person receiving a prohibition order include repeated failure to adequately clean premises and equipment, and blatant disregard for health risks.

A proprietor has the right of appeal to a Crown Court; similarly a manager can appeal where an order has been made against him or her personally.

Prohibition orders last indefinitely but they can be lifted. An order in relation to premises, a process, treatment or equipment must be lifted once the local authority is satisfied that the risk of injury to health no longer exists. A prohibition order on a person can only be lifted after an application to the court, but not earlier than six months from the date of the original order.

Figure 3.6 summarises the procedures under sections 10 and 11 of the Act.

*Section 12 — Emergency Prohibition Notices and Orders*

This section allows for immediate action to be taken by EHOs where health risk conditions exist to the extent that there is imminent risk of injury to health. This is a new power for the enforcement authorities, who can now serve an emergency prohibition notice immediately.

The issue of an emergency prohibition notice will immediately close a premises, or prevent a particular process or piece of equipment from being used. There is no right of appeal against such a notice.

Emergency prohibition notices can be issued without the intervention of the courts and only have a three-day life. Within this period the enforcement officers must make an application to the court for an emergency prohibition order.

If satisfactory measures are taken to remove the imminent risk to health before the court hearing, the enforcement officer may issue a certificate lifting the emergency prohibition notice.

An emergency prohibition order cannot be made against a person. Figure 3.7 summarises the procedures under section 12.

*Section 13 — Emergency Control Orders*

Section 13 provides power for a minister to make an order prohibiting the carrying out of a commercial operation in respect of food, food sources or contact materials which may involve imminent risk of injury to health.

## Consumer Protection

*Section 14 — Selling Food not of the Nature, Substance or Quality Demanded*

The offences under section 14 and section 15 are mainly consumer protection offences and are judged in relation to consumers' expectations.

## Figure 3.6: Summary of Procedures under Sections 10 and 11 of the Food Safety Act 1990

```
┌─────────────────────────────────┐
│     INSPECTION OF PREMISES       │
└─────────────────────────────────┘
┌─────────────────────────────────┐
│  CONTRAVENTIONS OF HYGIENE       │
│  OR PROCESSING REGULATIONS       │
└─────────────────────────────────┘
┌─────────────────────────────────┐
│  NO IMMINENT RISK TO HEALTH      │
│  Subsequent action may follow one│
│  or more of the routes below at  │
│  the discretion of the local     │
│  authority                       │
└─────────────────────────────────┘
```

**IMPROVEMENT NOTICE ISSUED***
including details of:
1. Offences
2. Reasons for Notice
3. Measures to be Taken
4. Time Limit

**INFORMAL NOTICE**
Letter requesting certain works to be undertaken

**MEASURES NOT COMPLETED**

**MEASURES COMPLETED**
No further action

**SUMMONS ISSUED**

**MAGISTRATES COURT**
Prosecution under hygiene or processing regulations and/or for non-compliance with an improvement notice

**CASE DISMISSED***

**CONVICTION***
Penalty

**PROHIBITION ORDER***
if risk to health remains against:
1. Premises
2. Process
3. Equipment

**PROHIBITION ORDER***
if risk to health remains against the person

**APPLICATION FOR LIFTING OF ORDER**
to the local authority

**APPLICATION FOR LIFTING OF ORDER**
made to magistrates court after 6 months' minimum

**CERTIFICATE ISSUED**

**CERTIFICATE REFUSED***
Notice issued giving reasons

**APPLICATION REJECTED**

**ORDER LIFTED**

**RE-APPLICATION**
after 3 months' minimum

* An appeal may be made at this point.

Source: Croner's Practical Food Hygiene

## Figure 3.7: Summary of Procedures under Section 12 of the Food Safety Act 1990

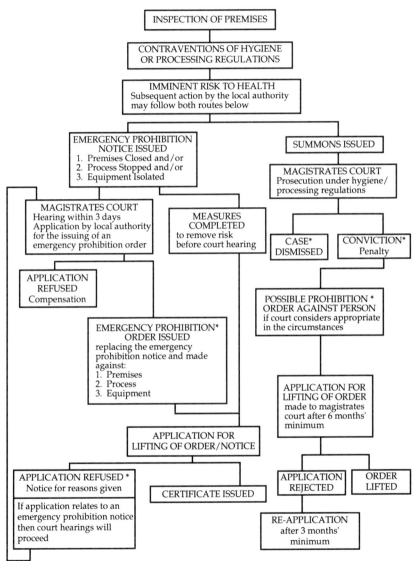

* An appeal may be made at this point.

Source: Croner's Practical Food Hygiene

Section 14 makes it an offence to sell to the purchaser's prejudice any food which is not of the nature, substance or quality demanded, for example:

Nature     –    Different kind or variety, eg cod instead of haddock
Substance   –    Not containing proper ingredients, eg foreign bodies
Quality     –    Inferior to that demanded by the purchaser, eg battery eggs sold as free range eggs

*Section 15 — Falsely Describing or Presenting Food*

This section prohibits false and misleading descriptions of food by way of labelling and advertising. Falsely describing a food item on a menu would be a contravention under this section. It is also an offence to present foods in such a way that it is misleading.

## Regulations

*Sections 16 to 19 — Regulations*

The Food Safety Act allows regulations to be made controlling a number of situations. Examples are:

–   to ban substances for use in food production
–   to require food to meet microbiological or quality standards
–   to require, prohibit or regulate processes or treatments
–   to require owners of food businesses to observe hygienic practices
–   to prohibit, or to impose standards for labelling, marking, presenting and advertising food
–   to control materials which come into contact with food.

Regulations will also cover the enforcement of EC provisions without the need for primary legislation.

## Defences

*Section 20 — Offences Due to Fault of Another Person*

An enforcement officer is able to bypass the immediate offender where in fact the offence was committed by another party. An example would be where a foreign body was found in a food item sold but not prepared by the caterer, for instance a pre-packaged sandwich.

*Section 21 — Defence of Due Diligence*

A statutory defence is provided where the defendant can prove that he or she took all reasonable precautions and exercised all due diligence to avoid committing an offence.

For offences against sections 8, 14 and 15, special provision is made for persons who neither prepared the food themselves nor imported it into the UK. Such persons will have exercised all due diligence if they can prove that:

- the offence was committed by some person not under the control of the defendant
- the offence was the result of information provided by a person not under the control of the defendant
- checks were carried out or it was reasonable to rely on the supplier's system of checking
- there was no knowledge of the offence
- the offending product was not sold under the defendant's brand name and the first, second and fourth points above can be proved.

If it is alleged that the offence was due to a third party, information in writing must be made available to the court concerning the third party.

The Food Safety Act has introduced many changes to food legislation, but probably the most significant is the "due diligence" defence, together with the abolition of all of the defences in the 1984 Food Act.

Prior to the Food Safety Act, food law offences in the UK were "absolute offences". This regime of strict liability caused injustice where a person was held to have committed an offence for which he or she had no responsibility at all, or because of an accident or some cause completely beyond his or her control. Proof of quality assurance systems only served to reduce the penalty after conviction.

With the fast progress of the food industry now involving many links in a chain, often divorced from each other by distance, the "absolute offence" was no longer deemed to be fair or appropriate in all cases. Therefore, although offences committed under sections 7, 8, 14 and 15 of the 1990 Act are still strict liability offences, a defence of due diligence is now permitted.

Also prior to the Food Safety Act, food legislation contained the so-called "warranty" defence. A person accused of an offence needed to prove that when purchased the product had a written warranty, that there was no reason to believe that the product could not be legally sold or dealt with and that the product was the same as when first purchased, if conviction was to be avoided.

The defence of due diligence is not new; it appears in the Trade Descriptions Act 1968 and the Weights and Measures Act 1985, two other Acts that are concerned with consumer protection.

Therefore, although the due diligence defence is not very familiar to the food industry, it is a well known defence in consumer protection law, and there is a considerable body of case law, with much having already been written and discussed about the defence. It is not within the scope of this book to expand fully on the subject, but it is perhaps worth commenting that there are no infallible paths to making out a defence.

However, it is very pertinent to the purpose of the book that a well documented quality assurance system will most likely attract the defence, although this cannot be guaranteed. In many instances, the catering industry is using section 21 of the Act as the means by which resources can be channelled into the design and implementation of an appropriate quality assurance system, such that in the event of an offence being committed, due diligence will be easier to prove.

## Miscellaneous and Supplementary

*Section 22*

This provides a defence for advertising, printing or publishing businesses which publish an offending advertisement in good faith during the normal course of their business.

*Sections 23 to 26*

Section 23 enables local authorities to run food hygiene training courses and to contribute to the costs of such courses run by other people.

Under section 25 powers are given to ministers to obtain samples from food businesses or to gain information regarding food substances or contact materials.

## Administration and Enforcement

*Sections 27 to 31 — Sampling and Analysis*

Authorised officers may purchase or take samples of food or any other substance used in the preparation of food or of any contact material. These samples are then sent to either a public analyst or microbiologist. Code of Practice No. 7 provides guidance on sampling for analysis or examination.

*Sections 32 to 33 — Powers of Entry*

Authorised officers can enter food premises at all reasonable times for the purpose of enforcing the law. "Reasonable" normally means when the business is operational. Provisions also exist for forcible entry, including powers to inspect, seize and detain records.

It is an offence for any person to obstruct intentionally enforcement officers during the course of their duty, or to provide false or misleading information.

*Sections 34 to 39 — Prosecutions*

Offences may be tried at either a magistrates' court or by a jury at the Crown Court, but the first hearing is always at a magistrates' court.

Penalties for offences under the main provisions of the Act are up to £20,000 per offence. For other offences, fines are up to £5,000 per offence and a prison sentence of up to six months when tried in a magistrates' court. Fines are unlimited in Crown Courts and prison sentences are up to two years.

## Codes of Practice

*Section 40*

Under section 40 of the Food Safety Act ministers may issue codes of practice to guide food authorities on the execution and enforcement of the Act and regulations made under it. The codes of practice aim to ensure that some degree of consistency is achieved across all local authorities.

The catering industry will find them useful in understanding how the enforcement authorities intend to apply the law and copies are available from the HMSO. (See Appendix 1 — Sources of Advice and Useful Addresses.)

To date, 13 Codes of Practice have been issued under section 40:

No. 1   Responsibility for Enforcement
No. 2   Legal Matters
No. 3   Inspection Procedures
No. 4   Inspection, Detention and Seizure of Food
No. 5   Use of Improvement Notices
No. 6   Prohibition Procedures
No. 7   Sampling for Analysis or Examination
No. 8   Food Standards Inspections
No. 9   Food Hygiene Inspections
No. 10  Enforcement of the Temperature Control Requirements of Food Hygiene Regulations
No. 11  Enforcement of Food Premises Registration Regulations
No. 12  Division of Enforcement Responsibilities for Quick Frozen Foodstuffs Regulations 1990
No. 13  Enforcement of Food Safety Act 1990 in relation to Crown Premises*

* Crown premises, which include the offices of Government Departments, prisons, canteens in magistrates' and Crown Courts, messes in military establishments and restaurants in Royal parks became subject to food legislation under the Food Safety Act 1990 in April 1992.

# MAJOR REGULATIONS AFFECTING THE CATERING INDUSTRY

Under section 19 of the 1990 Act, ministers can make regulations covering a wide range of food safety and consumer protection matters. There are many regulations which are pertinent to the food industry, but the catering industry is primarily concerned with the regulations relating to food hygiene, which include:

- Food Hygiene (General) Regulations 1970
- Food Hygiene (Amendment) Regulations 1990
- Food Hygiene (Amendment) Regulations 1991

The Government's White Paper identified a number of proposals which would have an impact on the food industry. Many of the proposals have been incorporated into the Food Safety Act itself, whilst others will form secondary legislation in the form of Regulations.

The catering industry will be greatly affected by at least two of these proposals. The first of these proposals was to introduce registration of food premises, which would enable local authorities to identify premises more readily; the Food Premises (Registration) Regulations 1991 came into force on 1 February 1992.

Second, proposals were included for the introduction of training for all food handlers. A consultative document was issued in 1990, but to date no firm recommendations have been made. It is however expected that training for food handlers will become mandatory, undoubtedly having a substantial impact on the catering industry. Regrettably, the Government have not communicated with the industry on the likely format of the proposed regulations.

Recent studies have found a clear link between good training and lower health risk. The Audit Commission/EHO *Food Premises Condition Survey* (Audit Commission Report No. 2, June 1990) specifically addressed the issue of training and concluded that there was a marked difference in the extent of staff training in the different types of premises. Those operations which presented a high health risk invariably had very poor assessments of training. Figure 3.8 illustrates the training in the different types of premises.

The main provisions of the food hygiene regulations and the registration of food premises regulations are outlined below.

# FOOD HYGIENE (GENERAL) REGULATIONS 1970

These regulations are concerned with the hygienic operation of food premises and relate to the majority of food premises including shops, restaurants, canteens, food factories, hospitals and takeaways.

Amendments to these regulations were made by the Food Hygiene (Amendment) Regulations 1990, which came into force on 1 April 1991, and

## Figure 3.8: Training in Different Types of Premises

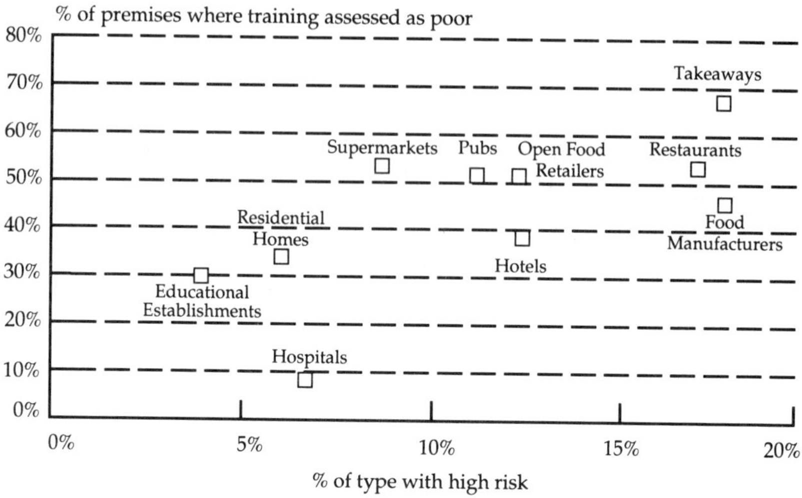

% of premises where training assessed as poor

% of type with high risk

Source: Audit Commission survey 1990

the Food Hygiene (Amendment) Regulations 1991, which came into force on 5 July 1991. The main changes are in respect of temperature controls. The main objective of the food hygiene regulations is to prevent food poisoning.

Part I of the regulations deals with the interpretation of certain words and phrases. Part II is concerned with general requirements; Part III relates to the handling of food and food handlers, and Part IV deals with food premises.

## General Requirements

*Regulation 6 — Insanitary Premises*

Food businesses must not be carried on at any insanitary premises or place where the condition, situation or construction is such that food is exposed to the risk of contamination.

A breach of this regulation may result in the issue of an emergency prohibition notice of the Food Safety Act 1990 (see above).

*Regulation 7 — Cleanliness of Articles of Equipment*

Food equipment and containers must be maintained in good condition, kept clean, be impervious and should not expose food to risk of contamination.

*Regulation 8 — Restriction on the Use of Premises*

Caterers cannot give out any food to be prepared or packed by any person in domestic premises (other than their own) where the food is to be subsequently sold on the caterer's premises.

## Food Handlers

*Regulation 9 — Protection from the Risk of Contamination*

Food handlers must take all reasonable steps to protect food from the risk of contamination, in particular:

– food must not be put in any place that endangers its safety, ie cooked food placed in contact with raw food
– unfit food must be separated from other food and appropriately labelled
– in any forecourt or yard, food must be stored 48cm above ground level, unless it is adequately protected
– open food, where reasonably necessary, must be kept covered or screened from possible sources of contamination when exposed for sale, during sale, or during delivery
– animal feed must not be kept in a food room unless it is in a closed container.

*Regulation 10 — Personal Cleanliness*

Food handlers must keep themselves and their clothing clean. Cuts must be covered with a waterproof dressing. Spitting and the use of tobacco is prohibited in food rooms.

*Regulation 11 — Protective Clothing*

Persons handling open food must wear clean and washable overclothing. This regulation does not apply to waiters, persons only engaged in the carrying of unskinned rabbits, hares, unplucked game or poultry and in the transport of food by rail or other carrier when the vehicle does not normally carry food. Persons carrying meat which is liable to come into contact with their head or neck must also wear head and neck coverings.

*Regulation 12 — Carriage and Wrapping of Food*

Food must not be carried in a container together with any article that may contaminate the food.

Materials used for wrapping or containing food must be clean and not liable to contaminate food.

*Regulation 13 — Persons Suffering from Certain Infections*

Food handlers with certain infections must report them to their supervisor who must notify the local authority. Infections which are notifiable include:

- typhoid fever
- paratyphoid fever
- other salmonella infections
- amoebic dysentery
- bacillary dysentery
- staphylococcal infections such as septic cuts, boils, throat or nose infections.

*Regulations 14, 15 and 16 — Drains, Cisterns and Sanitary Conveniences*

These regulations require drains and sanitary conveniences to be clean, operate efficiently and not expose food to risk of contamination. "Wash your Hands" notices must be displayed.

Under the Health and Safety at Work etc Act 1974 there must be an intervening ventilated space between a sanitary convenience and a food room.

*Regulation 17 — Water Supply*

Food premises must have an adequate clean, wholesome and constant supply of water.

*Regulation 18 — Wash Hand Basins*

All food premises must have suitable and sufficient wash hand basins placed in accessible positions. These basins must be supplied with hot and cold water, soap, nailbrushes and drying facilities. They must only be used for personal hygiene.

*Regulation 19 — First Aid Materials*

Adequate first aid materials must be provided. Antiseptic cream is no longer permitted.

*Regulation 20 — Accommodation for Clothing*

Provision must be made for the storage of outdoor clothing and footwear not being worn whilst working.

*Regulation 21 — Facilities for Washing Food and Equipment*

Suitable and sufficient sinks for washing food and equipment must be supplied.

*Regulations 22 and 23 — Lighting and Ventilation of Food Rooms*

Satisfactory standards of lighting and ventilation must be provided and maintained in all food rooms.

*Regulation 24 — Food Room not to be a Sleeping Place*

No food room can be used as a sleeping place.

*Regulation 25 — Cleanliness and Repair of Food Rooms*

The structure of food rooms must be kept clean and in good repair, such that they can be effectively cleaned. Food rooms must also be free from pests.

*Regulation 26 — Accumulation of Refuse*

Adequate space must be provided for the storage of waste. Waste must not be allowed to accumulate in a food room except for the proper carrying on of the business. All waste must be removed from the food room as often as is practical.

*Regulation 27 — Food Storage Temperature Controls*

The original Regulation has been amended, largely by the Food Hygiene (Amendment) Regulations 1990 and to a lesser extent by the Food Hygiene (Amendment) Regulations 1991.

The provisions now provide a more comprehensive scheme of temperature controls for high risk foods. Certain named foods must be kept at either below 8°C or above 63°C. From 1 April 1993 certain foods will be required to be kept below 5°C.

To assist caterers, the Department of Health issued a series of guidelines on the Food Hygiene (Amendment) Regulations 1990. This document provides a comprehensive interpretation of the Regulation and lists the relevant foods to which the Regulation specifically refers.

It is important that accurate temperature records are maintained as enforcement of Regulation 27 will take place through a series of normal hygiene inspections and measurements.

Delivery vehicles are covered by the Food Hygiene (Markets, Stalls and Delivery Vehicles) Regulations 1966. The temperature control requirements of these Regulations have also been amended by the Food Hygiene (Amendment) Regulations 1990. The Department of Health guidelines clarify the exact requirements.

Code of Practice No. 10 details guidelines on the enforcement of the new temperature control requirements.

## Administrative Provisions

*Regulation 28 — Exemption of Premises from Certain Requirements*

Certain food premises may receive a certificate of exemption where, due to circumstances, Regulations 17, 20 and 24 cannot be reasonably met.

*Regulation 29 — Offences*

Offences may be committed by owners, managers or individual food handlers. Food handlers are guilty of an offence if they fail to comply with

Regulations 9–13. Proprietors are guilty of an offence if any regulation other than 10 and 13 are contravened. In addition, they are guilty of an offence if they do not take all reasonable steps to ensure that their employees comply with Regulations 10 and 13.

Managers or supervisors of food handlers are guilty of an offence if they fail to take all reasonable steps to ensure that the food handlers comply with Regulations 9–13.

*Regulation 30 — Penalties*

Fines of up to £5,000 and/or six months' imprisonment can be levied against a person found guilty under these Regulations at a magistrates' court. If convicted at a Crown Court, the penalty is an unlimited fine and/or imprisonment for not more than two years.

# FOOD PREMISES (REGISTRATION) REGULATIONS 1991

These Regulations require that food premises (including vehicles and moveable structures) can only be used for the purpose of a food business if they have been registered by a local authority.

The purpose of the registration regulation is to provide local authorities with up-to-date information on the number and type of food premises by area which are subject to the Food Safety Act 1990. It will allow for resources and premises inspections to be planned more efficiently.

*Regulation 2 — Requirement for Registration*

All premises must be registered unless they are used for less than five days, whether consecutive or not, in any five week period.

An application for the registration of a new business must be made at least 28 days before the business opens.

*Regulation 3 — Exceptions*

Exemptions from the requirement to register may be given for certain types of premises. A full list is provided in the Regulations.

*Regulation 4 — Applications for Registration*

The registration process is outlined in Figure 3.9. Normally an application form must be completed by the proprietor of the business.

The content of the application form is specified by Regulation 4 and completed forms must be returned to the district council within whose area the food premises are situated. No forms or certificates of registration are issued.

*Regulation 5 — The Register*

Each district council must keep a register of all food premises which is to be made available to the public.

*Regulation 6 — Supplementary Records*

District councils are allowed to keep supplementary records of information relating to registered premises, eg the number of staff, types of food handled, etc.

*Regulation 7 — Supply of Information and Alterations to the Register*

New registration forms must be completed where there is a change in proprietor.

If there is a change in the nature of the business, the change must be notified within 28 days of it taking place.

*Regulation 8 — Offences*

There are a number of offences under this Regulation, such as failure to apply for registration, failure to notify any change to the business, etc.

Offences are dealt with by a magistrates' court and, on conviction, a fine is imposed.

The Richmond Report, Part 1 recommended that a system of formal licensing involving prior inspection should be introduced to cover a wide range of food operations, including all catering operations. However, the Government has not adopted this full recommendation and has opted for

## Figure 3.9: Registration of Food Premises

A flow chart to explain the registration provisions of the Food Premises (Registration) Regulations 1991 — what premises need to be registered and by whom

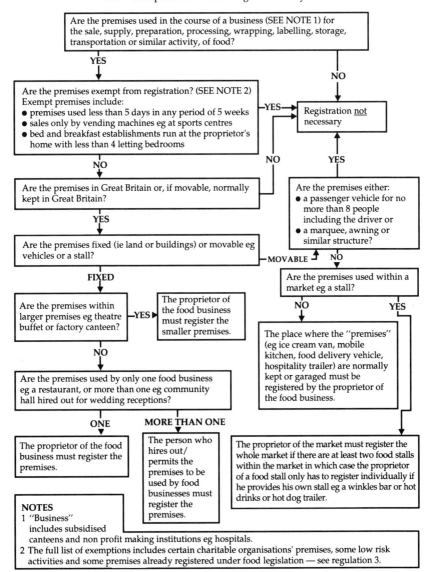

Source: Roger Peters, in *Hospitality*, April 1992

registration only. Licensing will be restricted to irradiation plants, dairy farms and dairies at the present time.

Whilst registration is certainly a welcome progression, the opportunity for businesses to start trading and yet not fully comply with the food laws is still a reality.

# THE WAY FORWARD FOR THE CATERING INDUSTRY

The Food Safety Act is now well established but there is still concern as to the number of catering businesses who do not understand fully the content and implications of the Act.

Larger catering organisations often have internal resources which enable time to be spent understanding, interpreting and implementing the necessary changes required. Others, particularly the small businesses, find it difficult to afford such resources or time to keep up-to-date and invest in the changes required.

The changes to the legislation have, on the whole, been welcomed by the industry, the major impact being that the customer can be assured that greater effort is being made to prevent food safety problems from manifesting themselves. Unfortunately, food poisoning will continue, but it is hoped that the enforcement powers of the local authorities will be sufficient to curb the rising food poisoning statistics. The onus is now definitely with the caterers to ensure that their operations are managed and run effectively and meet the current legislation.

Keeping up-to-date with the legislation, both actual and proposed changes, is not easy. MAFF commissioned a survey which investigated the general public's knowledge and perception of various aspects of food poisoning and food hygiene (*Food Hygiene — Report on a Consumer Survey* 1988). The results demonstrated that half of the respondents felt that they did not have easy access to information on the subject, with knowledge being gained mainly from friends, magazines, and schools.

Various initiatives have been taken to provide the catering industry and the public with more information on the changes to food law and their implications. Appendix 2 details a list of useful leaflets, guidelines and brochures which have been produced to assist with this process. Some are free to the public but others attract a small charge.

Food safety is vital to the success of a catering business and enforcement officers now have the power to prevent businesses that do not satisfy the food safety requirements from operating.

The catering industry has definitely been active in taking on board the new food legislation, some sectors more prominently than others. New legislation always brings with it a surge of enthusiasm, and resources are found to make sure that the necessary changes are implemented. Caterers must guard against the often natural reaction to relax the system and standards once the original impetus of meeting the new challenges laid down by the legislation has passed.

Food safety should, however, be an integral part of any catering business, not an add-on function. It is with this in mind that the implementation of a quality assurance system can be of real benefit, as not only are the requirements of the legislation fulfilled, but also a quality product in the widest sense is provided for the customer. Systems such as HACCP have been quoted by the Richmond Committee and other bodies, as being one of the ways that the catering industry can tackle the issue of ensuring that operating standards are sufficient to meet the food safety requirements. This subject is discussed fully in Chapter 4. HACCP is a system primarily related to food safety, but there is an increasing trend for it to form part of a more widely developed quality assurance system encompassing the whole business.

Developing and implementing a quality assurance system is one method whereby food safety can be integrated, monitored and controlled as part of the total business. Quality assurance systems move with the business, and as new food safety regulations are issued by the Government the mechanism and vehicle for change is already in place. In addition, the system prevents a relaxing of standards — this is vital if the catering industry is to strive to improve its image and reputation regarding food safety.

Food law in the UK is no longer agreed and introduced solely at national level. Increasingly, food law is being harmonised within the EC, and decisions made at a very high level by the Council of the European Communities.

The UK Government will face a vital task in ensuring that the controls now apparent under the Food Safety Act and subsequent Regulations are not compromised by EC decisions, particularly in respect of food hygiene.

# Chapter 4

# HACCP — The Concept, Development and Application

Hazard Analysis Critical Control Point (HACCP) is a structured approach to assessing the potential hazards in a catering operation and deciding which are critical to the safety of consumers. The main aim of HACCP is to control the safety of the final product eaten by the customer.

This chapter examines why the technique of HACCP is now considered to be an essential tool in controlling food safety, and looks at a suggested approach to its application in the catering industry. The technique has only really been applied to the control of food safety and not to the wider control of other quality related issues, although it certainly has wider applications. Whilst HACCP is a quality system, it is narrower in its application than, say, BS 5750 or TQM, both of which embrace the wider aspects of an operation. HACCP's main aim is to control operational hazards related to food safety. Nevertheless, for many caterers, the implementation of the HACCP system will be the first step down the quality route, and is therefore a positive step towards improving the industry's food safety record.

## THE EVOLUTION OF HACCP

The catering industry has been at the forefront of much publicity and concern relating to the safety of food which culminated in the Food Safety Act being introduced by the Government. With the rising incidence of food poisoning outbreaks, managers operating in the industry have a real responsibility to the public to make more determined efforts to curb this trend.

Approximately 40,000 cases of food poisoning were reported in 1988, almost three times the total for 1982 (see Figure 4.1). Caterers were quoted as being responsible for over 70% of general outbreaks in 1988 by the Communicable Disease Surveillance Centre. Whilst there are many critics who challenge the validity of the figures produced, the picture is, nevertheless, not good and one which needs urgent action to reverse the trend.

The technology now available to operators throughout the food chain from farmer to chef have advanced considerably to meet consumer demands. Customers are demanding the all year round supply of fruit and vegetables from across the world, extended shelf-life and a wider choice of prepared foods and complete meals. Consequently, production, distribution and the service of food has undergone rapid change, bringing with it a host of unknowns. Micro-organisms, such as listeria monocytogenes, are now a threat, to the extent that in 1989 the Chief Medical Officer issued

## Figure 4.1: Notifications of Food Poisoning
## England and Wales 1980-1988

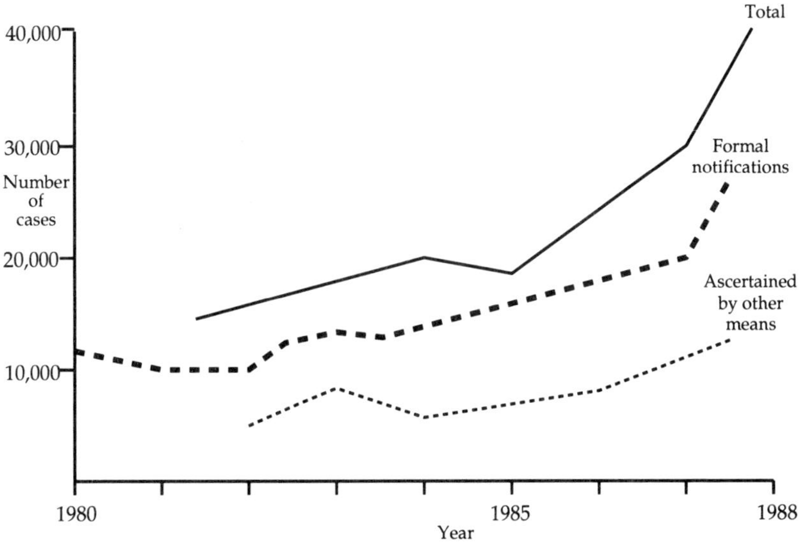

Source: Office of Population Censuses and Surveys.

a statement to the public warning pregnant women and other vulnerable groups of people to avoid eating certain foods which were known to contain the micro-organism. In addition, new pathogens are being introduced into the UK from foreign countries as a result of a large influx of people from all over the world, particularly Asia, and these are presenting the food industry with new challenges.

All of these factors are increasing the pressure on the catering industry, as part of the wider food industry, to control sufficiently the production and service of food so that the safety of the products can be assured. Unfortunately, too many catering operations rely on outdated operating manuals, distant training and good luck to control food hygiene and safety. Some even operate without any written information whatsoever!

Conventional approaches to controlling food safety rarely constitute a complete control system because they can be haphazard, fragmented, and only operated when there is "time" or when pressure is applied as a result of, say, a visit from an Environmental Health Officer. Most operators have cleaning schedules (supplied by the cleaning materials supplier), stated standards of personal hygiene, rules for reporting illness and other traditional controls, but very few have a total, fully comprehensive and practised control system.

The Richmond Report Part 1, referred to in Chapter 3, was published in 1990 and comments were made on the HACCP system. The Committee endorsed the general consensus outlined in the 1980 World Health Organisation report and other international documents, stating that "this is a sensible approach to good manufacturing practice if properly carried out".

The second part of the Richmond Report, published in 1991, recommended that

> caterers should follow a disciplined and carefully structured approach to the identification of hazards and control points; and that advice to caterers should emphasise the importance of this approach for the safe management of catering operations.

The Report finally recommended that the Government should take the lead in drawing up a set of guidelines for the catering industry, with the onus being placed on the enforcement authorities to ensure that the guidelines reached individual caterers.

Towards the end of 1991, the Department of Health published a leaflet entitled *HACCP — Practical Food Safety For Businesses* which outlines briefly what HACCP is, its advantages and how to set up a HACCP system. The leaflet has been distributed via the enforcement authorities but can be obtained direct from the Health Publications Unit. (The address is given in Appendix 1.) In addition, the Hotel Catering and Institutional Management Association published a revised Technical Brief—Sheet No. 5, in 1991, which provides an overview of the system.

A great deal of work has been published on the subject of HACCP and other references are included in the Bibliography, but it has been recognised that the implementation of a full HACCP system for many smaller caterers may be inappropriate. Nevertheless, what the Government is suggesting is that a form of HACCP should be operated in all catering establishments.

# THE HACCP CONCEPT

The original development of the HACCP concept was the result of a joint effort between three American organisations, the Pillsbury Company, the National Aeronautics and Space Administration (NASA) and the US Army Natick Laboratories, to produce zero-defect foods for astronauts. It is actually based on an engineering system which consists of examining all of the components and processes involved in making a product and establishing what can go wrong within the total system. Since the early 1970s, its application has been expanded within the various sectors of the food industry, particularly in food manufacturing, but as already explained, it is only very recently that its application in the catering industry has become a reality.

Understanding the terms used in the HACCP system is important and they should be precisely defined and used if the analysis is to be of real value. Furthermore, anyone who is involved in the HACCP process must understand the terms and use them correctly. Some definitions are given below.

– A *hazard* is a potential cause of harm to the customer from physical or microbiological contamination of the food product.
– A *control point* is a location, stage, operation or raw material which prevents safety hazards being realised.

- The *risk* is the chance that the hazard would be realised.
- *Hazard Analysis* is the identification of all ingredients, stages in processes, environmental features and human factors that are potentially hazardous to the safety of what the customer receives.
- *Critical Control Points (CCPs)* are the points at which control is essential to guarantee that potential hazards cannot at some time become actual hazards (not all possible points of control are CCPs).

HACCP is a logical, systematic approach for monitoring and managing effectively the hygiene and food safety aspects involved with food production. It can in fact be applied to every aspect of the food chain, but its application here will be restricted to food production in the catering industry. The benefits of implementing a HACCP system are wide ranging, but the financial benefits are more difficult to assess since it is hard to put a price on food safety other than the extreme of life itself. The most obvious benefit will be compliance with the food safety legislation and guidelines, which in turn will lead to increased customer confidence and the development of a good reputation.

# HACCP AND THE CATERING INDUSTRY

The benefits to be gained from introducing a HACCP system are significant, but the development work and commitment required by all levels of staff should not be underestimated. The Department of Health recognises that the implementation and application of a full HACCP system is not an easy task, and recommends that advice be sought from experts to assist with the process.

The limited application of the HACCP system in the UK catering industry is now set to change; but undoubtedly management will come up against a number of issues with their own operation which may need extensive changes to be made if an effective quality system is to be introduced and maintained. The catering industry does have a number of features which may cause teething problems to the introduction of a HACCP system, and a number of these are discussed below.

*Non-standardised working practices and methods* are often found in catering establishments. It has only recently become more common to see operations' manuals which document procedures and practices. These are invariably found in systemised operations such as cook-chill and cook-freeze. The use of standard recipes and methods is not a common feature in the majority of catering operations other than perhaps in systemised operations and public sector operations such as hospitals and schools. Many caterers advocate the use of standard recipes, but the reality of the situation is that prestigiously clean copies are held on file in the office which have never seen the light of day except at the printer's! This situation is improving, but it is a feature of better cost control as well as quality control.

*The use of inefficient equipment and poorly designed facilities* is a serious concern and one which will not disappear overnight. It is widely recognised that major capital expenditure is required across the catering industry. Many operations are riding on the back of the current legislation in an attempt to encourage the release of funds for expenditure on kitchens and support areas. The large, over-equipped kitchens of the past are now causing problems. The equipment does not function effectively and operators are forced to improvise. The distances that have to be walked by the operators is excessive and leads to short cuts being taken — one journey is taken to the refrigerator instead of several, leading to the improper storage of foods for extended periods of time. New designs are taking modern approaches to catering into consideration but there are still many caterers who are facing the future in less than satisfactory premises.

*Extensive handling of food products* is a common feature of every-day catering. There is definitely a move towards the use of more prepared foods such as meat and vegetables, but the actual preparation of a product which comprises many ingredients still involves a lot of handling, for example, the preparation of a mixed salad. Where the handling of foods is excessive the risk of contamination is increased. Tight vigilance concerning personal hygiene is therefore of utmost importance if the preparation and production of food items is to be controlled and the risk of contamination reduced. Many products and dishes also require a staged approach to complete the dish. An example would be the preparation of a chicken and mushroom pie, which involves many distinct stages: the cooking and cooling of the chicken, the preparation and cooling of the mushroom sauce, the making of the pastry, the combination of the ingredients and the final cooking. Such a multi-process operation needs very careful planning and control to avoid the real possibility of a food safety problem.

*An inadequately trained workforce* is a frequent problem in the industry as has already been shown in earlier chapters. Insufficient training is frequently a cause of standards not being attained. However, for training to be effective, it is also important that the correct procedures and standards to be achieved are clearly stated and communicated. This is further complicated by the excessive use of casual and part-time seasonal staff that the industry relies on to cope with peak periods of trading. Investing in the training of this category of staff is often neglected with the hope that common sense and help from the permanent staff will resolve any problems.

*Time constraints imposed by set service periods* is common in conventional kitchens where production is geared up to meet set service times and demands from the customer. Whilst demand is forecasted, the desire to avoid waste by over-production often leads to pressure and stress when demand exceeds expectations but where a service still has to be provided. Planning does not enter into the criteria for success, but any action is taken to cope with the demand, often involving short cuts being taken such as the inadequate cooking of food items to avoid "keeping the customer waiting" — a naive and dangerous practice. One of the advantages of systemised operations is the separation of production from service and hence the removal of the service hysteria.

*The requirement for flair and innovation* is what attracts and retains many chefs and cooks in the industry. Removing the craft element of the job is, to many, the end of the craft. Standardising practices and procedures is not about removing flair and imagination, but just about making sure that food is produced in the correct, safe way every time. Trends and fads in the industry also crop up from time to time, such as nouvelle cuisine. Regardless of whether the trend is good or bad, the associated beautiful presentation of the food must pose serious questions regarding the amount of handling involved and, therefore, the time element involved when foods must be either going cold, or getting warm.

Putting these potential problems to one side, there is no doubt that the concept of HACCP has a guaranteed future in the catering industry. The degree to which a full HACCP system is introduced will vary from operation to operation and will depend on the resources available and the style of the operation.

The development of a full HACCP system is complex and requires skilled input from specialists such as microbiologists, as well as from management, chefs and equipment engineers. Whilst HACCP is attainable by most caterers, the reality is that many operators would not invest the necessary resources required. Most caterers may not be in a position to set up such teams of people or be able to undertake the development work in the detail required. Lack of time and the availability of resources is not a valid argument against putting in a full HACCP system, particularly since the objective is to produce safe food. However, the realities of the industry are that many operators struggle to adhere to the food safety legislation and would find the concept of HACCP even more difficult.

Caterers who operate cook-chill, or other forms of systemised catering, may find the introduction of a full HACCP system easier than other caterers, as cook-chill systems already operate within a series of strict guidelines laid down by the Department of Health (*Guidelines on Cook-Chill and Cook-Freeze Catering Systems* 1989). The successful implementation of the technique across the catering industry is going to be a very long process, but of greater importance is that caterers are assisted in the development of a control system which is easy to operate and to maintain, but which achieves the end goal of producing safe food. It may be, therefore, that an appropriate starting point for many caterers, particularly the smaller operators, is to develop and introduce a simplified HACCP system and that on-going developments will build on and strengthen the system for the future

# SETTING UP A HACCP SYSTEM

The process outlined in this chapter examines a simplified approach to HACCP. For organisations in food manufacturing, it is vital that a comprehensive, detailed system is implemented. Campden Food Preservation Research Association in Technical Manual 19 — *Guidelines to the Establishment of HACCP* sets out such an approach. For many catering operators, these Guidelines are too technical and require interpretation by experienced and qualified experts in the field of microbiology. For many catering organisations, such an approach would be impractical, complex and off-putting. What must be remembered is that any system introduced must be understood by those who have to operate it.

The catering industry is not as fully automated as food manufacturing, and therefore many tests and inspections carried out as part of a quality assurance system will be undertaken manually by operators with basic food hygiene skills. Food manufacturers often have the benefit of a full quality assurance team to develop, implement and maintain a system such as HACCP. The majority of caterers are not in such a position. It could be argued that such a full, comprehensive system as found in food manufacturing is not required by the catering industry, because of the quick turnover of food products and the small scale of most catering operations. However, the catering industry is reported as being responsible for 70% of food poisoning outbreaks and this must surely suggest that a relatively comprehensive quality assurance system is required by those operating in the industry. Ultimately, it is for each organisation to decide on the complexity of the system to introduce; the objective will always remain the same, ie to ensure that a safe product is produced. The approach outlined here will enable any catering organisation to establish a sound, practical system based on the principles of HACCP.

## HAZARDS

Before moving on to describe the stages involved in setting up a HACCP system it is worth examining the typical types of hazards which are most common in the catering industry.

In terms of ensuring safe food, the emphasis is on trying to prevent the contamination of food by micro-organisms or foreign objects that could cause the customer some harm, examples being the bacteria salmonella or a foreign body such as a fly. It is unrealistic to expect a caterer to prevent all contamination but what is expected is that further contamination is prevented and the potential for bacteria to grow is minimised. A good knowledge of food hygiene and food safety is needed to be able to identify and analyse the hazards within an operation.

The technique of hazard analysis in the catering industry should reveal where the main hazards are likely to occur and the main sources of contamination.

The category of hazards most likely to be revealed by analysing the operational processes include:

– potentially hazardous foods, for example raw poultry
– pathogenic foodborne organisms, for example salmonella
– employee practices which may cause or fail to prevent the transfer of pathogens to foods, for example sneezing over food will transfer staphylococcus

- time/temperature conditions that permit the survival of, promote the multiplication of, or fail to destroy foodborne pathogens, for example failing to cook chickens to a minimum of 70°C for two minutes
- procedures that may contaminate foods after reheating, for example serving utensils which have been used on raw foods and then on a reheated product
- environmental conditions that may permit the maintenance of foodborne pathogens, for example the use of contaminated water for washing salads and vegetables.

Given that any one or a combination of the hazards described above may be present in a catering operation, the HACCP process will, if carried out properly, identify:

- potentially hazardous foods or ingredients
- likely sources and points of contamination at each stage of the various catering processes
- the potential for micro-organisms to survive at each stage of the catering process
- the potential for micro-organisms to multiply in food products by establishing time/temperature relationships.

In catering establishments, the areas where problems are most likely to occur include:

(a) incoming raw materials and their storage
(b) time and temperature control at all stages of the operation
(c) people hygiene, and
(d) equipment and environment hygiene.

## Raw Materials and Ingredients

Raw materials and ingredients must be examined on delivery because they are a possible source of contamination, for example raw poultry carries salmonella. Extra care must be taken to separate raw from cooked food at this stage. For the caterer, observation and thorough checking of packaging, labels and the food itself will help to reduce the risk of contaminated food being accepted and transferred into storage.

## Time and Temperature Relationships

Storage, cooking and holding times and temperatures of food products are critical to ensuring food safety. Clear standards must be set to prevent the survival or subsequent growth of pathogens. Certain time and temperature restrictions are laid down in the Food Safety Act, but time limitations including date coding must be addressed by the operators.

## People Hygiene

People as a source of contamination represent a significant hazard to the product as people carry pathogens naturally, for example everyone carries staphylococcus on their hands. In addition, people may have food poisoning themselves and not realise it and can therefore transfer pathogens from one place to another by cross-contamination from hands and protective clothing. High priority must be given to personal cleanliness, medical status, protective clothing, personal habits and working practices.

## Equipment and Environment Hygiene

The design and layout of kitchens and production areas has improved tremendously with the impact of new technology. However, many kitchens are not ideally designed and contamination can occur because of the way premises are laid out and hence operated. Particular attention must be paid to the structure of buildings, layout and workflows, ventilation, water supply and drainage, pest control, cleaning and waste and rubbish disposal. Consideration must also be given to the design of equipment, the materials the equipment is made of, the method of use and the way it is cleaned.

# HACCP APPROACHES

The development and implementation of a HACCP system requires a great deal of dedication and commitment from the whole workforce if its implementation is to be a success. It is important to understand that guidance can be given on how to introduce HACCP, but each catering operation is unique and therefore a purpose designed package will need to be developed to reflect each situation. A HACCP system is not something that can be bought off the shelf.

The choice of approach to implementing a HACCP system will be influenced by the expertise and resources available within the organisation. There are a number of different approaches to planning and implementing HACCP — three different options are described below.

## Option 1

Employ a specialist consultant to undertake most of the research, including identifying the hazards and critical control points of the operation. The consultant will assist the operator to set up the necessary control procedures and advise the operator of any problem areas to rectify. Regular surveillance visits would be carried out by the consultant to check on the systems and working practices.

## Option 2

As for Option 1 but the operator would undertake the main monitoring of the system in-house, once the system was in place, with limited back-up and support from the consultant.

## Option 3

Establish a full HACCP system in-house with the help of external experts to verify the system if necessary.

For many smaller caterers, Options 1 and 2 are likely to be more cost effective and workable than Option 3. However, it is likely that the larger the operation, the more important it becomes to consider the benefits of Option 3. In-house systems (such as Options 2 and 3) are invariably more effective than those which are controlled by a third party. This is due mainly to the commitment which will have been built up and the continual pressure to adhere to the system. The main drawback of Option 1 is that operators are likely to perform better prior to and during a visit from the consultant — this obviously defeats the object. However, the adoption of any one of the three options shows a commitment to the production of safe food for the customer. Ultimately, operators must seek advice to ensure that the most effective approach is selected for their business.

Whichever option is chosen, the work programme will be similar; the people carrying out the process will be the variable factor.

# THE HACCP PROCESS

The establishment of a HACCP programme falls into a number of discrete stages. These are illustrated in Figure 4.2.

**Figure 4.2: The Establishment of a HACCP Programme**

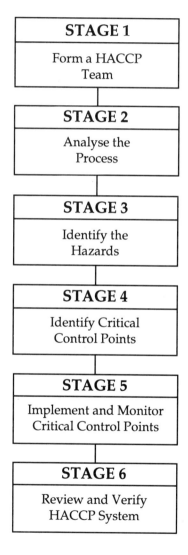

| STAGE 1 |
|---|
| Form a HACCP Team |

| STAGE 2 |
|---|
| Analyse the Process |

| STAGE 3 |
|---|
| Identify the Hazards |

| STAGE 4 |
|---|
| Identify Critical Control Points |

| STAGE 5 |
|---|
| Implement and Monitor Critical Control Points |

| STAGE 6 |
|---|
| Review and Verify HACCP System |

## Stage 1 — Form a HACCP Team

Establishing and implementing a HACCP system is a senior management responsibility. Before the development of the system can begin, senior management must agree the objectives for proceeding with the work and issue a policy statement to all members of staff. Management commitment is primarily one of accepting responsibility and leading from the top — without this commitment, the system may well fail. The major task facing managers is the need to persuade all levels of staff to adopt the correct attitude towards food safety. This may involve changes to working practices away from the easiest and quickest method, to a more time consuming but safe method. Figure 4.3 illustrates management's responsibilities to achieving high food safety standards.

Management alone, however, cannot develop and introduce HACCP. There is a tremendous amount of information to be collected which will form the framework of the system and, therefore, people working in the various parts of an operation will need to be involved. It is recommended that a team is set up to plan and implement the system as many different skills are required. Involving as many people as possible will assist in the process of gaining commitment to the system and its ultimate success. This is not to say that a large team should be formed, but a team which reflects the size and complexity of the operation.

In a food manufacturing operation it is likely that the team would include the production manager, microbiologist, an engineer, and cleaning specialist. In the majority of catering operations it is unlikely that such a team could be pulled together from internal resources. It is important, however, for the team to include members who understand the business, such as the manager responsible for the operation, the head chef, and maybe the restaurant manager. What is of utmost importance is that the team has a sound understanding of food hygiene, without which the system cannot be developed.

It may be appropriate in the first instance to seek advice from external experts to help put together a planned approach and to provide essential knowledge of microbiological issues, as required. Depending on the nature of the business, other disciplines may need to be involved at particular points in the development such as purchasing, marketing, product development and (where appropriate) distribution.

It must be remembered that for many catering operations, the manager

## Figure 4.3: Food Safety — Management's Responsibilities

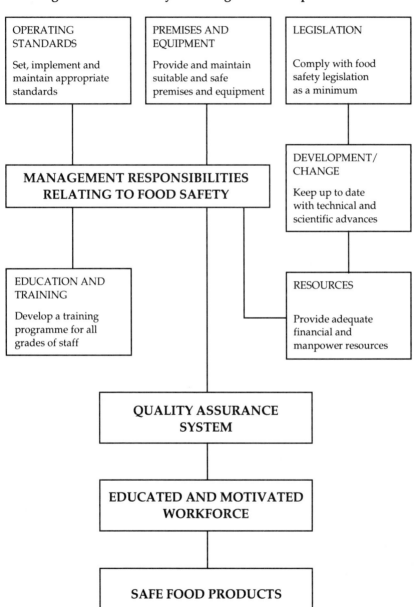

OPERATING
STANDARDS

Set, implement and
maintain appropriate
standards

PREMISES AND
EQUIPMENT

Provide and maintain
suitable and safe
premises and equipment

LEGISLATION

Comply with food
safety legislation
as a minimum

**MANAGEMENT RESPONSIBILITIES
RELATING TO FOOD SAFETY**

DEVELOPMENT/
CHANGE

Keep up to date
with technical and
scientific advances

EDUCATION AND
TRAINING

Develop a training
programme for all
grades of staff

RESOURCES

Provide adequate
financial and
manpower resources

**QUALITY ASSURANCE
SYSTEM**

**EDUCATED AND MOTIVATED
WORKFORCE**

**SAFE FOOD PRODUCTS**

and head chef are jointly responsible for all functions of the business. For operations with limited resources, it is advisable to involve the local Environmental Health department as soon as possible — they will provide assistance on how HACCP should be approached for a particular type of operation.

Before embarking on Stage 2, the analysis of the process, the team's first job will be to inform all the other employees of the plan to introduce HACCP. Reference has already been made to the need for commitment to the implementation of HACCP from all employees. This can be achieved in a number of ways, both formally and informally, but the information given to all staff must include:

- a simple outline description of HACCP
- the benefits of introducing the system
- who will be involved
- an overview of how the development work will be done
- how long it will take
- how much it will cost (if appropriate)
- how each member of staff can participate and how the system will affect them.

The method by which this information is communicated will depend on the size of the operation and the number of employees involved. One of the most effective methods of communicating this fairly complex topic is a simple verbal presentation or chat followed by an open question forum. It is unlikely that a bulletin or newsletter is likely to be effective, although this method of communication is more suitable as a means of updating people on progress. Small groups or one-to-one discussions are far more likely to be effective in the early stages.

The aim of the presentation must be to assure staff that introducing a HACCP system will be of benefit to the business and therefore to them personally. Staff must not be frightened or be put off by the terminology used — the words used to describe the system are difficult, unusual and appear very technical to the average catering person. Communicating effectively to the staff will make it easier to gain the commitment and co-operation needed to make the system work. It must not be forgotten that the whole process will be extremely difficult for many operators to understand fully and implement successfully in a short space of time. In addition, it must be impressed on staff that the system is for life and is not just another management fad which in time will go away. With this in mind, the team must plan to introduce a system which suits their operation and which is simple and understandable. A simple system can be further developed at a later date, a complicated system that fails is very hard to resurrect.

## Stage 2 — Analyse the Process

The first task that the team has to undertake is a thorough analysis of the process of producing each food product or group of products. The objective of this task is to identify where there are hazards to the product.

The analysis work should be undertaken by a member of the team who understands each process fully and a specialist, for example a microbiologist, who can observe the processes, identify sources of contamination, assess the levels of risk to the product and consumer and collect all the information relating to the product.

Given that most catering operations produce a wide range of products, an analysis of every product could, potentially, be an enormous, time consuming exercise. A suggested method for caterers with a multi-product operation is illustrated in the two-step process below.

*Step 1 — Product/Dish to be Analysed*

Decide which product or dish or similar groups of products or dishes to analyse first and then set priorities. Consideration should be given to:

1.  Raw materials where pathogens are commonly found, eg raw poultry, other raw meats, eggs, raw vegetables and rice.
2.  Bought-in foods (that have received some processing) which can support the growth of pathogens, eg cooked meats, dairy produce, mayonnaise and shellfish.
3.  Known problem areas with the production of particular items, eg those products that have been shown by microbiological analysis to be "suspect".
4.  Complicated processes for handling particular products, eg the preparation of composite pies such as steak and kidney which involve many processes.

The first step is to decide which products are high risk and which are not. Priority should be given to analysing products which include ingredients with a known potential hazard. Products which present a low risk should be analysed as a lesser priority.

*Step 2 — Evaluate the Process*

For each product identified in Step 1, information must be collected and documented for each stage of the production process.

In the first instance it is useful to draw a simple flow diagram of the process undertaken for each product without attempting to identify hazards or other issues which may emerge. This will enable the total production process for each product to be illustrated on one sheet of paper. An example of a flow diagram for the production of Beef Bourgignonne in a conventional catering system is shown in Figure 4.4.

## Stage 3 — Identify the Hazards

The next step is to evaluate each stage of the process flow to identify all the operations which occur when making the product. What needs to be documented is exactly what happens, not what the operators say happens. This can only be achieved by practical observation, which will involve following the product through its entire life-cycle. For products with several ingredients, each ingredient will have to be followed and documented separately to the point where they come together to form the finished product.

A suggested chart for the collection of data is illustrated in Figure 4.5(a). The complete hazard analysis process can be documented on this chart. A simple worked example is illustrated in Figure 4.5(b).

The information which needs to be collected at this stage includes:

(a) activity – the part of the process, for example, ingredient issue
(b) area – the area where the specific activity is taking place, for example, main dry goods store
(c) time started – the time the activity started
(d) time finished – the time the activity finished
(e) hazards identified – the identification of hazards perceived during the observation of the activity.

## Figure 4.4: Flow Diagram — Production of Beef Bourgignonne

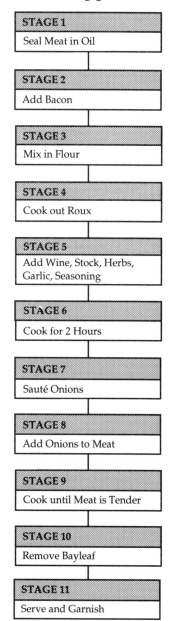

| INGREDIENTS | |
| --- | --- |
| Beef | Red Wine |
| Onions | Herbs |
| Oil | Flour |
| Stock | Seasoning |
| Bacon | Garlic |

**STAGE 1**
Seal Meat in Oil

**STAGE 2**
Add Bacon

**STAGE 3**
Mix in Flour

**STAGE 4**
Cook out Roux

**STAGE 5**
Add Wine, Stock, Herbs, Garlic, Seasoning

**STAGE 6**
Cook for 2 Hours

**STAGE 7**
Sauté Onions

**STAGE 8**
Add Onions to Meat

**STAGE 9**
Cook until Meat is Tender

**STAGE 10**
Remove Bayleaf

**STAGE 11**
Serve and Garnish

**Figure 4.5(a): Hazard Analysis — Product Process**

Company/Site _____     Date _____

Product _____     Compiled by _____

| ACTIVITY | AREA | TIME STARTED | TIME FINISHED | HAZARDS IDENTIFIED |
|----------|------|--------------|---------------|--------------------|
|          |      |              |               |                    |

**Figure 4.5 (b): Hazard Analysis — Product Process**

Company/Site ___Expert___  Date ___8/8/92___

Product ___Egg & Cress Sandwiches___  Compiled by ___Mr Expert___

| ACTIVITY | AREA | TIME STARTED | TIME FINISHED | HAZARDS IDENTIFIED |
|---|---|---|---|---|
| Boil eggs | Kitchen | 8.00 | 8.15 | — |
| Put eggs into cold running water | " | 8.15 | 8.30 | — |
| Shell eggs | Sandwich Room | 9.00 | 9.15 | Eggs still warm 35°C. |
| Mash eggs with salad cream, add seasoning & cress | " | 10.30 | 10.40 | Time delay – eggs not refrigerated. No hand washing. Stored in deep bowl. No opportunity to cool down. |
| Butter bread and fill sandwiches | " | 10.40 | 11.15 | Eggs still warm 15°C. |
| Cut, wrap & label | " | 11.15 | 11.30 | Not put into refrigerated display cabinet until 12.00. |

The identification of the hazards will need to be undertaken by a member of the team who is qualified to at least the advanced food hygiene certificate level.

At this stage it is also worth recording any other relevant information that could have a bearing on assessing the risk to the product, for example, working practices.

When identifying potential hazards, reference should be made to whether the hazard is direct process contamination, for example, hand contact, or indirect process contamination, for example, cracked floor tiles leading to inadequate floor cleaning.

Initially, this process must be followed for all products which were identified as high risk, and thereafter for all other products. This will ensure that whilst low risk products are less important, a thorough check is made to ensure that the processes involved do not constitute a potential hazard.

*Examination of Product Process Charts*

The next stage of the hazard identification process involves the thorough examination of the completed Product Process Charts. At this point the process has been clearly documented and the potential hazards identified.

Every stage of the process must be considered in turn. At each stage, the significance of each hazard identified must be discussed thoroughly. The questions to be addressed include:

– what is the possibility that contamination might occur at this point?
– what is the possibility that growth may occur for microbiological hazards?
– what is the possibility that microbiological or chemical hazards will be destroyed?

Once the true picture of the complete process is known and understood, every effort must be made to eliminate as many hazards as possible. This may simply mean changing working practices, changing suppliers, altering recipes and methods. In some instances, it may mean more fundamental changes such as re-investment in new equipment. An example of where new equipment would be required is for chilled products. Traditionally, products requiring chilling have been allowed to cool down in an ambient atmosphere or "next to the window''. This practice has now been deemed unacceptable. Investment in a blast chiller is now considered to be essential where hot products need to be chilled prior to consumption.

In some instances the hazard identified may have occurred because the member of staff involved had not carried out the task according to the laid down instructions. This may be due to inadequate training, a misunderstanding, staff shortages, an equipment fault or simply as a result of a short-cut having been taken.

It should be expected that these types of deviation from the correct method of carrying out a task will happen. What the HACCP team must do is identify clearly the best methods of controlling these deviations and prevent them from becoming serious hazards.

*Final Process Flow — Standards and Specifications*

After all the necessary changes have been made to the current practices and procedures to remove as many hazards as possible, a final process flow should be established for each of the products or groups of products.

This final process flow must identify the standards and specifications to be achieved at each stage of the process, for example, purchasing specifications and cooking times and temperatures.

To ensure the safety of the final product, every aspect involved in the production of the product needs to be specified with the standards to be achieved. It is not sufficient to assume that thorough cooking and chilling will eliminate the hazards. The environment, equipment, people and ingredients will all need to be controlled to minimise their hazard to the product. By establishing standards and specifications, the operation is establishing *control points.*

This is probably the most difficult part of the HACCP process and will take considerable time and discussion to agree the standards and specifications for each product and the processes involved.

Some standards are already available, for example, the temperature restrictions laid down in the Food Hygiene (Amendment) Regulations 1990 and 1991. The Department of Health guidelines for cook-chill and cook-freeze operations also lay down a series of standards to be achieved. Other standards and specifications may not be so easy to specify. It is at this point that HACCP needs the input from team members with expertise in microbiology, since consideration has to be given to food poisoning and foodborne pathogens, their growth characteristics and sources. This is not an area where many caterers would have the necessary knowledge to tackle this aspect of the process.

The catering industry has been governed by certain standards for very long periods of time and not surprisingly most caterers, if asked, would state that their operation follows set working practices, adheres to the food safety legislation and the employees are regularly trained. It is probably quite true that managers and operators do know what standards are expected of them — what is not perhaps so clear is why such standards are really necessary.

The setting of standards and criteria for a HACCP system forces caterers to think about the real meaning and worth of standards and, therefore, why they must enforce them at all times. Certain standards are so ingrained in every day working, such as cleaning equipment after use, handwashing and storing food at the correct temperature, that the real meaning as to why those practices are performed become lost. HACCP re-establishes the meaning of standards and their importance.

## Stage 4 — Identify Critical Control Points

The new process flow chart must identify clearly where the potential hazards still remain and the standard to be achieved which will prevent the potential hazard ever becoming a real hazard.

Each hazard identified on the final process flow chart then needs to be reviewed and a judgment made on its severity. It is important to assess the severity of each hazard and the associated risk. Where there is a high risk that the hazard could be realised, this point in the process becomes a *Critical Control Point* (CCP).

A critical control point can be a procedure, a process, a location or any operation which, if not controlled, could result in an unacceptable safety risk to the ultimate consumer.

The setting of standards throughout the process will identify a wide range of control points. With the HACCP system it is only those that are *critical* which need to be controlled. It may not be necessary, desirable or practical to attempt to exercise tight control over every hazard and potential risk identified. Determining which hazards to control, how and how often is the key to an effective HACCP system. The factors which need to be taken into account when determining which hazards are critical and which are not will include:

- the point in the process where the hazard occurs, eg where a product is to be cooked, contamination after cooking is probably more important than contamination occurring prior to cooking
- the ultimate consumer, eg pregnant women are advised to refrain from eating certain foods known to be susceptible to listeria monocytogenes
- the type of hazard, eg certain bacteria are more harmful than others
- legislation and guidelines: everyone must abide by the law of the land.

Some problems do arise at this stage when attempting to determine which hazards are critical and which are not, because of the way in which certain foods have been traditionally served in the UK. The classic example is "hot" rare roast beef. Where a customer requests a rare sirloin steak, should it be served or not? What is the level of risk? What about legislation, 63°C being the temperature at which hot food should be served? All of these questions would need to be addressed.

It is important not to exaggerate the potential risks from hazards. The absolute meaning of the word critical is important here — it is desirable to have the minimum number of critical control points which are required to ensure effective control over the product range.

It has already been stated that standards should be set, where appropriate, at each stage of the product process. These standards must reflect the acceptable limits within which the critical control points identified are to be controlled. Appropriate standards must be of a nature and level which will prevent the hazard from being realised at the critical control point and which can easily be checked to show whether control is being maintained.

Due to the limited resources available to most caterers, it is important that the standards and the critical control points set are realistic and as straightforward as possible. It is probably unrealistic for most caterers to set microbiological standards for finished products — controls would be expensive, retrospective and not understood by the majority of people. However, when setting up a new catering operation, or introducing a new product, it is often advisable in the first instance to undertake microbiological analysis to provide assurance that a satisfactory product can be achieved. Given acceptable results from the analysis, strict control of the critical control points is a reliable method of achieving product safety.

For the catering industry, suitable standards can be derived from legislation, codes of practice, guidelines and other recognised published information. Objective standards such as "cook to 70°C for two minutes" are much easier to understand and enforce than standards such as "total aerobic colony count after incubation of agar plates for 48 hours at 37°C — less than 100,000 per gramme". This is not meant to infer that microbiological standards are not useful, they are, but there are more useful preventative measures and standards which caterers can use.

It is essential to define some form of standard for each critical control point and the exact nature and complexity of the standard must reflect the severity of the hazard, the type of operation and the resources available.

Tables 4.1(a)-(i) (adapted from Bryan 1981) illustrate a typical food production and service work flow and highlight a series of hazards, critical control points, preventative measures (standards) and monitoring procedures. Whilst these are general examples, not specific to any product or range of products, the aims and objectives of a HACCP system are demonstrated clearly.

## Stage 5 — Implementation and Monitoring of Critical Control Points

At this point in the process, the following information for the HACCP model for each product or group of products will have been collected:

- activities
- potential hazards
- critical control points
- standards/preventative measures.

Having agreed the standard to be achieved at each critical control point, the next stage is to establish and implement procedures which will check that each critical control point is under control. It is important that each critical control point must be capable of being monitored.

For each critical control point established, a clear procedure must be drawn up which states clearly how the critical control point is to be monitored.

The monitoring procedures should measure accurately the factors which control the critical control point, should be simple to carry out and give quick results.

For the HACCP system to function properly, critical control points must be monitored by the people involved in the operation. This will help to ensure that everyone is involved in the system and committed to its success.

**Table 4.1(a): HACCP — Typical Food Production and Service Workflow**

| TASK | HAZARD | CRITICAL CONTROL POINT | PREVENTIVE MEASURES | MONITORING PROCEDURES |
|---|---|---|---|---|
| Purchasing and Receiving | Pathogens on raw food or ingredients | Incoming food | Separate delivery point for raw and cooked food | None practicable because many raw foods are contaminated with a variety of foodborne pathogens |
| | Foods obtained from unsuitable source | Food at source | Obtain food from approved and vetted suppliers | Check credibility of suppliers and their quality assurance system |
| | Food delivered at incorrect temperature | Incoming food | Reject | Take temperature of food and delivery vehicle |
| | Food and packaging shows signs of spoilage | Incoming food and packaging | Reject | Observe condition of food and packaging |

**Table 4.1(b): HACCP — Typical Food Production and Service Workflow**

| TASK | HAZARD | CRITICAL CONTROL POINT | PREVENTIVE MEASURES | MONITORING PROCEDURES |
|---|---|---|---|---|
| Food storage | Frozen Food | | | |
| | Thawing of frozen food | Temperature of food | Keep frozen foods frozen | Measure temperature of freezer and food. Should be –18°C |
| | Prolonged storage of frozen food | Time between freezing and use of food | Good stock rotation | Check use by date, texture of product |
| | Frozen food shows signs of spoilage | Temperature of food | Discard | Check condition of food for mould, smell, freezer burn, etc |
| | Chilled Food | | | |
| | Spoilage due to prolonged storage | Temperature of refrigerator | Maintain chilled food between 0-5°C | Check temperature of equipment and food and observe condition of food for signs of food spoilage |
| | Cross-contamination | Storage practices in refrigerators | Store foods separately or above raw foods, cover and label all foods | Observe storage practices |

**Table 4.1(c): HACCP — Typical Food Production and Service Workflow**

| TASK | HAZARD | CRITICAL CONTROL POINT | PREVENTIVE MEASURES | MONITORING PROCEDURES |
|---|---|---|---|---|
| Food storage | _Dry Stores_ | | | |
| | Physical damage to packaging | Check temperature and humidity of stores | Store in dry area, handle packaging carefully | Look at packaging for entry of moisture |
| | Poisonous substances contaminate food | Storage practices in storerooms | Store poisonous substances in separate room | Look for substances such as pesticides and cleaning materials in storerooms |
| | Contamination from pests | Storage practices, structure and condition of storerooms | Protect storerooms from entrance of pests, eg insects, rodents | Look for evidence of pest infestation, check areas where dirt may be harboured, check for food spillage |
| | Excessive heat causes food spoilage | Physical attributes of store area | Protect foods from excessive heat, maintain good air circulation | Look for evidence of heat sources, poor air circulation, foods on floor against walls |

**Table 4.1(d): HACCP — Typical Food Production and Service Workflow**

| TASK | HAZARD | CRITICAL CONTROL POINT | PREVENTIVE MEASURES | MONITORING PROCEDURES |
|------|--------|------------------------|---------------------|-----------------------|
| Preparation | Cross-contamination, hands and clothing become contaminated with foodborne pathogens | Handling raw foods | Wash hands and change protective apron after handling raw foods | Check if workers are washing hands, occasionally swab workers' hands and test |
| | Cross-contamination, equipment and utensils become contaminated with foodborne pathogens | Equipment and utensils that come into contact with raw foods | Clean and disinfect equipment, separate raw food areas and operations from cooked food areas and operations | Observe flow of raw foods and check that they do not go into areas used for cooked foods, check that equipment and utensils used for raw foods are washed and disinfected after use and before use for other foods, swab surfaces and test for pathogens |
| | Cross-contamination, cleaning cloths become contaminated with foodborne pathogens | Cleaning cloths used to clean raw food preparation areas | Use separate cleaning cloths in raw and cooked food areas, identify by different colours, use disposable cloths and destroy after each major use | Observe use of cloths and discard cloths after use |

**Table 4.1(e): HACCP — Typical Food Production and Service Workflow**

| TASK | HAZARD | CRITICAL CONTROL POINT | PREVENTIVE MEASURES | MONITORING PROCEDURES |
|---|---|---|---|---|
| Preparation | Growth of bacteria during room temperature storage | Time foods are exposed to room temperature | Refrigerate foods to be served cold, immediately after preparation | Check that food not to be cooked or to be served cold is kept refrigerated |
| Cooking | Survival of pathogens because of inadequate cooking | Temperature of food at completion of cooking | Cook potentially contaminated foods thoroughly, eat cooked food immediately after cooking | Insert thermometer into centre of cooked food, foods must reach 70°C for 2 minutes. Microbiological testing of food before and after cooking to check if heat process was effective |
| | Time delay between cooking and storing food; if storage practices are poor, bacteria multiply | Foods after cooking | Eat hot foods immediately after cooking or hold hot above 63°C or rapidly chill to 0–3°C | Check that hot foods are eaten soon after cooking, held hot or chilled rapidly |

**Table 4.1(f): HACCP — Typical Food Production and Service Workflow**

| TASK | HAZARD | CRITICAL CONTROL POINT | PREVENTIVE MEASURES | MONITORING PROCEDURES |
|---|---|---|---|---|
| Hot Holding | Growth of bacteria when temperatures are too low | Temperature of cooked food during hot storage | Hold cooked foods at temperatures higher than those at which pathogenic bacteria multiply | Test with probe thermometer, check to see that foods are above 63°C. Microbiological analysis of food if necessary |
| Room Temperature Holding | Rapid growth of bacteria | Temperature of cooked food during room temperature storage | Never hold cooked foods at room temperature for more than 30 minutes. Hold foods at temperatures higher than pathogenic bacteria multiply at or rapidly chill foods | Check that no foods are held at room temperature |
| Handling Cooked Foods | Contaminated by operators during handling | Cooked foods during preparing, slicing, handling or while in contact with equipment | Minimum handling of cooked foods, use utensils to handle food | Observe if cooked foods are handled by workers, check for poor personal hygiene or other poor food handling practices which may subject foods to contamination |

**Table 4.1(g): HACCP — Typical Food Production and Service Workflow**

| TASK | HAZARD | CRITICAL CONTROL POINT | PREVENTIVE MEASURES | MONITORING PROCEDURES |
|---|---|---|---|---|
| Handling Cooked Foods | Cross-contamination via equipment, utensils, cleaning cloths or hands | Cooked foods during handling and preparation | Use clean and sanitised utensils and equipment to process, hold or handle cooked foods | Look for possible routes of cross-contamination from raw foods to cooked foods. Swab surfaces and analyse as necessary |
| Cooling Cooked Foods | Growth of bacteria during long periods of room temperature cooling before refrigeration | Temperature of food during cooling | Chill rapidly | Look to see if cooked food is stored at room temperature. Check centre temperature of food, food should ideally chill down to 3°C within $1^1/_2$–2 hours. |
| | Growth of bacteria in large masses of foods during refrigerated storage | Size of storage container | Store foods in shallow containers during refrigeration | Check refrigerators to ensure that foods are not stored in deep containers |
| | High temperatures of refrigerators | Temperature of refrigerator air | Set refrigerators to run at low temperatures, check that air circulation is good | Record refrigerator air temperatures regularly |

**Table 4.1(h): HACCP — Typical Food Production and Service Workflow**

| TASK | HAZARD | CRITICAL CONTROL POINT | PREVENTIVE MEASURES | MONITORING PROCEDURES |
|---|---|---|---|---|
| Cooling Cooked Foods | Contamination of cooked foods from raw foods during improper refrigerated storage | Storage practices in refrigerators | Cover foods to prevent contamination. Locate foods to prevent contamination from drippage or direct contact. Store cooked foods in separate refrigerators or areas from raw foods | Check refrigerator to see if any cooked foods are stored in such a way that could lead to contamination from raw foods |
| Reheating | Survival of pathogens | Temperature of reheated foods | Reheat cooked left-over foods thoroughly to at least 70°C for 2 minutes | Check centre of food with probe thermometer to check that 70°C for 2 minutes has been reached |
| Cleaning of Equipment and Utensils | Cross-contamination | Equipment surfaces | Clean equipment and utensils thoroughly. Disinfect cleaned and rinsed equipment and utensils | Check that equipment is clean to sight and touch. Check for evidence of practical cleaning schedules, observe cleaning practices. Swab clean areas to check compliance with microbiological criteria |

**Table 4.1(i): HACCP — Typical Food Production and Service Workflow**

| TASK | HAZARD | CRITICAL CONTROL POINT | PREVENTIVE MEASURES | MONITORING PROCEDURES |
|---|---|---|---|---|
| Management and Operators | Poor operational procedures leading to contamination of foods and survival or growth of foodborne pathogens in foods | Procedures performed | Train and supervise workforce | Look for operations that contribute to foodborne diseases and for poor hygiene practices |
| | Contamination of foods by operators | Control of operators' health and work practices | Do not work when ill with diarrhoea, colds, infections, etc | Observe whether operators work when ill. Sign declaration of health when returning to work after illness |
| | Contamination of foods by operators | Standards of personal hygiene | Practise personal hygiene | Observe personal hygiene practices and ways in which foods are handled. Check hand washing procedures particularly after handling raw foods, visiting the toilet, coughing and sneezing. |

There are a number of questions to be addressed in designing the monitoring procedures, including:

(a) *how* are critical control points to be measured?
(b) *who* will carry out the monitoring procedure?
(c) *how often* will the critical control point be measured?
(d) *how* will the results of the monitoring procedure be recorded?
(e) *what* happens when there is a deviation from the standard?

*How* critical control points are measured may take many different forms, such as:

–   making observations
–   taking measurements, such as manual or automatic temperature monitoring
–   collecting and having food samples analysed
–   weighing products
–   time measurement
–   swabbing of surfaces for cleanliness.

It is important that any equipment which is used for measurement purposes is checked regularly for accuracy. It is recommended that any temperature monitoring equipment, such as hand-held probe thermometers or integral temperature monitoring systems, are calibrated at least six-monthly. Time clocks on equipment and weighing scales should also be calibrated regularly.

*Who* carries out the monitoring process is important to the success of the system. It is always more satisfactory if the operators involved with a certain process actually undertake the monitoring role, be it by observation or measurement. Supervisors and managers must also be involved with monitoring by reviewing the operators' results. This will ensure that the monitoring is being carried out effectively.

*How often* monitoring takes place will vary. It would be practically impossible to check every item at a critical control point and the principle of random sampling may be more appropriate. Where final cooking temperatures are considered to be a critical control point, it may be agreed that a temperature taken from the top, middle and bottom shelves of a product being processed in an oven, would be a reasonable sample for that batch. Similarly, when checking raw ingredients from suppliers, it would be impossible to check every item, but to take a random sample from a box or batch would be more reasonable. Operators are also more likely to carry out the monitoring function correctly if the monitoring frequencies stipulated are sensible. The frequency of monitoring critical control points may also vary over time. For instance, if a new supplier is used, or a new practice introduced into the production process, it would be advisable to monitor the set critical control points more frequently until a satisfactory trend is established.

The ultimate aim must be to monitor the critical control points as often as is necessary, to check that the standards which have been agreed are effective in controlling and preventing potential hazards from becoming actual hazards.

The frequency of monitoring, be it by observation or measurement, must be clearly laid down and communicated to the relevant personnel to avoid there being any misunderstandings as to the exact requirements.

*How results* of the monitoring process are recorded will vary according to the type of operation. For management to be confident in the safety of the final food product, there must be evidence that controls at critical points have been executed correctly. In addition, documents can be vital in providing evidence in the case of legal proceedings.

There are a number of different ways to record the information for each different type or group of products. The two most common are:

(a)  a log sheet which follows each individual product or group of products through its entire process flow; and
(b)  static log sheets which are positioned at the critical control points, on which information relating to all products is recorded.

The advantage of individual product log sheets is that information relating to each product is on one sheet of paper and can be easily reviewed. If a problem should arise, it is also easier to trace the process and identify where the problem may have occurred. The main disadvantage is that where there are a wide range of products to be produced which cannot easily be grouped together, the paperwork can be substantial. In addition, there is always the risk of paperwork being held up in the system, or indeed it presents an opportunity to mislay the log sheets! The static log sheets are easier to complete and manage, particularly in very busy operations. The main disadvantage is the difficulty in reviewing the paperwork and identifying exactly what happened to a particular product during its process flow.

Typical examples of static log sheets used for the production and chilling functions in a cook-chill operation are illustrated in Figures 4.6(a) and 4.6(b).

The nature and complexity of each operation will determine which method is the most effective and easy to manage. But, whichever method is used to record information, the use of paper should be avoided where possible. Paper disintegrates, gets wet, dirty and eventually becomes illegible. Laminated log sheets and the use of permanent marker pens are more practical. The information recorded throughout the process can be photocopied at the end of the working day to ensure that a hard copy of the log sheets is kept on record. The laminated cards can then be cleaned off (using an alcohol based solution) ready for use the next day.

The records should be kept on file for at least one month, if not longer. Records are very useful to analyse as part of the review and verification process.

*Action is required* whenever the results of the monitoring process indicate that the standards defined have not been met. Immediate action must be taken to rectify the situation. Typical catering problems likely to be experienced include:

-   inadequate re-heating of foods
-   hot foods dropping below the statutory 63°C
-   inadequate chilling of hot foods to an acceptable storage temperature
-   raw materials being delivered at unacceptable temperatures
-   faulty equipment.

Whatever the problem identified, the course of action will ultimately be dictated by assessing the level of risk at the particular critical control point.

In many catering situations, production and service are very close together and therefore any failures in the system must be brought to the attention of management quickly. In the food manufacturing industry,

## Figure 4.6(a): Time and Temperature Control Record Sheet

Date: _____

| ITEM | COOKING | | | | SIGNATURE |
|------|---------|------|------|------|-----------|
| | NO. OF PORTIONS | START TIME | FINISH TIME | FINISH TEMP. | |
| | | | | | |
| | | | | | |
| | | | | | |
| | | | | | |
| | | | | | |
| | | | | | |
| | | | | | |
| | | | | | |
| | | | | | |
| | | | | | |
| | | | | | |
| | | | | | |
| | | | | | |
| | | | | | |
| | | | | | |
| | | | | | |
| | | | | | |
| | | | | | |
| | | | | | |
| | | | | | |
| | | | | | |
| | | | | | |
| | | | | | |
| | | | | | |
| | | | | | |
| | | | | | |
| | | | | | |
| | | | | | |
| | | | | | |
| | | | | | |
| | | | | | |
| | | | | | |
| | | | | | |
| | | | | | |

## Figure 4.6(b): Time and Temperature Control Record Sheet

Date: _____

| ITEM | CHILLING | | | | | |
|---|---|---|---|---|---|---|
| | INTO CHILLER | | | AFTER CHILLING | | |
| | TIME FROM COOKING | TIME INTO CHILLER | TEMP INTO CHILLER | TIME OUT OF CHILLER | TEMP OUT OF CHILLER | SIGNA-TURE |
| | | | | | | |
| | | | | | | |
| | | | | | | |
| | | | | | | |
| | | | | | | |
| | | | | | | |
| | | | | | | |
| | | | | | | |
| | | | | | | |
| | | | | | | |
| | | | | | | |
| | | | | | | |
| | | | | | | |
| | | | | | | |
| | | | | | | |
| | | | | | | |
| | | | | | | |
| | | | | | | |
| | | | | | | |
| | | | | | | |
| | | | | | | |
| | | | | | | |
| | | | | | | |
| | | | | | | |
| | | | | | | |
| | | | | | | |
| | | | | | | |
| | | | | | | |
| | | | | | | |
| | | | | | | |
| | | | | | | |

where there is a degree of concern about a product batch, microbiological testing can sometimes be undertaken before the product is released. This would not, however, be possible for fresh and chilled products, which would probably be consumed before the results of any tests could be released. In conventional catering situations this is not achievable.

Even well organised catering operations experience problems of one kind or another where the standards required at a critical control point are not met. To ensure that the right action is taken, a clear reporting structure must be in place.

It is also important at this stage to consider how the results which do not require action will be used. If members of staff collect information which is never reviewed or discussed, the need and motivation to carry out the monitoring function may begin to lapse. Whilst the purpose for collecting the information at the critical control points should be known and understood by all members of staff, the HACCP team and senior management must respond by carrying out a similar monitoring function of the results. It is as significant to comment on the results when the system is working well as it is when there are problems. It is always easier to highlight deficiencies rather than strengths. Supervisors and managers should take an active part in providing feedback to the staff on how the system is operating. Additionally this gives the staff an opportunity to suggest improvements to the system or to share any concerns they may have.

At the end of Stage 5, all the necessary development and implementation stages will have been completed. All the information collected and the procedures agreed form part of a final document for each product or group of products. This is often referred to as the HACCP Product Chart or Model. An example illustrated in the Richmond Report Part 2 is shown in Figure 4.7.

The HACCP Product Charts will form the basis of the system and will be complemented by the Measurement Charts used at the critical control points. This documentation will form the basis of the training package for the staff.

## Stage 6 — Review and Verification of the HACCP System

A HACCP system should be thoroughly reviewed and verified to check that:

**Figure 4.7: HACCP Product Chart**

Product: Hamburger      Date of Issue:
Issued by:

| STEP | IMPORTANCE | HAZARDS | PREVENTATIVE MEASURE (CONTROL) | MONITORING |
|---|---|---|---|---|
| 1. Raw materials | CCP | Foodborne illness-causing bacteria in ingredients. | Purchase good quality beef patties from reputable supplier. Proper storage conditions. Stock control. | Check deliveries for quality and temperature. Temperature of storage units. |
| 2. Raw material storage | | Failure to control may lead to significant growth. | Hygienic design of equipment and preparation area. Effective cleaning and disinfection. Control of temperature. Controlled thawing if to be defrosted before cooking. Control of time and temperature of thawed patties. | Visual check on effectiveness of cleaning. Temperature of storage units. Time of storage of perishable materials. |
| 3. Cooking | CCP | Survival of infectious foodborne illness-causing microorganisms if cooking inadequate. | Efficient well maintained cooking equipment. Well established cooking procedure capable of achieving a minimum food temperature in excess of 70°C for 2 mins. | Check temperature of cooking equipment correctly set. Check food temperature where practicable. |
| 4. Post cook handling and hot holding | | Recontamination with foodborne illness-causing bacteria. Bacterial proliferation. | Hygienic design of equipment and utensils. Effective cleaning of same. Personal hygiene of staff. Cleanliness of garnishes. Minimise hot holding period. Hot holding must maintain food temperature above 63°C. Clean, hygienic packaging material. | Visual monitoring of cleaning. Check staff hygiene. Check hot holding temperature. |

Source: Richmond Report Part 2

- all the known hazards have been identified
- the risks of the hazards have been assessed correctly
- the critical control points selected are still relevant
- the correct standards and specifications have been set down
- monitoring procedures and measurement checks are in place
- production and service processes and procedures are in place.

The records which have been maintained will be needed as part of the review process. They will enable a person or team of people to check that the monitoring is working well and that the correct action has been taken when deviations from standards have occurred. It is recommended that at periodic intervals a totally independent and unbiased review of the system is undertaken. For many caterers, this will involve the use of an external body to carry out the verification process. However, internal supervisors and managers have a very important role to ensure that the monitoring of the system takes place and that the records are correctly maintained.

Updating the system is very important. If any part of a process or procedure changes, then the HACCP Product Charts affected should be changed accordingly.

Where a new product is introduced, then the total HACCP process should be undertaken and the appropriate HACCP Product Chart produced.

## STAFF TRAINING

The success of a HACCP system is dependent on total commitment from the staff, supervisors and management.

Training is a key to the success of HACCP and should be on-going as part of the HACCP process and not just a one-off occurrence when the system is being developed and implemented. All members of staff must understand fully the purpose and meaning of HACCP within the operation and recognise and understand the importance of the critical control points.

All staff must be familiar with all HACCP Product Charts and Measurement Charts for the relevant products or group of products and understand exactly how the log sheets are to be completed. The training and communication network must be flexible to enable existing and new staff to be updated when operational or procedural changes are made to the system.

Two-way feedback from supervisors and management to staff and *vice versa* will play a key role in maintaining commitment to the system and will encourage all staff to strive for continuous improvement of the HACCP system.

# THE FUTURE OF HACCP IN THE CATERING INDUSTRY

There is no doubt that the HACCP concept, if applied sensibly, will provide caterers with a high degree of assurance that the products produced are safe to consume.

An American expert in HACCP, Frank L. Bryan, states:

HACCP is:

- **rational**, because it is based on historical data about causes of illness and spoilage;
- **comprehensive**, because it takes into consideration ingredients, processes and subsequent use of products;
- **continuous**, because problems are detected when they occur and action is taken then for correction;
- **systematic**, because it is a thorough plan covering step-by-step operations and procedures.

The Government in the UK is actively pursuing this route for the catering industry. However, it may be some time before many catering organisations understand the HACCP concept sufficiently to implement it into their own operation. Unfortunately there are still plenty of operators who are only just beginning to understand the implications of the Food Act. There will need to be a concerted effort by the experts to educate the catering industry to appreciate the benefits, both short term and long term, of introducing a HACCP system.

Financing the introduction of a HACCP system will be a stumbling block for many of the smaller catering operators. The Government, through the Department of Trade and Industry (DTI), has supported organisations wishing to introduce BS 5750 by offering a grant-aided scheme, whereby a percentage of the consultants' fees are paid for by the DTI. In its bid to improve the food poisoning statistics, the Government may well need to consider a similar scheme to assist in the introduction of the HACCP concept.

HACCP systems have been introduced successfully by a small number of catering organisations in the UK and its future development can only be seen as a positive step forward in the need to provide consumers with safe food products.

# Chapter 5

# BS 5750

BS 5750 is the UK standard for quality assurance systems and as such has created much discussion and interest amongst caterers in recent years. The aim of this chapter is to provide an understanding of the following:

- how the Standard has evolved
- the reasons organisations give for gaining BS 5750 and the benefits they believe it offers
- what the requirements in the Standard mean, and what an organisation needs to do to comply
- quality auditing — what it is and how to do it
- the costs of going for BS 5750
- how to approach BS 5750 certification and the maintenance of the standard, once certified.

## THE BACKGROUND TO BS 5750

The Ministry of Defence was one of the first purchasers to demand that its suppliers operate a quality assurance system to guarantee the quality of goods provided. They needed to be sure that the product would be fit for the purpose intended. As it was impossible for them to test every item, they developed an approach where inspectors examined the manufacturing process and assessed whether the process used assured the quality of the product. This approach, called second party assessment, has been adopted by many purchasers, perhaps the most notable being Marks and Spencer.

From this desire to check manufacturers' systems as a means of assuring quality, grew the British Standard for quality systems, BS 5750. BS 5750 is assessed by an independent third party and is just one of thousands of Standards published and controlled by the British Standards Institute (BSI). BS 5750 was first introduced in the UK in 1979. As a result of the UK's trade and technical connections with other countries, national quality standards were introduced in other parts of the world. Many of these standards were based on the British Standard.

This worldwide interest in quality standards led to the International Organization for Standardization (ISO) starting work on an International Standard in 1983. This work was completed in 1987 with the publication of the ISO 9000 series. The ISO standards are based on the UK standard BS 5750: 1979 but reflect international requirements and the experience of UK organisations. BS 5750 was revised in 1987 to align with the International Standard ISO 9000 and the European Standard EN 29000.

BS 5750 identifies the basic disciplines, procedures and criteria required to make sure that the services provided meet the customers' requirements. The Standard sets out how a supplier can establish, document and maintain an effective quality system, which will demonstrate commitment to quality and the ability to supply the required quality. However, it is important to realise that BS 5750 does not specify actual service quality standards, nor does it specify the correct methods to use to achieve the desired standards. The aim of BS 5750 is to provide confidence that a predetermined acceptable level of quality will be achieved every time the product or service is provided.

Since its introduction, BS 5750 has been adopted primarily in the manufacturing industries. The BSI *Annual Report and Accounts 1990-1991* states that there are in excess of 10,000 BS 5750 certified organisations in the UK — a complete list is set out in the *Register of Quality Assured UK Companies*, published by the Department of Trade and Industry. Currently, only a very small proportion of these certified companies operate in the food and hospitality industries, and most of these are in the food processing sector.

There has been much discussion recently about the suitability of the Standard for the catering industry and many have criticised it for being "product" rather than "service" orientated. Whilst the catering industry is generally thought of as a "service" industry, it must be remembered that many of the services provided are indeed "products", for example, a function, a meal or a drink. As long as the Standard is read sensibly, and not taken too literally, it can be used effectively by the catering industry, and this has been proven by those who have already gained certification; for example, Girobank, Newcastle Health Authority, Enfield School Meals and Crownpoint Foods. Whilst there are some who disagree, there is a strong belief within the industry that BS 5750 is a way forward to demonstrate commitment to quality assurance.

As a result of this strong interest in BS 5750 and the criticisms raised regarding its unsuitability for service industries, the BSI are currently reviewing the Standard and will publish a revised document specifically for the service industries. A set of guidelines has also been prepared by the BSI, in conjunction with the Hotel, Catering and Institutional Management Association (HCIMA) and other industry bodies, to assist operators with the interpretation of the Standard as it exists.

# REASONS FOR GAINING BS 5750

The most common reasons for organisations wishing to introduce quality assurance systems are marketing related, and include the desire to meet customer demands and to gain a competitive edge. A further reason which has been put forward is the need to comply with the requirements of the Food Safety Act 1990, and in particular, section 21, which relates to "due diligence". BS 5750 can help to achieve these objectives in the following ways.

## Meeting Customer Needs

Many major companies will only purchase from suppliers who have a recognised quality assurance system. This is becoming more and more common as companies improve their supplier control. Suppliers must respond to this pressure or risk losing customers. Customers are becoming more discerning and are demanding that the service is provided "right first time". Therefore, to stay in business it is necessary to have a system which will facilitate getting it right first time — BS 5750 can help.

## Competitive Edge

Marketing people look for the factors within their organisation which will give them an edge over the competition. This is certainly true in the catering industry, and as noted above, there is a widely held belief that BS 5750 can provide that desired competitive edge. Consequently, several operators are well on the way to gaining certification. Some industry cynics are putting forward the view that it is pointless to go for BS 5750, because eventually all suppliers of catering services will be certified and therefore no one will have a competitive edge. This view should not put off suppliers keen to pursue certification, because it is unlikely to occur, even in the long term, unless BS 5750 becomes mandatory.

The British Government is also a driving force behind BS 5750 — its programme to promote the importance of quality as a means of strengthening the competitiveness of UK companies in international markets, encourages third party assessment.

The European Commission faces the difficult problem of resolving how to harmonise official food inspection procedures once the Single Market is in operation. It is believed that BS 5750 could help resolve this dilemma, as it is accepted as the European Standard EN 29000. If this is the case, BS 5750 certified companies will have a "head start" in the Single Market. This potential edge is further reinforced by the fact that the European Commission intends that quality assurance will play a significant role in the future of the food industries in the Community. This is reinforced by Article 6 (92/C24/13) which says that Member States should encourage food operators to adopt EN 29000.

## Food Safety Act

The Food Safety Act 1990 has tightened up on existing food safety requirements, has enforced changes and has given greater power to Environmental Health Officers. One of the most discussed aspects of the Act relates to what will be accepted by the Courts as evidence of "due diligence". It is generally believed that BS 5750, particularly when linked with HACCP principles, which have been discussed in Chapter 4, will form a very good basis for meeting the "due diligence" requirements. In order to prove that all reasonable precautions had been taken and that "due diligence" had been exercised, the defendant must provide, amongst other things, documented evidence of a control system — a BS 5750 certified company will have such a system.

# BENEFITS OF BS 5750

The benefits of introducing a quality assurance system have already been discussed in Chapter 2. The key additional benefits which BS 5750 attract are:

- the Standard is internationally recognised
- "British Standards" represent a mark of quality in the eyes of the customer
- the requirement for reassessment provides the discipline and motivation to maintain quality consciousness.

# BS 5750 — THE PARTS AND THE REQUIREMENTS

## THE PARTS

BS 5750 is set out in six parts — Parts 0, 1, 2, 3, 4 and 8.

### Part 0

Part 0 explains the principles of the Standard. Section 0.1 is a guide to the selection and use of the appropriate part of the Standard. Section 0.2 is a guide to the overall management and quality system elements within the series.

### Part 1

Part 1 sets out the specification for design/development, production, installation and servicing and comprises 20 different requirements. It is intended for use in the production and manufacturing industries.

## Part 2

Part 2 sets out the specification for production and installation and comprises 18 requirements. It is intended for use by organisations who offer a service or a product to a published specification or to a customer's specification. This is the part considered appropriate for the catering industry.

## Part 3

Part 3 sets out the specification for final inspection and testing in 12 requirements. It is intended for use by companies such as distributors of goods.

## Part 4

Part 4 is a guide to the use of Parts 1, 2 and 3.

## Part 8

Part 8 is a guide to quality management and quality systems elements for services.

# THE REQUIREMENTS

Set out below are the key elements of the 18 requirements of Part 2 of the Standard, which an organisation is required to fulfil if certification is to be achieved, together with the author's interpretation of what the requirement means for the catering industry. The interpretation takes the form of issues to consider when developing the quality system. The following pages must be read in conjunction with the Standard, as the text is not intended to be definitive summary of the Standard's content. The Standard is, at first reading, a difficult document to understand and it does not provide an explanation of its meaning. Therefore, the aim of this text is to provide an overview of what is required and to set out the scope of work to be undertaken. Throughout the Standard, there is reference to the "supplier" and the "purchaser". To clarify these definitions, the "supplier" is the organisation offering the product or the service and the "purchaser" is the person or organisation buying the service or product.

## Management Responsibility (Requirement 4.1)

A *quality policy* (4.1.1.) must be prepared. This policy is a written statement setting out the organisation's intentions with regard to quality, its objectives and its commitment to the achievement of quality. The content of the policy will vary immensely from organisation to organisation, but whatever the content, it should be clear and concise, certainly no longer than one A4 page. Most policy statements make reference to fulfilling the requirements of the customer and some highlight specific areas of interest to the customer: in catering this could be food safety, health and safety or service to the customer. The quality policy should be signed by the Chief Executive to show that commitment to it is from the very highest level. Commitment must come from all levels of the organisation, top and bottom, and must be real and visible. The quality policy must be understood, implemented and maintained at all levels in the organisation. Every employee should be able to quote the quality policy, albeit in shortened "motto" form.

It is appropariate to draw up an *organisation chart* (4.1.2) shows clearly the personnel responsible for quality and how they fit into the overall management structure of the organisation. The authority of and the interface between these people must be stated clearly. It is vital that those who have responsibility for quality have the necessary authority to take whatever action is required to maintain the quality system. A detailed description of responsibilities for quality must be given for each person in the structure — this could be provided in the form of a job description.

It is a role of management to ensure that suitable *verification resources and personnel* are available to inspect, test and monitor all processes undertaken by the organisation. These personnel must be identified, must be trained appropriately and must be available to carry out checks at the designated time. As these personnel will come from within the organisation, for example head chef, restaurant manager, supervisor, and will have other responsibilities, it is vital that their role as "verifiers" is not compromised in any way. The greatest problem facing caterers will be finding "spare" resources to fulfil this function; time and resources must be found, because this requirement is critical to success, not only in achieving certification, but also in the on-going maintenance of the quality system. A *management representative* must be appointed. Depending upon the size of the organisation, this person may have other duties as well as their quality responsibilities. The quality management representative must have the authority to ensure that the requirements of the Standard are fulfilled at all times. This person will be a senior member of the organisation, should report directly to the Chief Executive and may be given the title Quality Assurance Manager.

The Standard requires that the quality system is *reviewed by management* (4.1.3). This review is normally carried out by the management representative with the support of other senior managers. In most organisations, an annual review is considered appropriate, but whatever the frequency decided upon, it must be clearly defined. The objective of the review is to check that the quality system is still effective and right for all the operations of the organisation and that it keeps abreast of change. With this in mind, it is sensible that the review involves all relevant line managers, for example restaurant managers, head chefs, purchasing managers, administration managers, as these people are concerned with the day-to-day execution of the quality system and will know if it needs to be changed. Records of the reviews must be kept and the results reported to senior management for action. Records are usually kept in the form of minutes, recording those participating, the parts of the system reviewed, the conclusions reached and any corrective actions recommended.

## Quality System (Requirement 4.2)

ISO 8402 defines a quality system. The abbreviation given in Part 8 states that a quality system is:

> the organisational structure, responsibilities, procedures, processes and resources for implementing quality management.

In other words, a quality system is the means by which quality is managed. It must be remembered that quality does not just happen, it has to be made to happen, and this is where the quality system comes in. The quality system is the mechanism by which the quality policy will be implemented. Therefore, the system must be an integral part of the organisation's management system, not an "add-on".

**Figure 5.1: The Quality Triangle**

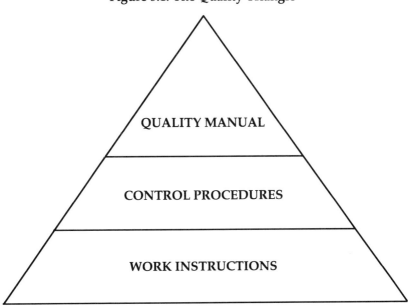

The Standard requires the caterer to establish and maintain a documented quality system to ensure that the service or product required by the customer meets the specification every time.

The quality system must cover adequately each of the requirements of the standard and be pulled together into a cohesive document. There is no standard format for the presentation of the quality system — the documentation must reflect the exact requirements of the organisation, ie be tailor-made. Thus, it is unlikely that two identical quality systems will be found. For this reason, it is not advisable to take another organisation's quality system and try to adapt it to your own — this approach will be fraught with difficulties and it will be more effective to take a clean sheet of paper and develop what is right for your organisation. The documentation required to demonstrate the quality system can most easily be demonstrated using a triangle (see Figure 5.1).

At the tip of the triangle is the *quality manual,* a short document of some 15 to 20 pages, which outlines the organisation's approach to satisfying each of 18 requirements of the Standard. This document is normally prepared by senior managers.

In the middle of the triangle are the *control procedures*, which are fundamental to satisfying the Standard's requirements. Procedures are detailed statements specifying what has to be done, by whom, where and when; for example, the procedure for the service of breakfast will consider what is to be done (table laying, order taking, service of food, table clearing), by whom (breakfast waiting staff), where (in the breakfast room), and when (between 0700 and 0930 hours). Given that the procedures must reflect accurately what happens, it is sensible for those personnel responsible for the activity to write their own procedures. Therefore, procedures are generally prepared by middle management, probably with the help of "ground floor" operators. All procedures must have a common format and numbering system. An example is shown in Figure 5.2.

At the bottom of the triangle are the *work instructions*. These are the "nitty gritty" details of precisely how the job is done, for example how a table is to be laid, how an order is taken from a customer, how the food is served on the plate, the recipe with measured ingredients and methodology, when and how the table is cleared, etc. By the nature of the content of the work instructions, the only people who can prepare these effectively are the people who do the jobs, that is, the "ground floor" operators. When work instructions are prepared, there is often conflict over which is the right way to do a job. It is inevitable, particularly in the catering industry where flair, imagination and initiative are encouraged, that there will be as many different ways to do a job put forward as the number of people asked. Where there are different methods of doing the same job, a consensus must be reached on the right way, and this must be communicated to all concerned. If a job is to be done "right first time", it must be done the same way each time. Perhaps two of the best examples of this approach in the catering industry are McDonald's and Little Chef, where clear procedures and instructions are provided for every element of the system.

Thus, the quality system is made up of three key components:

- the quality manual
- the control procedures
- the work instructions.

The control procedures and work instructions may be bound into just two manuals or a number of manuals. For example there may be separate

**Figure 5.2: Procedure Layout**

| XYZ Co. | Procedure No: | Issue: | Date: | Procedure: | Title: |
|---|---|---|---|---|---|

1.0 *Purpose*
   A statement of the specific purpose of the procedure.

2.0 *Scope*
   Identification of all departments, personnel etc to which procedure applies, including all interfacing departments.

3.0 *References*
   To other procedures which interface with this procedure.
   All forms and documents used in operating the procedure to be listed.

4.0 *Definitions*
   Of any terms whose meaning is not immediately apparent.

5.0 *Procedure*
   Details of action to be taken, by whom, where and when. As procedures are mandatory, the word "shall" must be used.

| Prepared by: | Approved by: | Page 1 of 1 |
|---|---|---|

manuals for training, food safety and Health and Safety or it may be possible to incorporate working instructions into one manual.

As the drawing up of the quality system requires employees from all levels of the organisation to be involved, an understanding of the Standard and, more importantly, a commitment to quality, will be developed at an early stage. It is important to nurture this commitment to make sure that it does not wane.

Once the quality system has been developed and documented, it has to be implemented effectively. The Standard makes reference to a number of activities which need to be considered in the development and implementation of the quality system. In summary, the Standard is making the caterer aware of all the implications associated with the implementation of the quality system, such as the need for potential investment, the clarification of standards, the preparation of quality records, etc.

The Standard also refers to the use of *quality plans*, although these are not mandatory. A quality plan would normally be used where a customer has specified requirements which are not covered by the quality system; for example, a restaurant is asked by a regular customer to provide a wedding reception, a service not normally offered. The purpose of the quality plan is to reflect the particular requirements of the job. Quality plans offer the opportunity to "extend" the scope of activities as described in the quality system, in a planned and structured way. A quality plan will be a scaled down version of the full quality system — it will address all of the requirements in the Standard which are pertinent to the job. It has been suggested that quality plans could be used by organisations such as catering contractors and restaurant chains, to bring new outlets under the wing of BS 5750 without having to go for separate certification. There is much debate currently about whether or not this is acceptable and what is the best way for large, multi-site organisations to proceed with BS 5750 certification. More discussion is required between companies pursuing BS 5750 and the various certification bodies to gain an authoritative view on the use of quality plans.

The quality system must not be thought of as a static document, which once prepared will hold good forever. It will not. The quality system must be reviewed, as already discussed, and updated as necessary. Perhaps of greatest importance is the fact that the quality system must be implemented and, in particular, the control procedures and work instructions must be available at the work place, they must be understood and they must be followed. At this point it is worth remembering that the aim is to get all systems and processes under control, but at the same time, not to create unnecessary bureaucracy. There is a temptation to create a mountain of paperwork — this must be avoided.

## Contract Review (Requirement 4.3)

The requirement for contract review is quite straightforward — all contracts must be reviewed to check that the purchaser's requirements are clear and that the organisation can supply in line with the specification. Where formal contracts are used, the review process must take place prior to the contract being agreed in final form and signed. In the catering industry, many transactions between the customer and supplier are verbal, for example, placing an order for food in a restaurant. In these circumstances, the contract review process must still occur and must be carried out by the organisation's employee who has direct contact with the customer, for example, the restaurant manager. It is the responsibility of this person to make sure that they understand what the customer is seeking and verify that the organisation can supply. Whilst many transactions are purely verbal, some verbal requests are followed up with written confirmation, for example, function bookings. Where written confirmation is provided by the customer, it is critical that the customer's specifications are once again reviewed to ensure that supply can be provided. Records of any formal contract reviews must be maintained.

## Document Control (Requirement 4.4)

Document control is a vital element of the Standard. It requires that all documents and data which relate to the operation of the quality system are controlled. This means that any document which may affect the quality of the service and all other documents which may affect the running of the quality system must be put under control. Procedures will need to be established which document how this control will be maintained. In theory, all control procedures, all work instructions and all supporting policy manuals will be subject to control. It should be noted that there is a school of thought which states that work instructions need not be controlled — the control of the system is much simpler if they are not under control.

The objective of controlling documents is to ensure that operations are undertaken following the most up-to-date version of the procedure, work instruction, etc. With this in mind, the control mechanism must make sure that documents are generated, maintained and distributed to the right places, and that all old versions are removed.

To achieve effective control necessitates a systematic approach.

1. Documents must be identified uniquely.
2. Documents must be reviewed and approved prior to issue.
3. The issue of documents must be controlled.

To *identify a document* uniquely requires a numbering system of the sort used by banks to identify individual customer accounts. The following is a suggested numbering system:

- identify the document by a *code*, for example, K for kitchen, RS for restaurant, ST for stores
- give each document a *unique number*
- identify the department originating the document with a *code*, for example, QA for Quality Assurance
- identify the *revision status* of the document, for example, 1, 2... or A, B...
- if there is a need to relate to a particular customer specification, because this is not the normal specification for the service, identify a *contract number.*

Thus, a document number could be as follows:

C23/KP-01-QA/3
C23 - unique contract number
KP  - code for kitchen procedure
01  - unique number
QA  - code for Quality Assurance
3   - revision status

The Standard requires that all documents are *reviewed and approved* prior to issue (4.4.1). The nature of the document will determine who should be the approving authority, for example documents relating to the operation of the quality system would be approved by the quality assurance manager, whilst documents relating to the production of food would be approved by the restaurant manager or head chef. It is possible that some documents will require approval by more than one person.

The review and approval process must be seen to be done. This is normally achieved by the approving authority counter-signing the revised document. The identity of the originator is already part of the unique numbering system and so this does not need to be duplicated.

The last stage in the document control cycle is the issue of new and revised documents (4.4.2). As a principle, documents should only be released on a "needs to know" basis. In this way, the potential mountain of paper is contained, and the retrieval of obsolete documents is made easier because fewer people are involved. It is a requirement of the Standard that obsolete issues of documents are removed and disposed of promptly, so that the danger of out-of-date procedures being followed is reduced to a minimum.

It is useful to keep, with each document, a summary of revisio.:s done (see Figure 5.3). This is usually shown in tabular form detailing the revision status, the date, the reason for the change and the authorising signature. It is also useful to keep a master list of all documents which sets out the revision status of each document at a point in time. The main purpose of the master list is to act as a double check for users of the documents, to ensure they have the correct version.

## Purchasing (Requirement 4.5)

It is the responsibility of the supplier to make sure that all materials or services provided by sub-contractors meet the specification set by the purchaser (4.5.1). Materials and services from sub-contractors must not compromise the quality of the service (4.5.2). This requirement applies to all sub-contractors even where the sub-contractor may be part of the supplier's parent company; for example, Forte would apply the same checks to Puritan Maid (an in-house Forte supply company) as they would to other suppliers not forming part of the Forte organisation. All sub-contractors must be included. In the catering industry, in addition to all raw materials, this will include, for example, the provision of staff through agencies, the supply of linen and laundry services, security services, pest control services, courier services, and any other specialised services bought in by the supplier.

## Figure 5.3: Document Revision Status Page

| XYZ Company | | Procedure No . . . . . . . . . | |
|---|---|---|---|
| Document Title . . . . . . . . . . . . . . . . . . . . . . . . . . . . . | | | |
| Issue No. | Date | Reason for change | Authorised by |
| | | | |
| | | | |
| | | | |
| | | | |
| | | | |
| | | | |

Sub-contractor assessment must consider the ability of the sub-contractor to meet certain quality, technical and commercial criteria. The suitability of the sub-contractor may be assessed in a number of different ways, namely:

– a review of previously demonstrated capability and performance
– visits to premises to assess the appropriateness of systems in use
– independent testing of raw materials samples
– approval by means of a third party assessment, for example, the sub-contractor has BS 5750 certification.

The assessment may use one or more of the above techniques depending upon the nature of the product involved. The basis of the assessment must be stated in the appropriate procedures and records of compliance must be kept. The records should include sufficient data to substantiate

the decisions made. A list of all acceptable sub-contractors must be kept —
this is generally known as an approved suppliers list.

It is not uncommon for caterers to use local wholesalers, local retailers
and specialist markets. The continuation of such practices could compromise the achievement of certification as it would be difficult to uphold the
guarantees of sub-contractor suitability. While some organisations may
see this as a problem, it should be noted that the practice of using only
nominated approved suppliers is the rule for most large caterers.

It is a requirement of the Standard that all purchase orders should include
data describing clearly the items to be provided (4.5.3). Such data will include
all raw material specifications and specific criteria relating to size and
packaging. For most approved sub-contractors, it is unlikely that their
complete range of products will be available to suppliers, for reasons of cost
and quality, and therefore it is essential that only those nominated products
can be purchased. The best way of ensuring the right products are purchased
is for the sub-contractors to prepare special order forms for their customers,
setting out the agreed products with details of brand name, precise product
description, size and packaging. In this way, the customer will not be required
to write out detailed descriptions of each product, but will be assured that the
right product will be provided. Unfortunately, this approach will not be
practical for smaller operators, and it will be necessary for clear product
specifications to be written on each and every order. It has been assumed so
far that all orders placed are written. This is unlikely to be the case in the
catering industry, where orders are placed daily for perishable items and very
often orders are made over the telephone. In these circumstances, the same
principles must be applied; clear but simple product specifications must be
given and full records kept of orders placed.

It is also a requirement of the Standard that all purchasing documents
must be checked for adequacy of specification prior to the order being
placed with the sub-contractor. In most catering organisations, this will
add an extra "layer" to the purchasing process, but it could easily be
accommodated by a nominated person making a final check. This checking must also be built into the procedure for telephone orders.

Where specified in contract agreements, the purchaser may reserve the
right to check purchased products at source, ie at the sub-contractor's
premises (4.5.4). This checking does not release the supplier from his
responsibilities to check products, nor is it proof of effective quality
control by the sub-contractor.

## Purchaser Supplied Product (Requirement 4.6)

It is the responsibility of the supplier to ensure that any products supplied directly by the customer will not compromise the quality of the service ultimately provided to the customer. The supplier must define the procedure for the receipt, storage and maintenance of purchaser supplied products, and must alert the purchaser if any supplied product is unsuitable.

Where the supplier is employed to provide a service on the purchaser's premises, for example, contract caterers, the premises themselves could be considered to be a purchaser supplied product. In these circumstances, the supplier must make sure in the first instance that the facilities provided can do the job required, and having established this, the supplier must then ensure that the facilities are used and maintained properly. Where maintenance is the responsibility of the purchaser, the supplier must ensure that this cannot compromise their performance. Other examples of purchaser supplied products include wines, flowers and wedding cakes.

## Product Identification and Traceability (Requirement 4.7)

The Standard requires that the product/service can be identified during all stages of storage, preparation, production and service. The level of identification required by the Standard is not generally provided as a matter of course in catering establishments, other than in large scale central production facilities. The best way to achieve the requirement is to consider what information will be required to document the progress of a product or service from "goods in" to "goods out". Taking the example of a shepherd's pie, the following information could be gathered:

- details of when each of the ingredients came into the premises and where they were stored
- reference to the recipe and methodology followed
- details of the timing of preparation and production and who carried out the work
- details of the equipment used
- details of time and temperature checks throughout the process
- details of who served the pie and the timing of consumption.

It would be wholly impractical to collect all this information for every product offered every day, and therefore it is appropriate to consider the vital elements of information required. So long as appropriate procedures are in place to check:

- raw materials on arrival at the premises
- that recipes and methodologies are followed
- that storage times and temperatures are adhered to

the author recommends that the keeping of daily production schedules, detailing what was produced by whom and the labelling of all products with production and "use by" dates, should provide a sufficient level of product identification. Where a service is provided which mainly involves the provision of staff (for example, cleaning of rooms, portering services), daily records must be kept of who was on duty and assigned which tasks.

This is an area where the use of HACCP may be very useful, as critical stages of any operation are monitored against set standards.

## Process Control (Requirement 4.8)

The supplier must identify all processes which directly affect quality and make sure that these processes are carried out under "controlled conditions" (4.8.1). In terms of the Standard, "controlled conditions" mean that for each process there should be:

- documented work instructions
- monitoring and control procedures
- written standards.

To keep processes under control will necessitate the following key activities:

- setting targets in the form of written standards
- measuring actual performance against the targets
- comparing actual performance with the targets
- taking action to bring actual performance in line with targets where there is a difference.

The Standard also requires that continuous monitoring and/or compliance with documented procedures are necessary for special processes

145

(4.8.2). Special processes are those activities where deficiencies in the process may only become apparent after the product is in use, for example food which has an acceptable visual appearance, but which has been contaminated with food poisoning bacteria. The author proposes that all food production falls into the special process category and, accordingly, must be monitored throughout its life.

The supplier must determine which aspects of the total organisation ultimately affect the quality of the products and services being offered. There is a potential dilemma here, because it is arguable that all the workings of the organisation, from the accounting and purchasing departments to the switchboard operator, will have some bearing on the perceived quality to the customer. More and more organisations are seeing the benefit of incorporating all activities into the quality system, because then there are no opportunities for loop-holes. Whichever route is chosen, procedures and relevant work instructions must be written for all activities deemed to affect quality. Work instructions must be very clear statements setting out precisely:

- the work to be done
- the correct sequence of activities
- the materials and equipment to be used
- specific conditions, eg temperature, hygiene
- standards for the process and the finished product, eg yields, photographs, recipe ingredients and methodologies.

In order to minimise the number of work instructions to be written, it is worth considering whether the job would be done to a lesser standard if no instruction were available. If the answer is that a competent operator would still achieve the required quality, then the work instruction is not necessary.

At first glance, it may seem that this requirement is particularly difficult and time consuming to comply with. However, it should be remembered that the requirement is seeking the introduction of a systemised approach to catering, which, it is recognised, is easier to operate than the more traditional methods.

## Inspection and Testing (Requirement 4.9)

Inspection and testing procedures must be established at each of three stages: receiving (4.9.1), in process (4.9.2) and final inspection (4.9.3). The aims of these procedures and the process monitoring and control procedures are similar — to check the process to ensure that the product or service is not served or sold unless it meets the specified requirements. Therefore, the two sets of procedures must link together and be balanced. In other words, they should complement not contradict each other.

Set out below are some brief examples of inspection and testing requirements in the catering industry:

(a) *Laying table linen*

| | |
|---|---|
| Receiving | – check linen from laundry for cleanliness, colour, tears, marks |
| In process | – check linen in store for cleanliness |
| | – check waiting staff take correct size and quantity of linen |
| | – check laying of linen to ensure tablecloths, napkins, etc are put on table correctly, the overhang is even, napkins are folded and positioned correctly |
| Final | – check visual appearance of table |

(b) *Preparation of ham sandwich*

| | |
|---|---|
| Receiving | – check quality of raw materials (ham, bread, butter, garnish) on receipt from suppliers |
| | – check storage conditions and temperatures, "use by" dates |
| In process | – check quality of raw materials on receipt from stores |
| | – check correct amounts of raw materials drawn from stores |
| | – check adherence to recipe and methodology |
| | – check for hygienic practices |
| Final | – check visual appearance of ham sandwich on plate |

(c) *Silver service of vegetables*

| | |
|---|---|
| Receiving | – check all service implements ready on dumb waiter |
| | – check visual appearance of cooked vegetables provided by kitchen |
| | – check temperature of vegetables |
| | – check vegetables in correct dish |

| In process | – check correct implements are chosen for service |
| | – check dish and service implements are held correctly |
| | – check service implements are used correctly |
| Final | – check vegetables are positioned correctly on plate. |

Given the nature and frequency of the example checks set out above, it is clear that it would be impractical for a team of quality control inspectors to carry out these functions, other than on an *ad hoc* basis. In terms of BS 5750, it is wholly acceptable that such inspection and testing can be carried out by those doing the job, provided they are authorised to do so, are suitably trained and provided with appropriate equipment. If the inspection and test process relies on the operators, it is sensible to have an independent inspection team to carry out random checks to ensure that the self-inspection system is operating effectively.

It is a requirement of the Standard that records of all inspections and tests must be maintained, demonstrating that the product has passed inspection (4.9.4). Careful thought must be given as to how these records can be completed without over-burdening the day-to-day running of the operation with paperwork. If the HACCP system is introduced, the records kept may well be sufficient to meet the needs of this requirement.

## Inspection, Measuring and Test Equipment (Requirement 4.10)

The supplier must control and calibrate any equipment used for inspecting, measuring and testing, whether or not the equipment is owned by the supplier. In the catering industry, the best example is temperature probes — this equipment must be accurate because of the legislative requirements to serve foods above or below certain critical temperatures. Another example is weighing scales. Calibration must be carried out in line with national standards, where these are applicable. The need for calibration applies to equipment used for precise measurement. Where equipment is used for indication purposes only, for example oven probes, formal calibration may not be necessary.

There are a number of tasks the supplier has to undertake:

(a) identification of measurements to be made
(b) agree frequency of calibration
(c) establish, document and maintain calibration procedures

(d)  labelling system to identify calibration status
(e)  maintain calibration records
(f)  agree handling and storage facilities for the equipment.

## Inspection and Test Status (Requirement 4.11)

The inspection and test status of a product/service must be identifiable at any stage throughout the process. The most practical way of achieving this in the catering industry is by the use of inspection records. The purpose of identifying inspections and test status is to ensure that only those products/services which have passed inspection are used. HACCP records may be useful here.

## Control of Non-conforming Products (Requirement 4.12)

The Standard requires that a product which does not meet the specification must not be used. There are a number of ways in which such non-conforming products can be identified, namely, by process control, by inspections, by internal quality audits or by customer complaints. The supplier is required to identify, document, evaluate, segregate (where practical) and dispose of non-conforming products and notify relevant persons. Non-conforming products must be reviewed (4.12.1) and a decision made by a nominated representative:

(a)  to reject and dispose of the product
(b)  to regrade the product for alternative use, for example overboiled potatoes could be used for mashed potatoes
(c)  to use the product having asked the customer if they will accept the product
(d)  to rework to meet requirements, for example re-lay a table.

Repaired and reworked products have to be re-inspected in accordance with documented procedures.

With regard to non-conforming services, a decision must be made either to reallocate the duty or to retrain the member of staff.

Records of all non-conforming products and services must be kept (see Figure 5.4).

**Figure 5.4: Non-conformance Report**

| NON-CONFORMANCE REPORT |
| --- |
| Product: |
| Batch number:          Date: |
| Problem: |
| Action Taken: |

## Corrective Action (Requirement 4.13)

Corrective action is the action taken to put right a product or service which has not met the specification. There are two stages to corrective action — the cure and the prevention. The control of a non-conforming product, as described above, is the cure for the immediate problem. Once the problem has been cured, it is then important to take a wider view of the conditions which caused the product to fail to meet the specification, to identify its root cause and to make the necessary corrections. This latter element is the prevention stage.

To achieve this prevention ability, the Standard requires the supplier to set up procedures to:

- investigate why non-conformity has occurred
- analyse all processes within the quality system to detect and eliminate possible causes of non-conformity
- agree on preventative action to be taken
- ensure preventative action has been effective
- record changes to procedures resulting from corrective action.

It is important to note that corrective action is not necessarily something that has to happen as a result of a non-conformance. The aim of an effective corrective action system will be to identify adverse trends and to take appropriate action to avert non-conformances occurring. One of the major problems to achieving this pro-active approach will be getting staff to highlight problem areas and thus seeing adverse trends in time to take action. The best solution is for the management to encourage, by example, the recording of errors, which will help to resolve and prevent problems in the future.

The most common reasons for non-conformance are that operators follow incorrect working methods or that they do not comply with the work instructions. Working methods may have been adjusted because the correct procedure is difficult to achieve, for example, the use of disposable gloves when handling raw poultry when the wrong type of gloves have been provided. The author proposes that most non-conformance in the catering industry falls into the second category — non-compliance with work instructions. The main justification given for non-compliance with work instructions is that there are quicker ways to do a job and speed is of the essence. If it is to be effective, the corrective action process has to be handled sensitively to ensure that it does not alienate the operators. The operators must take an active role in the corrective action process and must understand that the aim is to help them to provide products and services to the specified standard, not to hinder them.

## Handling, Storage, Packaging and Delivery (Requirement 4.14)

The aim of this requirement is to ensure that product quality is not reduced by poor handling, unsuitable storage, inappropriate packaging or delivery procedures (4.14.1). The procedures to cover this requirement will link in closely with the procedures for process control monitoring and inspection and testing.

Handling and packaging procedures must ensure that the product will be protected whilst "in process"; this will include the use of suitable containers for movement around catering areas, consideration of optimum temperature requirements and the correct handling practices by staff, particularly of food, but also of equipment (4.14.2 and 4.14.4).

Storage procedures must ensure that products are kept safe and secure, at the correct temperature and, in the case of food, that cross contamination is prevented. Procedures must be drawn up relating to the receipt of goods into and the issue of goods out of stores, and for the regular inspection of products whilst in storage to establish that the product is not deteriorating (4.14.3).

Delivery procedures for food products must ensure that the product reaches the customer at the correct temperature and in an acceptable state. This will involve, for example, checking the temperature control of vehicles, other delivery containers and service counters, checking the standards of service provided by staff and checking the quality of the product given to the customer (4.14.5).

Where there is no tangible product involved, for example, the service elements of a meal in a restaurant, the "delivery" procedures will check purely the standard of service offered by the staff.

## Quality Records (Requirement 4.15)

Quality records must be maintained to demonstrate achievement of the required quality of the product and the effective operation of the quality system. Two types of records will be required:

(a) product quality records, and
(b) quality system management records.

Product quality records will include:

- inspection and test records
- details of non-conforming products and their disposal.

Quality system records will include:

- all quality procedures; for example, contract review, purchasing, process control, inspection and testing, etc
- internal quality audit reports
- staff training and qualification records
- sub-contractor approvals information
- calibration records
- management review of quality system records
- corrective action records.

BS 5750 requires that all elements of the quality system are implemented in line with documented procedures. These procedures provide the first evidence to a client that the organisation has a workable quality system. The quality system itself is required to produce records which will illustrate its effective implementation and maintenance. Therefore, the records are vital to demonstrate that procedures are being complied with, and that corrective action is taken when the product is not up to specification. The records of quality system reviews and internal quality audits assist with proving that the system is being maintained, because it can be shown that updating and amending happens as required to reflect changes from the organisation, the product or the customer.

All records kept must be legible and, therefore, if hand-written records are the only practical option, guidelines must be given in terms of style of writing, for example capital letters only, size of letters, colour of ink, etc.

All records must be stored so that they can be retrieved easily and they must be protected from loss, deterioration and damage. Storage periods must be determined for each type of record — these may relate to legislative requirements, customer requirements or specific organisational needs. Disposal of records at the appropriate time must be carried out in a controlled manner. A procedure should be drawn up stating who can dispose of records and how the disposal should be undertaken.

To facilitate easy retrieval from storage areas, all records should be indexed so that they are readily identifiable. It is also useful to state clearly on the identification label when the record can be disposed of.

It is important that storage areas are reviewed on a regular basis to check that storage conditions remain acceptable.

## Internal Quality Audits (Requirement 4.16)

The purpose of internal quality audits is to establish whether:

- procedures are documented and comply with the requirements of the Standard
- procedures are in place and used correctly
- the system of procedures achieves the quality objectives of the organisation.

It is important that a systematic approach to quality auditing is followed. Audits should be carried out in line with a pre-planned schedule ensuring that all requirements of the Standard and all parts of the organisation are covered within a set period of time, usually one year. How often certain aspects are audited will be determined by their importance.

The most common way of presenting the quality audit programme is in the form of a table showing:

- the part of the organisation to be audited
- the planned date of the audit, on a month-by-month basis
- the relevant requirements of the Standard which will be looked at.

The responsibility for auditing usually rests with the quality assurance manager/team, but it is important to realise that internal quality audits can be conducted by anyone in the organisation, so long as they are independent of the function being assessed, but have experience of it, and are suitably trained in auditing. There are a number of courses available to train personnel in the skills of quality auditing — details of suitable companies can be obtained from the Institute of Quality Assurance.

The aim of an internal quality audit is to provide an independent assessment of how well the quality system is operating. With this in mind, it is important that the audit is carried out with the co-operation of the department being audited. Therefore, appropriate notice of the audit should be given, in writing, to the management of the department and, if possible, a member of the department should accompany the auditor during the audit process. Details of how internal quality audits should be conducted are discussed later in this chapter.

Records of internal audits must be kept and a summary of the audit findings presented at management review meetings. It should be remembered that the role of the audit is not only to establish where the quality system is not functioning as it should be, but also to put forward recommendations as to how any deficiencies can be overcome with appropriate corrective action.

## Training (Requirement 4.17)

The Standard requires that a systematic approach to training is adopted. Training needs must be identified and this training must then be provided. The best way to identify training needs is to review all activities in the organisation which affect quality and pose the question: do the staff have the right qualifications, skills and experience to do the job to the standard required? If the answer is no, then the staff must be trained suitably. In the catering industry, particular consideration must be given to how temporary, casual and agency staff will be checked to make sure they are suitably trained to do the job. A possible solution to this problem is to prepare a skills list which each prospective employee is checked against prior to their engagement. This checking could be carried out by the agency or the organisation's personnel department.

Training may be internal or external, on-the-job or off-the-job; the type of training used should be the most suitable to fulfil the need. Records of all training carried out must be kept. It is useful if the training records are made available to all supervisors so that they can allocate jobs to staff who have had the right training.

## Statistical Techniques (Requirement 4.18)

The Standard requires that, where appropriate, adequate statistical techniques should be used to verify the product and the process. Statistical techniques should be employed where they provide an effective means of assessing objectively the level of quality of the product or service.

Statistical techniques of the nature intended in the Standard are not used in the catering industry. However, statistics of the operation are maintained; for example, hotel bed occupancy, average spends per head, average room rack rate, food cost percentages, gross and net profit percentages, etc. Consideration should be given to whether these statistics could help the organisation to assess the level of quality achieved. If they can, it would be useful to include them as part of the quality system. If statistical techniques are used, procedures for their use must be prepared and records of the results kept.

# QUALITY AUDITING

A quality audit of a quality system is like a financial audit of an accounting system — it checks that everything is in place, is understood and is used properly. It helps to make sure that the organisation's commitment to quality is grasped by all employees and that the commitment is maintained. A quality audit is not designed to "catch out" people not doing their jobs properly, but to identify where the quality system and its procedures are lacking. Figure 5.5 shows the quality audit process.

There are two levels of audit — a systems audit and a compliance audit. A systems audit checks whether procedures exist and are available to the right people in the workplace. A compliance audit checks that the procedures are being followed.

### Audit Planning

Quality audits must be planned. There are five key stages to planning an audit:

(a)  an audit schedule must be produced (see Figure 5.6)
(b)  the function to be audited must be notified
(c)  all relevant documents must be obtained and reviewed
(d)  checklists identifying key questions must be prepared
     and
(e)  a schedule for the audit must be agreed.

## Figure 5.5: Quality Audit Process

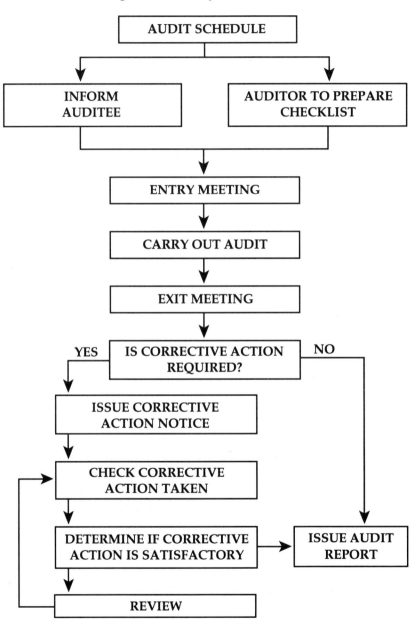

### Figure 5.6: Quality Audit Schedule

| XYZ Company | Year 1993 | | | | | | | | | | | |
|---|---|---|---|---|---|---|---|---|---|---|---|---|
| Department | Jan | Feb | Mar | Apr | May | Jun | Jul | Aug | Sep | Oct | Nov | Dec |
| | | | | | | | | | | | | |
| | | | | | | | | | | | | |
| | | | | | | | | | | | | |
| | | | | | | | | | | | | |
| | | | | | | | | | | | | |
| | | | | | | | | | | | | |
| | | | | | | | | | | | | |
| | | | | | | | | | | | | |
| | | | | | | | | | | | | |
| | | | | | | | | | | | | |

As noted earlier in this chapter, the audit schedule must cover all functions within the organisation and must address all 18 requirements of the Standard. A schedule will normally be prepared for one year at a time and it is not anticipated that the schedule, once announced, will change. If there is a need for additional audits, these must be carried out in addition to the planned schedule.

The function to be audited, the "auditee", should be informed formally in advance. The usual notice period given is between 7 and 14 days.

The next stage of the planning process involves the gathering together of all necessary documentation; for example, the quality manual, procedures relevant to the function, specifications, previous audit reports and corrective action reports. This data must then be reviewed by the auditor and a full understanding gained of how the function operates.

The auditor will then prepare a checklist covering all the questions which he/she will ask the auditee (see Figure 5.7). The checklist will have space to record whether the answer to the question is satisfactory or not and also sufficient room for comments to each question. The checklists should be seen as a framework around which the auditor will pose questions and tease out where the problems lie.

**Figure 5.7: Quality Audit Checklist**

| Date.......... | Department........................... | |
|---|---|---|
| Auditor.................. | Auditee ............... | |
| Requirement No:....................... | | |
| Questions | Compliance | Comments |
| | | |

The last stage of the planning process is to agree a schedule and itinerary for the audit with the auditee. The auditee should know where the auditor will be at all times during the audit. It is preferable for both parties if representatives of the auditee, for example supervisors, can accompany the auditor throughout the audit.

**The Audit**

There are three stages to the audit proper:

- an "entry" meeting
- the audit
- an "exit" meeting.

The "entry" meeting will take place before the audit starts. It will be a brief meeting between the auditor and his or her team and the auditee to discuss the scope of the audit, the auditor's approach and administrative arrangements.

The audit must be carried out in a formal manner and the prepared checklists should be used. The auditor must be ready to follow up on issues as they become apparent and to collect only objective evidence. Any non-conformances must be recorded. The auditor should discuss his or her findings with the auditee during the process of the audit, so that any misunderstandings can be cleared up immediately. The findings and conclusions of the auditor, as presented in the final audit report, should not be a surprise to the auditee, as all issues raised will have been discussed fully at the time they were discovered. This approach avoids debate after the event when it may be more difficult to verify the facts.

After the audit, the auditor must review the findings and determine which will be included as audit findings. The audit findings must be recorded formally on corrective action notice or request forms (see Figure 5.8). The auditor and the auditee, together with relevant representatives from the auditee's function, should be present at the exit meeting. The purpose of this meeting is:

- to discuss and review the findings of the audit and obtain any clarifications
- to provide copies of the corrective action notices
- to discuss appropriate corrective actions to be taken
- to advise the date of issue of the audit report and the expected date of response to the corrective action notices.

## The Audit Report

The presentation of the audit report should be determined by a procedure. It is normal practice for the report to have the following content:

- a front sheet summarising the audit findings together with a list of the corrective action notices
- report sheets covering the entry meeting, the audit, the exit meeting and follow up audits
- copies of the corrective action notices.

### Figure 5.8: Corrective Action Notice

| XYZ COMPANY | CORRECTIVE ACTION NOTICE |
|---|---|

Audit Ref. No . . . . . . . . . . . .     Department . . . . . .
Auditor . . . . . . . . . . . . . . . . .     Auditee . . . . . . . . .     Date . . . . . . .

**FINDINGS**




Signed by Auditor . . . . . . . . . . . . . . . . .
             Auditee . . . . . . . . . . . . . . . . .

**RECOMMENDATIONS**




Signed by Auditor . . . . . . . . . . . . . . . . . . . .

**CORRECTIVE ACTION**



Effective Date . . . . . . . . . . . .     Responsibility for Action . . . . . . . . . . .

Implementation of corrective action has/has not been satisfactory

Signed by Auditor . . . . . . . . . . . . . . . . . . . .     Date . . . . . . . . . . . .

*Comment*

The audit report should be signed by both the auditor and the auditee.

Follow up action must be taken to ensure that responses to the corrective action notices are received by the due date and that the responses are satisfactory. If the responses are not received or are not satisfactory, the auditor should discuss the matter with the auditee to resolve any difficulties and to establish the way forward. Whatever happens, corrective action notices must not be left "unfinished" and must not be allowed to become dormant.

## The Auditor

The size of the organisation will determine whether one auditor will be able to cope with the internal quality audit programme on their own. In many organisations, there is a need for a team of auditors to be set up. Where more than one auditor is involved in an audit, a lead auditor must be designated who has overall responsibility for the audit's management.

Auditors must not only be trained in quality auditing techniques and procedures, but must also possess certain characteristics if they are to be successful in the role. An auditor must be diplomatic, patient, observant, impartial and honest — they must help auditees during the audit, not aim to catch them out. Auditors must have excellent observation, questioning and listening skills and must be able to put the auditees and employees they are observing at their ease. Given that much of the information and objective evidence they will collect will be from talking to employees in the workplace, the auditor must be suitably adaptable and sensitive to be able to draw out the necessary details from people who are nervous.

The role of the internal quality auditor is vital to the on-going success of the organisation and is a very interesting role. Where a team of auditors are required, it is very worthwhile encouraging volunteers from throughout the organisation to take on this role, because it helps to generate interest and thus maintain commitment to the quality objectives and the quality system.

# HOW MUCH DOES BS 5750 COST?

Some people take the philosophical approach and pose the question "How much will it cost my company if we do not become certified?". As Dr. W.

Edwards Deming states, "Defects are not free. Someone makes them and gets paid for making them." The implication of these statements is that if BS 5750 (or another quality assurance approach) is not pursued, indirect quality costs will continue to be incurred. It is almost impossible to quantify these indirect costs.

It is the aim of this section to give an indication of the direct, quantifiable costs which an organisation may expect to incur if the BS 5750 route is followed. There are six key areas of possible cost involved in gaining BS 5750 certification:

(a) the use of consultants
(b) the requirement for a quality representative
(c) the preparation of the required documentation
(d) the education and training of staff
(e) the introduction of necessary changes, and
(f) the certification costs.

## Use of Consultants

There are many consultants who offer a variety of services to organisations embarking on the BS 5750 route. Advice can range from general guidance on how to start to full assistance including development of quality manuals, procedures and work instructions, training, and the provision of support and implementation personnel. It is the view of the author that where consultancy advice is required, this should be as facilitators to the organisation's own management team, rather than as a team of outsiders who will come in and set up all the systems and procedures necessary without the real involvement of the in-house personnel. There is a temptation to bring in an expert outside team to do all the hard work, especially if timescales are tight. This approach is not recommended because the systems and procedures will always "belong" to the consultants, and not to the management team. This is not a good way to develop and maintain commitment to the system.

Under the Department of Trade and Industry's current Enterprise Initiative Programme, financial help is available to companies of up to 500 employees that are seeking consultancy assistance to improve quality. For those organisations located in Assisted Areas and Urban Programme Areas, two-thirds of the cost of consultancy (for projects up to 15 days) may be claimed. In other areas, up to half the cost of the consultancy may be sought. As with all DTI initiatives, this programme is subject to review and may change.

An alternative to the use of consultants is to seek help from the local Trading Standards Officer. Many TSOs have specific experience of BS 5750 and are happy to provide assistance in so far as their other work commitments will permit. Officers do not charge for their advice and therefore can be a very economical way of obtaining outside assistance.

## Quality Representative

The first requirement in the Standard states that there must be one individual who has direct responsibility for quality management. Whilst this person may have other, additional responsibilities, the fact that they must have sufficient time to dedicate to quality means that there is a direct cost attributable to BS 5750. Furthermore, the quality representative will require administrative support to assist with the processing of the documentation.

## Preparation of the Required Documentation

The Standard requires that the system is documented fully — this will incur cost for the organisation unless such documentation is already in place. Costs will be incurred to cover personnel time to prepare (writing, typing, checking, etc) the documentation, and also for the printing and production of the finished paperwork. On an on-going basis, there may well be additional costs in terms of stationery and administration to manage the paperwork load.

## Staff Education and Training

It is inevitable that the introduction of BS 5750 will necessitate the development of an education and training programme for all staff involved in the organisation's activities. The education and training programme should cover:

-   awareness training for *all* staff, from the managing director to the kitchen porter

- training in the specific requirements of BS 5750, for example how to write a procedure, how the documentation should be put together
- training of internal quality auditors
- training of staff in new or changed procedures and work instructions.

Training will undoubtedly be required for the four categories set out above, as the need for training is created specifically by BS 5750. However, the amount of training required for the last category will depend largely on how much change has to be made to the existing procedures and work instructions. If changes are significant, substantial re-training will be necessary. Even where little change is required, it may be necessary to embark on a comprehensive training programme if staff training in the past has not been thorough.

On the basis of the above, it is clear that the cost of training will be significant, particularly as every member of the workforce will require some form of training. When assessing the exact costs of the education and training programme, it is important to calculate not only the direct costs of providing the training, but also the indirect costs of cover for staff attending training sessions.

## The Introduction of Changes

BS 5750 will necessitate the introduction of new systems, for example document control, internal quality auditing, new procedures and work instructions and new monitoring and reporting procedures. This will cost money — the amount will depend upon the degree of change necessitated to comply with the requirements of the Standard.

## Certification Costs

It is difficult to obtain estimates of the likely cost of certification without specifically seeking a quote from one of the certification bodies.

The costs of certification may be broken down as follows:

- the application fee
- the assessment fee
- the fee for annual surveillance visits/continuous assessment
- the fee for re-assessment, as appropriate.

The certification bodies tend not to have standard charges for their services, stating that the cost will depend on the specific nature and size of the organisation. Most are happy to hold an initial meeting with a prospective client, free of charge, and having gained a good understanding of the work likely to be involved, will provide a fixed quote for carrying out the assessment work.

Suggested costs for an organisation comprising 150 employees on one site are as follows:

| | | |
|---|---|---|
| Application fee | – | £450– £500 |
| Assessment fee | – | £3,000–£5,000 |
| Annual surveillance fee/ continuous assessment | – | £1,000–£1,500 |
| Re-assessment fee | – | £2,000–£4,000 |

Additional costs may be incurred if the organisation's quality system does not meet the Standard's requirements, thus necessitating special visits. Furthermore, cancellation charges may be raised if agreed visit dates are cancelled by the organisation.

# A PLANNED APPROACH TO GAINING BS 5750

The starting point to a planned approach to gaining BS 5750 has to be the appointment of a manager who will "drive the process" and make sure that all targets are achieved. This person must be a senior member of the organisation and must have direct access to the senior management team to ensure that the decision making process happens speedily. This person may be given the title "Project Manager" or "Development Director" and may in time become the quality representative called for by the first requirement of the Standard. Alternatively, this person may undertake the role only for the period up to the implementation of the quality system, and at that point, hand over to a Quality Assurance Manager who will take the system through to certification and beyond. Here, the title Project Manager has been used.

The role of the Project Manager is to take the organisation through the work which needs to be done in a logical and time-effective manner. There are four key stages which the Project Manager must address:

Stage 1 — Making the decision
Stage 2 — Gaining commitment
Stage 3 — Planning and development
Stage 4 — Implementation of the system

A chart showing the key steps to be followed is set out in Figure 5.9.

## STAGE 1 — MAKING THE DECISION

The first stage involves going back to basics and asking the question "Why do we need a quality system?". It is essential that this question is asked afresh and that sound reasons are provided, for and against, so that everyone in the organisation can understand the logic for the decision to pursue BS 5750 certification. The answers, together with a summary of the findings, must be documented so that reference can be made to them if necessary at a later stage.

This question should be posed to senior managers — the initial decision must come from the top of the organisation. If possible the respondents should identify and quantify the anticipated benefits, although this may be difficult to achieve in practice. In addition to seeking the views of senior managers, it may also be appropriate to look outside the organisation to observe what the competition is doing. If the trend is to pursue BS 5750, the organisation may decide it must do the same, to keep up with its competitors, or it may decide that an alternative strategy would be more appropriate.

## STAGE 2 — GAINING COMMITMENT

Having established that the senior management of the organisation want to pursue BS 5750, the next job for the Project Manager is to sell the idea of a quality system to everyone in the organisation to gain total commitment. If the idea is not sold to everyone, it is very likely that the system will fail, because staff will not do their best if they are not committed to what they are doing. The best way for the Project Manager to achieve commitment is through a series of training sessions and workshops. This "awareness" training will be necessary for every single member of staff in the organisation.

## Figure 5.9: A Planned Approach to Gaining BS 5750

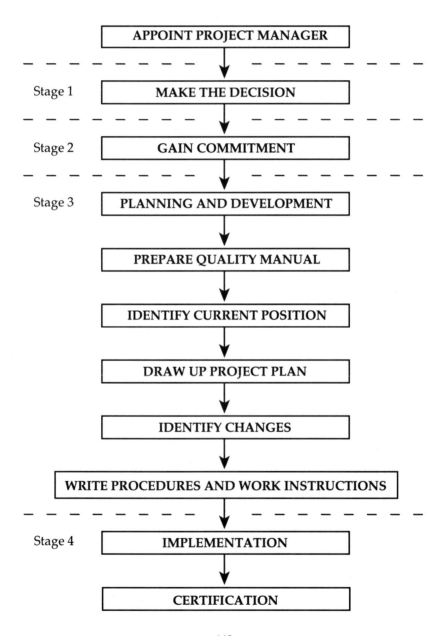

The awareness training package should explain clearly why the organisation is aiming to gain BS 5750 certification, describing the benefits which will materialise, and give a basic understanding of what BS 5750 is all about and what will be required of each individual. It is vital that the training is geared appropriately to the audience — the sessions must be understandable and move at a pace which maintains interest. It is useful at the awareness training sessions to give to all employees a summary of the organisation's quality policy in the form of a motto — something that can be remembered easily and instantly related to "quality" and to BS 5750. Given that the awareness training will take some time to complete, particularly in large organisations, it is sensible for work to commence on Stage 3 whilst the training is underway.

# STAGE 3 — PLANNING AND DEVELOPMENT

Having gained the commitment of all the staff, the Project Manager is now in a position to start on the detailed work of planning and developing the quality system. Within this stage, there are five key elements:

(a) the preparation of the first draft of the quality manual
(b) the identification of the current position
(c) the drawing up of a project plan
(d) the identification of any necessary changes
(e) the writing of procedures and work instructions.

### First Draft of the Quality Manual

It is a useful exercise for the Project Manager to put together quickly a first draft of the quality manual. As described earlier, this is a short document setting out the key policies of the organisation in response to the requirements of the Standard. The preparation of the first draft will provide a focus for the detailed work to be undertaken.

### The Identification of the Current Position

In order to be able to move forward, it is essential that everyone understands how the business works now and to what extent the requirements of the Standard are being met already.

The best way to achieve this is for the Project Manager to set up two series of workshops with employees from all parts of the organisation. In the first series of workshops, there should be groups set up to represent different activities in the organisation; for example, food production, storage, service, cleaning, hygiene, finance, administration, etc. These groups should include managers, supervisors and "ground floor" workers closely involved in the activity under examination. The aim of the workshop session will be for the group to identify all the jobs and tasks they undertake within the function and to state the current standards achieved for each job or task. In order to keep things simple, the description of jobs, tasks and standards should be kept short. With this in mind, the author proposes that each workshop is given the following pro-forma to complete.

*ACTIVITY:* . . . . . . . . . . . for example FOOD PRODUCTION

| JOB/TASK | CURRENT STANDARD |
|---|---|
| 1. | |
| 2. | |
| 3. | |
| 4. etc | |

Whilst not essential to fulfil the requirements of the Standard, the Project Manager may also ask the attendees at the first series of workshops to identify whether the current standards meet the demands of the customer. To assess this, it may be necessary to carry out customer surveys, look closely at complaints received and to consider what the competition is offering. A review of the organisation's market share and how this has changed over the past years will also give a good indication of whether the product or service offered is what the customer wants. If current standards do not match customer requirements, it may be desirable to use the vehicle of BS 5750 to introduce changes which will result in standards meeting customer expectations. The proposed pro-forma could be extended to include a third column titled "Customer Standard".

In the second series of workshops, there should be groups set up to look at the 18 requirements of the Standard and to identify where the organisation is in relation to the requirements and what work needs to be done. In determining who should be in which group, the Project Manager should include employees from all parts of the organisation and from all levels — the important qualification is that they should have an interest or possess some knowledge about the aspect of the business to be discussed. By having a cross-section of personnel, the output of the workshop group should not be biased towards the thinking of one specific element of the organisation. As with the first series of workshops' the author proposes that each group is given the following pro-forma to complete.

REQUIREMENT: . . . . . . for example PROCESS CONTROL . . . . . . . . . . . . . . . . . . . . . . . . .

| STANDARD REQUIREMENT | CURRENT PRACTICE |
|---|---|
| 1. | |
| 2. | |
| 3. | |
| 4. etc | |

Having held these two series of workshops, the Project Manager, in conjunction with other senior managers, department heads, etc, must make a decision as to which functions of the organisation will come within the proposed quality system. Whilst certain functions will obviously be included, for example restaurant service and food production, other "back of house" activities may not, for example finance, administration and personnel.

## The Drawing up of a Project Plan

Having identified the current position, the Project Manager must then draw up a project plan which sets out clearly the work to be done, based on the output of the two sets of workshop sessions. The project plan should also include tasks not specifically generated by the 18 requirements, but which are extremely important; for example, choosing a certification body, for a multi-site operation choosing how many and which sites will be included, and whether or not to set up a pilot scheme. In order for the project plan to be most effective, it is proposed that the plan is developed in the form of an action plan, detailing the following:

- tasks to be done
- by whom
- by when.

The project plan should be tailored to meet the timescale targets of the organisation. Timescale targets should not be too short as to be totally impractical, nor should they be too long. As discussed earlier in this chapter, if the process becomes too protracted, the commitment of the workforce will start to wane. An ideal timescale to aim for is 12 to 18 months from start to gaining certification.

The project plan must be agreed to by all those involved in carrying out the work as being achievable and realistic. If agreement is not reached, it is unlikely that the plan will be achieved — this situation must be avoided at all costs.

Depending upon the size and scale of work to be carried out, the person given responsibility for a task may decide to set up a working group to help them. They may divide the task up into smaller jobs and allocate relevant tasks to the working group members. This approach is a very sensible route to take, because it not only spreads the work load, it also ensures that many of the workforce are actively involved in the development of the quality system. This will help to guarantee their commitment and the commitment of those workers closest to them over whom they have an influence.

The Project Manager is responsible for monitoring the progress of the project plan against the timed plan and for giving support and help where needed. Inevitably, the Project Manager will be involved in much of the detailed work, but he or she must remember to "stand back" regularly and take an objective view of proceedings.

## The Identification of any Necessary Changes

One of the key questions which will be asked by each working group will be "Do we need to make any changes to the way we operate to achieve customer satisfaction?". If the answer is yes, this is the time to introduce the change. For this to happen effectively, it is vital that the full implications of any changes are thought through carefully and a plan of action drawn up. It may be helpful for working groups to complete the following pro-forma to help them identify the gap between "where we are" and "where we want to be".

| JOB | CURRENT STANDARD | GAP | CUSTOMER STANDARD |
|---|---|---|---|
| 1. | | | |
| 2. | | | |
| 3. etc | | | |

## The Writing of Procedures and Work Instructions

BS 5750 requires procedures and work instructions to be written for all tasks which will have an impact on quality. Procedures and work instructions should be written by the various working groups. The work instructions will include a statement of any new standards to be achieved and any changes to the method, equipment or raw materials to be used. Where different methods are used to do the same job, the task for the working group will be to establish which one is the best for the organisation. Procedures and work instructions must reflect any agreed changes and must be trial tested to ensure that they work in practice. If such a trial period is not run, the workforce are unlikely to be committed to the change — they need to be convinced of its merits and the benefits for them.

In order to assist with the writing of procedures and work instructions, the Project Manager should issue to all relevant persons instructions setting out how a procedure and how a work instruction should be prepared. The format for writing procedures is fairly strict and an example has been given earlier in this chapter. Work instructions can be prepared in whatever format is most appropriate for the organisation. However for ease of reference, the Project Manager should set up a pro-forma to be followed.

# STAGE 4 — IMPLEMENTING THE QUALITY SYSTEM

Once all the procedures and work instructions have been written covering all the requirements of the Standard, the next stage for the Project Manager is to implement the quality system or handover the system to the Quality Assurance Manager for implementation.

Implementation will involve putting into place all the procedures and work instructions, putting into action the document control system and introducing the concept of internal quality audits.

Throughout the implementation period, it is essential that all staff receive training relating to what they are being asked to do. The training must explain clearly the reasons behind any changes and the introduction of the changes must not appear to be imposed by senior management. If the suggested route described so far is followed, the workforce should not feel that any change is being imposed, because immediate colleagues will have been involved throughout and will have kept them updated on developments.

During the implementation stage, the internal quality auditors must be trained. Part of the training can include an initial assessment of the effectiveness of the quality system. However, to give the quality system a chance to "settle down", it is sensible to allow the system to run for at least two months before a full assessment is made. A full assessment must then be carried out and problem areas identified and rectified.

It is vital that communication to the whole workforce is excellent during the implementation period and thereafter on a continuing basis. Regular bulletins on progress should be displayed for all to see, showing the successes, but also the areas where more work is needed and where further changes will be necessary to achieve the requirements of the Standard.

Once the implementation is fully complete and any necessary changes made, it is now time for the Project Manager or Quality Assurance Manager to update the quality manual and to publish it in its final form. At this point, the organisation is ready for the assessment process by the certification body.

## PREPARING FOR CERTIFICATION

There is often confusion between the words "accreditation", "certification" and "registration". An organisation can gain either certification to BS 5750 or accredited certification to the Standard. Whilst both are nationally recognised, it is considered that an accredited certificate best provides the recognised assurance of quality.

The National Accreditation Council for Certification Bodies (NACCB) have set up a scheme to accredit certification bodies. The purpose of this accreditation scheme is to assess whether an independent certification body is fully competent and effective in assuring quality. In the UK, accreditation is awarded by the Secretary of State for Trade and Industry. The NACCB assesses the independence, integrity and technical competence of certification bodies which apply for accreditation and advises the

Secretary of State whether to grant accreditation or not. Bodies which successfully achieve accreditation can use the distinctive national mark — the tick, to denote their status.

A list of the current 25 accredited certification bodies is given in Appendix 3. The list includes certification bodies specific to certain industries, for example ready mixed concrete; obviously these bodies would not be able to certify catering organisations.

Ther term "registration" is a general term used to describe certification to BS 5750.

As noted earlier, it is generally accepted that the preparation period for certification should be between 12 and 18 months. This should permit sufficient time to prepare and develop manuals and procedures, etc, but does not allow time for the participants to become bored and stale. With this in mind, it is worth applying for certification as soon as a provisional date for the registration audit has been set.

The certification audit is in two parts: a theoretical assessment of the quality manual, and a practical assessment "in the field". The theoretical assessment is purely a paperwork exercise. The practical assessment will usually include a pre-assessment advisory visit to assess the organisation's state of readiness. This is an opportunity to ask questions of the certification body which may help with the practical assessment, for the certification body to sort out any queries they have from the assessment application and to establish the scale of the audit so that both parties know what to expect. The time taken to undertake the proper practical assessment will vary according to the number of sites involved and the size of the organisation. For a small, single site operation the assessment is likely to take approximately two to three days. Employees from every level of the organisation will be involved in the assessment. The assessors are used to dealing with "shop floor" workers and will ask their questions in such a way so that the operator is not confused or worried.

After the assessment, the certification body will prepare a report setting out unacceptable aspects — these will be detailed as "minors" and "majors", depending upon the severity of their unacceptability. The certification body will usually allow a set time for these "minors" and "majors" to be resolved. Often these can be dealt with by post.

The certification body will then register the organisation and issue a certificate. Having achieved certification, the certification body will carry out follow up visits — the number and frequency of which varies from body to body. A complete re-assessment is required by some certification bodies.

## MAINTAINING BS 5750

Internal and external quality audits should ensure that the quality system operates according to plan. However, some people believe that once certification has been achieved the work is finished.

Whilst the certification body will impose surveillance visits on an organisation at least yearly, effort will be required to ensure that the original enthusiasm and commitment of the workforce is maintained. In particular, difficulties will occur if:

- there is a lack of commitment from the senior and middle managers
- the Quality Assurance Manager's post is lost
- there is a change of the organisation's ownership.

Problems will continue to arise and it is unlikely that "getting it right first time" will always happen.

There are a number of actions that can be taken to help an organisation maintain the standards it has set itself:

- re-formulate action teams
- ensure that all new staff receive the appropriate training in the quality system
- make sure the internal audit reports are acted upon and problems solved
- review the systems and remove unnecessary paperwork.

BS 5750 is often seen as part of an approach to "quality" and many organisations go on to discover and use complementary techniques and tools to maintain quality within their organisation, for example Total Quality Management.

Maintaining BS 5750 is very important. Losing BS 5750 certification could have a devastating effect on the organisation. Senior management have a real responsibility to ensure that commitment to the system remains intact and they should be pro-active in their efforts to do so.

# GETTING HELP

There are a number of organisations who will provide information and literature on BS 5750, including:

- the Institute of Quality Assurance
- the Department of Trade and Industry
- the British Standards Institute
- the British Quality Association
- Trading Standards Officers
- consultants specialising in the field of quality.

Addresses of these organisations are given in Appendix 1.

# Chapter 6

# Total Quality Management

Total Quality Management is an all encompassing philosophy that involves and affects *all* aspects of a company and its business. It has been stated that the philosophy has an impact on all aspects of the life of an organisation and its people.

It is important not to confuse TQM with other systems such as BS 5750. TQM moves beyond the focus of meeting specifications, document control and internal non-conformance and inspection, to an environment that encourages continuous improvement, innovation and an obsession with delighting customers by exceeding their expectations. Unlike BS 5750, there is no certification process for TQM, and neither can there be. The only true measure of success can be given by the organisation's customers.

With TQM, customer orientation through continuous improvement becomes a "taken for granted" assumption shared by everyone in the organisation. The key to achieving this state is to develop an organisational culture totally dedicated to the customer, whether they be external or internal. For organisations who adopt TQM, the distinction between employee and customer is no longer valid — total quality means managing and serving the employee as well as the customer.

TQM relies completely on the attitude, understanding and commitment of the organisation's top management to embrace the philosophy and incorporate it into everything they do.

There is no end point to the implementation of TQM but it is vitally important that a clear structure and sound measures of improvement are in place. Training and education are vital, as are participation and the change in the behaviour of management which are invariably required.

This chapter aims to give a brief outline of TQM. The adoption of TQM in this country is relatively new and, at the time of writing, there is no evidence to suggest that a catering organisation has gone the full route of TQM. There is some evidence of catering departments who form part of a larger organisation becoming involved in TQM, but practical examples are not readily available. Catering in many large organisations is not the main business of the company and is often undertaken by catering contractors who are less likely to get involved in an organisation's TQM programme. Much, however, has been written about TQM and there is an increasing trend towards its development in this country. Examples of organisations who are committed to a TQM culture include Ind Coope Burton Brewery, Mercury Communications, the Rover Group and many other large companies.

# A BRIEF HISTORY

The concepts behind TQM are by no means new and are continuing to evolve. Contrary to popular belief, they are not Japanese but American. However, few would deny that the Japanese economic success in the second half of the twentieth century is based upon the statistical control of quality and the understanding that the customer is the most important part of the production line.

The history of TQM can be traced back to the early post-war period and to the impact of two major personalities, Dr. W. Edwards Deming and, later, Dr. Joseph Juran. Their teachings contributed enormously to the shaping of Japanese management practice. Whilst Deming and Juran were invited to advise on quality, their teachings influenced all aspects of management. In 1960, Dr. Deming was the first American to be decorated in the name of the Japanese Emperor, receiving the Second Order of the Sacred Treasure for his contributions to Japanese industry. (Dr. Juran has subsequently received this honour.)

It was not until the late 1970s that Western management began to think about quality and its application across the whole organisation. Quality had previously meant reliance on the mass inspection of products, not customer service. In the UK it has only been since the late 1980s that the teachings of Deming and Juran have become more widely listened to and practised.

· It is difficult to pinpoint the start of the quality explosion, but by the late 1970s it was becoming increasingly obvious that the tag of cheap and shoddy goods could no longer be applied to those from Japan. The alarming factor was that quality had risen dramatically but the price had remained low. As Derek Hornby, a former Chairman of Rank Xerox put it,

> It was only when we measured ourselves against the best of our competitors and realised that our manufacturing cost was about equal to their selling price, that we understood fully the fundamental nature of our problem.

Most organisations claim to have some form of quality initiative in place, but few are actually achieving their goal. In 1992, a survey carried out by A.T. Kerney indicated that eight out of ten quality programmes were failing.

# OBJECTIVES AND PRINCIPLES

For TQM to bring about real business improvements, it has to be applied throughout the whole organisation from the top to the bottom.

The top level of management must demonstrate clearly their commitment to TQM and that the issue of quality is a serious business concern which affects all employees. Within all operating departments basic changes of attitude will be required if TQM is to succeed. If top management do not recognise and accept their responsibilities for the development and implementation of TQM, the chances of failure are high.

Systems and techniques are important in TQM but they are not the main requirement. TQM is more concerned with attitudes of mind, teamwork, and a determination to do well all the time — in essence, a total commitment to delighting the customer and exceeding their expectations.

One of the objectives of TQM is to make every individual in the working environment accountable for their own performance and to bring about the necessary changes in attitude to ensure that each person is committed to attaining quality in a highly motivated way. If TQM is to succeed, it must be developed within the organisation, it cannot be imposed from outside. Continuous improvement is another key objective and if this is to be achieved, ideas for improvement must again come from individuals within the organisation and not from outside it.

TQM is about changing attitudes and skills so that all the work processes carried out by every individual in the chain of events are done "right first time, every time".

The introduction of a successful TQM programme is based on three key elements:

(a) a quality assurance system
(b) quality tools and techniques, and
(c) teamwork.

## Quality Assurance Systems

Meeting the customer needs and exceeding them can rarely be achieved without the development and implementation of a quality assurance system. The quality assurance system must ensure that the objectives set out by the management, often documented as the quality policy, are achieved every time.

Quality systems such as BS 5750 fulfil this requirement, and ensure that all practices and procedures which affect quality are controlled. This in turn assists in providing the consistency of product or service which the customer demands.

## Quality Tools and Techniques

Most quality problems occur because a variety of actions mean that standard procedures and processes cannot be adhered to, for example, variations in raw materials, late deliveries and variable individual performances.

TQM requires that the processes should be improved continually by reducing any variations to the set standards. This can be achieved by studying all aspects of the work processes and constantly searching for ways to improve them. In essence, it involves looking beyond checking that standards have been met to examining the effects of change on processes which may help eliminate any aspect likely to affect adversely the quality of the finished product or service required by the customer.

In addition to using normal control techniques to monitor and measure performance and conformance, all processes can be monitored and improved by gathering and using data more effectively. Simple presentation of data using diagrams, graphs and charts is a very effective way of communicating how things are going to the workforce. The use of statistical techniques can then assist in answering many questions such as, "if we changed this process, what would be the impact?".

There is a classical pattern in organisations that have adopted the TQM philosophy that, after about three years, improvement slows down. Continuous improvement requires the application of quality improvement tools and techniques. This is definitely an area where many organisations fail to understand what improvement techniques are available and how to use them. Continuous improvement demands continuous education in and application of the tools of quality improvement.

## Teamwork

Teamwork is an absolute essential of TQM. The use of a team approach to solving problems and striving for continuous improvement has many advantages over individuals working on separate problems. The benefits include:

- being able to tackle a greater variety of problems
- the opportunity to harness a pool of knowledge and expertise
- developing and building on ideas and suggestions more easily
- generating more diverse ideas
- a more rewarding and fun process.

When properly managed, teams improve the process of problem solving, producing results quickly and economically.

Teams should be work based and the first approach should be for teams to tackle those issues which are under their own control, not global issues. Where problems overlap with other departments, other teams can then be involved in the problem solving process.

Teamwork throughout any organisation is an essential component of TQM since it builds up trust and improves communication. If everyone is to be involved in the process of continuous improvement, then it is important that their efforts are recognised — this encourages teams and individuals to strive for continuous improvement and to continue to provide the necessary commitment to TQM. When ideas are taken on board, a feeling of importance and worth is generated: this aspect of teamwork recognises that people are very important to the ultimate success of the business. Every organisation must establish a structure which will allow everyone to be involved with quality improvement at their own level and have their efforts recognised.

# IMPLEMENTING TQM

The task of implementing TQM is daunting and is often further complicated by the extensive range of books, articles, theories and packages now available.

Before moving forward, top management need to understand what needs to be done to implement TQM. The quality gurus have summarised and documented a series of points which form the basis for moving forward and they include:

- total commitment to continuous improvement
- the requirement to "do it right first time"
- understanding the customer/supplier relationship
- recognition that improvement of systems must be managed
- a commitment to on-going education and training
- the instigation of teamwork and the improvement of communications
- the development of a systematic approach to the implementation of TQM.

As with all quality systems, the requirements needed to proceed must be discussed carefully and the reasons for implementing TQM established. There are many organisations who go down the quality route and fail. Whilst the reasons are often complex and numerous, it has been stated that often the initial planning, reasoning and thinking was inadequate. Adopting TQM for the wrong reasons will invariably lead to failure.

In the first instance, answering a number of simple questions will help to clarify the current position of the organisation and whether TQM is right or wrong for the business, namely:

- are the customers always delighted?
- are there customer complaints?
- is it known what the customers' needs really are?

– are the workforce committed to getting it right first time?

It may be that even after answering these questions, the way forward is still not clear. External help may well be required for an organisation to make the first decision on the right way forward.

## THE WAY FORWARD

There are two basic ways of proceeding, either alone or with the help of external advice from, for instance, external consultants.

Implementing TQM from within the organisation without any external assistance can be a tough and lengthy process. Not only is it time consuming, but often the internal resources with the knowledge and credibility to bring about change are not available.

Publications, videos and other training material are available which offer suitable advice. Organisations such as the Department of Trade and Industry also have a wide range of information which is available for companies wishing to implement TQM themselves. It is also helpful to visit and discuss TQM with other organisations which have already embarked on TQM. However, for many, the thought of this DIY approach is too risky.

The use of external consultants is often the route taken by many organisations, whether as a means of getting started, or to provide help throughout the main period of development and implementation.

If external assistance is required it should be understood that help can only be effective if it is in the form of facilitating the organisation and acting as a catalyst. A consultant in TQM who does not take this approach should be avoided. No consultant can introduce TQM alone — ownership and implementation must lie with the organisation itself.

## THE KEY ISSUES TO BE ADDRESSED

The process of development and implementation will vary from organisation to organisation. However, there are a number of key steps that should be taken in the process of adopting TQM. Very simply, these include the following.

1. The development of clear objectives which are published and communicated in the form of a quality policy or mission statement. Understanding and commitment to these objectives is essential if an organisation is to succeed.

2. The development of a clear plan of action to achieve the objectives. Members of the workforce from all levels should be involved in this process as the likelihood of gaining early commitment to them is increased.

3. Encourage the workforce to participate in the process. The management structure and responsibilities must be reviewed in the light of the objectives and the plan of action. An effective management structure is required to ensure the effective implementation of TQM.

4. Understand your customer requirements, needs and expectations. Encourage all employees to take part in this process for both external and internal customers.

5. Plan to do all jobs right first time.

6. Introduce a quality assurance system which identifies clearly the standards to be achieved.

7. Implement a quality improvement process to include the use of teamwork and the right tools and techniques. Measure how well the customer needs are being satisfied.

8. Demand and bring about continuous improvement, and recognise achievements when they occur.

The process of implementing TQM is never-ending. It takes years to see the benefits of adopting the TQM philosophy. Most people acknowledge that to achieve any sort of lasting change may take as long as five to seven years.

A recent article written by Paul Davies from TQM International Ltd states that there are three distinct phases which organisations go through in adopting TQM. These are illustrated in Figure 6.1.

The survival stage, with key problems being solved, teams being developed and training and education in progress, is unfortunately the stage that many organisations never progress from. Some organisations reach the prevention stage but very few UK companies would claim to be at the third stage of continuous improvement.

### Figure 6.1: Stages in the Development of TQM

| SURVIVAL | PREVENTION | CONTINUOUS IMPROVEMENT |
|---|---|---|
| Recognising competitive threat and the need for improvement | Bringing the business "under control" | Business an integrated process |
| Isolating key problems | Management ownership | Total customer orientation |
| Organising to solve them | Challenging existing roles and methods | Fully participative management |
| Solving them | Building quality into the business | Controlled improvement and change is the norm |
| | Developing capable and motivated people | |

Source: Paul Davies, TQM International Ltd.

Many organisations are adopting TQM as they see it as the key competitive strategy for survival for the long term future. For those organisations which have achieved certification to BS 5750, TQM is the next step.

There is no doubt that TQM is a long, difficult process to undertake. Its value lies in enveloping all aspects of an organisation and the requirement to develop a culture where quality is an integral part of everyday working life, not an add-on.

The growth of TQM in industry generally is expected to increase. Its value has been advocated by many as being the only way forward in this highly competitive world. Is it right for the catering industry? The answer to this question must be yes. The fundamental problem is that the industry is only just starting to think about quality as a real issue. Maybe TQM is for the future — at present very few catering operations will have heard about or understand TQM. As with many quality management systems, the cost may also be prohibitive to many. However, it is not beyond the caterer to understand the principles which represent the philosophy of TQM and start to consider the real benefits on offer.

In summary, TQM is all about:

- leadership from the top
- focusing on delighting and exceeding customer expectations
- continuous improvement in all aspects of the business
- teamwork to bring about quality improvements
- effective quality assurance systems to enable employees to "do it right first time".

A model illustrated in the DTI publication *Total Quality Management and Effective Leadership* is shown below, and provides a summary of the TQM philosophy and its key components.

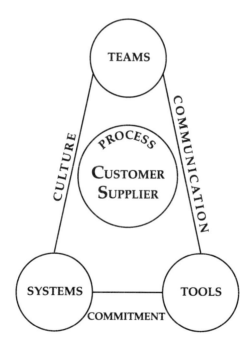

Further information on TQM is available from many sources and a list is provided in Appendix 1.

# Chapter 7

# Designing Your Own Quality Assurance System

Quality assurance is no longer considered a management fad and its future in the catering industry will be the difference between success or failure for many operators. The catering market is extremely competitive and with customers now more aware of value for money, quality is being demanded. Even within such sectors as hospitals and schools, which have a captive market, competition from the high street is real and is challenging the whole ethos behind "institutional" catering.

In a formal sense, catering is not at the forefront of industries who are acknowledged as operating quality assurance systems. However, many operations are further down the quality route than is often realised. It is encouraging to see that many catering operators have systems in place, but they have never been labelled formally as part of a quality assurance system.

This chapter aims to dissolve the mystique of quality assurance systems and assist caterers in designing and operating a simple, but effective system to meet their individual needs.

Earlier chapters discussed the more formal routes commonly recognised as acceptable quality assurance systems, for example BS 5750, but for many organisations these routes may not be suitable. The reasons can be numerous. It is recognised that many parts of the industry, particularly the smaller catering businesses, cannot afford to follow the route of BS 5750 or TQM, or indeed decide that neither route is appropriate.

This chapter outlines an approach to developing a system which is flexible in its approach, simple, and cost effective both in terms of financial and manpower resources.

It should be acknowledged that the implementation of any quality assurance system does take time and therefore by implication, incurs costs. The benefits of introducing a quality assurance system have already been extolled and whichever route is taken, the savings to be made from avoiding quality mistakes have been proven to outweigh the initial investment required.

# QUALITY ASSURANCE PRINCIPLES

The principles of quality assurance apply to all systems, although there are slight variations between the overall objectives and philosophy behind them.

One of the major differences between a tailor-made system and BS 5750 is that there is no formal assessment and certification process. The tailor-made system does not attract a nationally recognised mark of approval, and without this incentive it is essential that the principles of quality assurance must be firmly recognised and understood by all members of staff.

Top management support is absolutely critical, and commitment to the programme "for life" essential.

The major assets of a catering organisation are its people, the product it produces and, to a certain extent, the actual establishment. Without adequate care and attention to and from the workforce, implementing a quality assurance system will be difficult and sometimes impossible. Therefore, good communication is essential throughout the entire development and implementation programme, and beyond.

# TAILOR-MADE SYSTEM OBJECTIVES

Many internally designed systems have been based on the principle of control, not prevention. Inspections and checks have all focused on identifying and remedying problems after they have occurred.

The objective of the internally designed system is to develop processes and procedures which prevent quality mistakes from occurring in the first place. However, every quality assurance system needs controls to be developed and exercised in order to determine that the assurance system is working and is appropriate. Given that catering operations are very complex and often involve both elements of service and production, the approach to control for this quality system is based on setting standards and monitoring those elements which are *critical* to the customer receiving the quality of service or product required. It is impossible and not even necessary to monitor all aspects of an operation. This approach is similar to the approach advocated by the HACCP system of control which, experience suggests, works effectively.

The ultimate quality assurance system must include clear standards for every part of the operation (service and production elements, as well as finance, marketing, etc) and a monitoring system which not only includes tangible product checks but which also reveals customer perceptions, customer/staff interaction and customer satisfaction — the intangible considerations.

Figure 7.1 illustrates the key stages of development for the implementation of an internal, self-designed quality assurance system.

A practical approach to each stage of development is discussed and the process is illustrated with examples from key operating elements of a typical catering operation. No two operations are the same, but there are common elements in most catering operations. To illustrate the system, priority has been given to the main elements of food production and service.

# KEY STAGES OF DEVELOPMENT

At some stage, a senior management decision will have been made to introduce a quality assurance system and to appraise the available options. Undertaking this option appraisal is crucial to ensure that the right system is chosen.

Having confirmed that a self-design system is the most appropriate route to follow, the process of development can begin.

In the first instance, the staff need to be informed of the decision to proceed. Invariably, this announcement is merely a confirmation, since the original decision was made by a team from all levels within the organisation.

## Figure 7.1: Tailor-made Quality Assurance System — Key Stages of Development

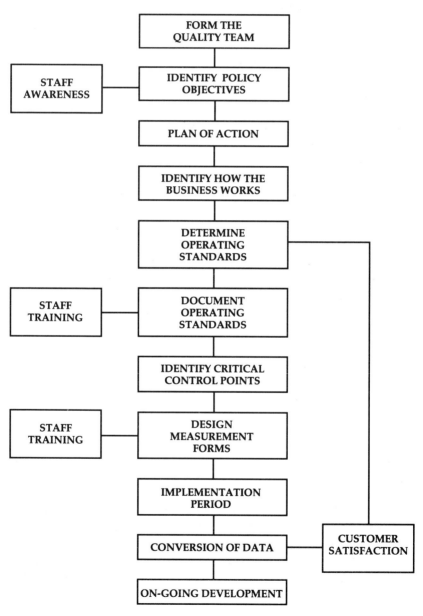

## Stage 1 — The Team

Introducing a quality assurance system successfully will involve time, commitment and dedication. The amount of time will depend on how far down the quality route the organisation is. Many catering operations, particularly in the last five years, have started to produce operating manuals, training programmes and have introduced computerisation; others will be starting from a less advantageous position.

Regardless of the starting point, the first task for the senior management team will be to set up a quality team to carry the programme forward.

Reference has already been made to the importance of commitment to quality throughout the entire organisation. Given that commitment is required from the top to the bottom of the organisation, the team must represent the various levels.

The size of the team will vary from operation to operation. Depending on how the process is to be planned and instigated, it may be appropriate to form a small team with representatives from each major department, which are supplemented with additional personnel as required; for example, a main quality team with departmental or specialist sub-groups.

The appointment and selection of a team leader is crucial. The quality team leader needs to possess certain characteristics. The organisation is effectively giving someone responsibility to change the culture of the organisation from one where quality is talked about to one where quality is a part of everyday working life. Personal attributes such as leadership, determination, motivation, persuasiveness, tact, patience, integrity and an understanding of quality assurance principles are essential.

Many organisations may not have suitable people readily available, except perhaps key managers who would not, due to operational constraints, be in a position to fulfil this role successfully. Careful thought needs to be given to these issues to decide whether help from another source is required. Options may include:

- the appointment of temporary personnel to allow a permanent member of staff to dedicate the necessary time required
- the use of external consultants to support and facilitate the process
- the appointment of the necessary personnel on a short term contract
- a short term internal reorganisation to make the necessary people available.

It may be possible to allocate the team leadership to an internal person as part of their job. This arrangement can succeed, but care needs to be taken to provide the necessary support to avoid any conflict of interest and the potential for work overload.

The quality team structure must be communicated to all staff as soon as possible.

## Stage 2 — Identify Quality Policy and Objectives

A quality policy or mission statement needs to be prepared by the most senior member of the management team. The policy or statement should demonstrate the organisation's commitment to quality and will be the basis on which the objectives are determined.

Setting clear objectives for the quality assurance system is important. They provide the focus for the planning, development and implementation of the quality programme to meet the main quality policy.

The objectives will vary from organisation to organisation and between departments. They may include gaining a competitive edge, increasing profits, meeting customer needs or just to comply with the Food Safety Act 1990. Conflicting objectives must be dealt with, but there is no reason why the introduction of a quality assurance system cannot meet a variety of objectives.

The agreed objectives must be documented and understood by all, as they provide the basis on which the whole programme will be developed.

## Stage 3 — Plan of Action

The team's first responsibility will be to plan the approach to developing the quality system. The range of issues for discussion will include:

- the current position regarding, for example, standards, systems, procedures and how well the customers' needs are met at present
- agreement on the stages of development required
- the manpower resources required
- the budget requirements and availability of financial resources
- the timescale involved.

To address all of the above issues is a time consuming exercise. Deciding where you are and what needs to be done must be tackled before sensible estimates on time, resources and budget requirements can be agreed.

The quality team need to agree the approach to gain this information. Sub-group workshops are an effective means of collecting data on the current position of each department. At this stage the team is looking for an overview of the operation sufficient to be able to detail a sensible plan of action.

Having assessed the current position, the work to be undertaken to meet the original objectives must be agreed. For the purpose of the tailor-made quality assurance system, it is likely that the key components of the process outlined in Figure 7.1 will form the basis of the way forward.

The gap identified between the current position and the work to be done will provide the basis on which manpower and financial resources can be discussed and estimated.

The key components of an action plan include:

– tasks to be undertaken
– individual responsibilities
– timescales for the completion of all tasks.

The output from this stage will be a long term action plan. An example of a summary action plan is illustrated in Figure 7.2. The number of days input shown in the plan are unlikely to be complete days or consecutive days. The extended shaded area indicates that it is a task which can be undertaken over a period of time. The amount of detail which is included in the action plan will vary. A summary action plan, as illustrated in Figure 7.2, may be appropriate for senior management, with additional, more detailed plans being produced for operational teams. The plan will be the management tool to control the progress of the implementation programme, particularly the target completion dates for individual tasks.

Approval to proceed with the plan must be obtained from senior management, particularly for the proposed timescale and budget.

Part of the initial planning process must be to agree how the staff will be kept informed of progress. The method and frequency of communication will depend on the size and complexity of the organisation. Useful methods of communication include:

# Figure 7.2: Quality Assurance Action Plan

| TASK NO. | TASK | DAYS INPUT | RESOURCE | JAN | FEB | MAR | APR | MAY | JUN | JUL | AUG | SEP | OCT |
|---|---|---|---|---|---|---|---|---|---|---|---|---|---|
| 1 | Form the Quality Team | 1 | XYZ | 2 | | | | | | | | | |
| 2 | Identify Objectives | 2 | Team | 2 | | | | | | | | | |
| 3 | Staff Awareness | 5 | Team | 5 | | | | | | | | | |
| 4 | Plan of Action | 20 | Team | | 10 | 10 | | | | | | | |
| 5 | How the Business Works | 10 | Teams | | | | 10 | 10 | | | | | |
| 6 | Operating Standards | 30 | Teams | | | | | 10 | 10 | 10 | | | |
| 7 | Staff Training | 10 | Teams | | | | | | 5 | 5 | | | |
| 8 | Documentation | 40 | Secretary | | | | | | 10 | 5 | 20 | 10 | |
| 9 | Identify CCP's | 10 | Teams | | | | | | | 5 | 5 | 10 | |
| 10 | Design Measurement Forms | 20 | Teams | | | | | | | | 10 | 5 | |
| 11 | Staff Training | 5 | | | | | | | | | | | |
| 12 | Implementation Period | | Teams | | | | | | | | | | |
| 13 | Conversion of Data | 5 | Teams | | | | | | | | | | 5 |
| 14 | | | | | | | | | | | | | |
| 15 | | | | | | | | | | | | | |
| 16 | | | | | | | | | | | | | |
| 17 | | | | | | | | | | | | | |
| 18 | | | | | | | | | | | | | |
| 19 | | | | | | | | | | | | | |
| 20 | | | | | | | | | | | | | |
| 21 | | | | | | | | | | | | | |
| 22 | | | | | | | | | | | | | |
| 23 | | | | | | | | | | | | | |

- verbal communication (suitable for very small operations only!)
- team briefings/meetings
- noticeboards, with space for quality issues identified
- written communication in newsletters/company magazines
- individual written communication via, eg, pay packets.

The method of communication is not as important as its effectiveness. The quality team must check that the information being disseminated reaches all employees in an understandable format. The catering industry employs a multi-national workforce with varying standards of experience and ability and the written word may not always be the most appropriate or effective means of communication.

## Stage 4 — Identify How the Business Works

There are three key issues to address at this stage—these will in turn shape the quality assurance programme.

The first issue is to address is what are the customers' needs and are they being met? The second issue is to understand fully the key operating activities that form the business, including the operating strengths and weaknesses. The third, to determine whether, from the outcome of the first two stages, the business needs to change to meet the identified customer needs.

### *Customer Needs*

The customer is the priority and there needs to be a process to ascertain the exact needs of the customer, specifically related to quality standards. Successful quality assurance systems are concerned with interpreting the customer needs correctly, designing the catering operation to conform to the standards required and monitoring the system to ensure that the desired quality is provided every time.

There has been a great deal of research undertaken into the interpretation and measurement of customer needs. It is outside the scope of this book to discuss the very complex issues surrounding the interpretation of customer needs, particularly intangible aspects such as "atmosphere", "ambience" and "social interaction".

Organisations such as McDonalds and other large multi-nationals, have spent excessive amounts of money on assessing customer needs in relation to product, style of service, opening hours, location and environment.

For the smaller catering operations, such investment is not feasible but some assessment of needs is essential. A number of simple methods will provide an insight into whether the quality standards are satisfactory or not, including:

- customer surveys
- local research and reviews of the competition
- investigation of complaints
- examination of external and market trends.

Assessing and interpreting customer needs is difficult and many common problems which are encountered include:

- management *thinking* they know what the customer wants
- management not interpreting the needs of customers correctly
- management not thinking about the customer at all!

Objectivity and independence are important in interpreting the results of the investigations.

*Key Operating Activities*

The size and complexity of the operation will determine how this process is tackled.

The main operational areas for catering businesses include a combination of those illustrated in Figure 7.3. It is unlikely in a small operation that separate departments would exist for each function, but each would be represented in some format.

Departmental workshops are an effective means of identifying how each function operates; in addition they delegate the data gathering process to the right people. Sub-groups should be formed with a team leader being appointed from each separate function. This is an excellent method of getting the staff involved and committed to the programme. The shop floor workers are, after all, the people who really know how the operation works.

The objective of the workshop is to brainstorm exactly what happens in that function. For example, the head chef would head a select team from the kitchen to identify all the key activities.

## Figure 7.3: Catering Business Functions

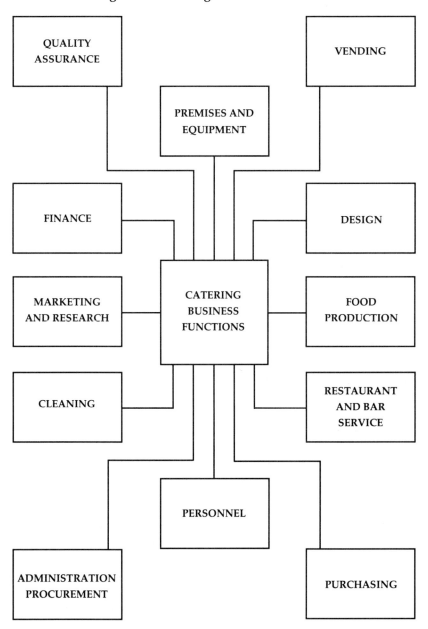

A simple method for identifying all the activities is to use a flow chart which identifies the process from start to finish. An example for a kitchen is illustrated in Figure 7.4.

The key activities for the whole business need to be identified and documented. Care needs to be taken to ensure that what really happens is documented, not what should happen!

The output of this stage of work should be an indication of whether the current operating standards are meeting the target customers' needs.

*Change Required*

The results of the needs assessment may identify a number of changes to be made. The extent of change needs to be verified and the implications thoroughly assessed both in operational and financial terms. Some areas of change will involve new products and services, others may be problems which had not previously been recognised as such.

The outcome of Stage 4 will provide the quality team with a thorough understanding of how the business works, the perceived customer needs and the key areas where change is required. The establishment of this information is critical to determining the operating standards required to meet customer needs.

## Stage 5 — Determine Operating Standards

The objective of this stage is to determine the operating standards which will meet those customer expectations.

Each of the key operating activities identified in the previous stage need to be re-examined and all tasks involved in every activity thoroughly reviewed.

For each activity, the current operating standard needs to be identified. Where the current standard is perhaps not the desired standard, the necessary changes should be discussed. Depending on the nature of any change required, implementation could be immediate, or considerable development may be required. For instance, an increase in the menu range may be relatively easy to implement, whereas a change from plated meals to silver service will include staff training, the purchase of additional service equipment, and a change to working practices. The operating standards need to be discussed and agreed within the functional teams, but it is advisable to have an independent assessment of the agreed

**Figure 7.4: Food Production – Overview of Key Operating Activities**

| MENUS | PURCHASING | RECEIPT/STORAGE | PREPARATION |
|---|---|---|---|
| Planning | Ordering | Check Goods | Mis en Place |
| Forecasting | New Suppliers | Accept/Reject | Salads |
| Research | Price Checks | Correct Storage | Sandwiches |
| Costings | Specifications | Document Invoices | Cleaning |
| | | Cleaning | |
| | | Stock-take | |

| AFTER-SERVICE | WASH-UP | SERVICE | COOKING |
|---|---|---|---|
| Clear-down | Pots–manual | Hot-plate | Cooking |
| Stock-take | Dishwasher | Replenishment | Cooling |
| Left-overs | Cleaning | Left-overs | Bain-marie |
| Cleaning | | Clear-down | Standard Recipes |
| | | Serve | Quality Checks |
| | | | Cleaning |

| PERSONNEL | TRAINING |
|---|---|
| Staff Rotas | On-job |
| Wages | Off-job |
| Casual/Agency | Records |
| Holidays | Planning |
| Disciplinaries | Doing |

standards. This will overcome any potential problems with the functional teams being too familiar with the operation and not seeing the opportunity for improvements. This objective assessment may be undertaken by a member of another team or by an external catering professional.

Figure 7.5 illustrates a suggested pro-forma for the identification of current and desired standards — the purchasing function has been used as a simple example of the work process to be analysed.

**Figure 7.5: Identification of Current and Desired Standards for Purchasing**

| CURRENT STANDARDS | DESIRED STANDARDS |
|---|---|
| Write in diary the list of goods to be ordered | Review menus and previous popularity |
| Phone through orders | Work out quantities from standard recipes/methods |
| Use nominated suppliers | |
| Quantities ordered – based on experience | Write out order in purchase order book |
| Order list – based on what is required | Telephone suppliers to get best price |
| Quantity purchased depends on price – buy more than required to get best price | Place order and give order number |
| | Orders to be in line with purchase specifications |

Once agreed, the actual operating standards need to be documented.

## Stage 6 — Documentation of Operating Standards

The operating standards need to be documented in a common format. Operating standards form the basis of the quality assurance programme, against which the provision of the service is measured.

It is common for all standards to be encompassed within a procedure or work instruction.

For ease of reference and future updating, each procedure should contain the following information:

- procedure title
- date of issue
- author
- issue number
- clear, concise procedure details.

The number of procedures produced will vary. Some organisations may want details and standards indentified for every single task, whereas other organisations may decide to only document procedures for key activities. The greater the number of procedures, the more complex the control and monitoring aspect of the system becomes.

All procedures can be filed together into a procedures manual. The adoption of the suggested format allows the manual to be updated regularly. As changes occur, a further issue can be produced to replace the obsolete issue.

A master sheet of all changes to procedures should be held centrally. This will ensure that all copies of the procedures are kept up to date. Old procedures should be destroyed immediately on receipt of the new procedure.

Figure 7.6 illustrates such a procedure for food storage.

*Staff Training*

At this stage all staff should receive refresher training for current operating procedures and standards. Where changes have been made, new procedures and standards can be introduced.

All training should be geared to incorporating the principles of quality assurance throughout.

## Stage 7 — Identify Critical Control Points

The use of critical control points is a system more commonly associated with HACCP. The HACCP system (as we have seen) is based on controlling those activities where there is a high risk of a health hazard occurring. HACCP is aimed primarily at food safety systems, but the principles are very useful in the context of the tailor-made quality assurance system.

## Figure 7.6: Procedure for Food Storage

| PROCEDURE TITLE Food Storage | ISSUE NO. 1 |
|---|---|
| PROCEDURE NO. 1 | AUTHOR JPE |
| | DATE 14 JULY 1992 |

1. All food stores including chilled and frozen storage must be maintained in a clean and tidy condition.

2. All spillages must be cleaned immediately.

3. Raw and cooked foods must be stored separately. Never place raw food directly above cooked food because of possible drip contamination.

4. Separate chilled and frozen storage cabinets are identified for each category of food as follows:

   | Refrigerator | 1 (a) | Salad Items |
   |---|---|---|
   | | 1 (b) | Cooked Foods |
   | | 2 (a) | Raw Meat |
   | | 3 | Vegetables |
   | | 4 | Dairy |
   | Freezer | 2 (b) | Meat and Fish |
   | Freezer | | Vegetables |
   | Chest Freezer | | Bakery and Ice-cream |

5. All refrigerators must be cleaned thoroughly at least twice weekly. All freezers must be defrosted monthly or in accordance with manufacturer's instructions.

6. All foods must be wrapped or stored in closed washable containers. All raw food must be labelled with the delivery date and name of the product. All cooked / chilled food must be labelled with the production date and use by date.

7. Food must never be stored with cleaning chemicals or other possible contaminants.

8. All foods which are delivered in bulk must either remain in the original packaging and be stored in a mobile food bin or be decanted into a suitable food container. In the latter case the product batch code number and any recommended use by date must be transferred to the food container.

| PROCEDURE TITLE    Food Storage | ISSUE NO.    1 |
|---|---|
| PROCEDURE NO.    1 | AUTHOR    JPE |
| | DATE    14 JULY 1992 |

9. Care must be taken to read and understand the manufacturer's instructions relating to storage.

10. The temperature of all food storage areas must be checked in accordance with measurement form QA3.

11. The storage temperature of certain foods is controlled by the Food Hygiene (Amendment) Regulations 1990. A copy of the document is available from the Group Head of Catering.

12. No foods must be stored on the floor in any store area. Mobile food containers must be used for bulk items.

13. Food stock must be rotated properly on the basis of first in, first out.

14. Any out-of-date stock must be destroyed immediately. Any such stock must be recorded and the head of the kitchen informed.

15. The refrigerators must not be used as a vehicle for chilling hot or warm foods.

16. Frozen foods which are to be defrosted should be stored for the appropriate length of time in a refrigerator. The core temperature of the food must be taken and recorded to ensure that the food item has been defrosted thoroughly. No defrosted food item must be re-frozen.

It is impossible to monitor all aspects of a catering service, so only those aspects where a lack of control would result in real customer dissatisfaction are monitored. These become the critical control points. This approach keeps the issue of quality in focus and leads to a simple, meaningful quality system.

The identification of the control points should be undertaken by the teams which agreed the operating activities and standards. In this way, agreement is reached quickly on which activities are critical and which are not. Certain critical control points will be the same for all catering operations, such as those related to food safety. Others will vary according to the type of establishment.

Every procedure should be reviewed and agreement reached on where control is vital. An example of a procedure for the cooking of food items is illustrated in Figure 7.7 and the suggested critical control points identified with a "C".

It is essential that the meaning of the word "critical" is emphasised. It is easy to end up with a system where everything appears critical and needs monitoring. The resultant quality assurance system would be unwieldy, meaningless and impractical to implement.

At the end of this process, each procedure will have been reviewed and points of control identified.

## Stage 8 — Design Measurement Forms

The next stage is to agree how the identified control points will be monitored to check that the standards documented in the procedures are met.

Checking that an identified critical point has been controlled may be undertaken in a variety of ways, for example, the use of temperature testing equipment, verbal communication, written communication and visual inspection.

Whatever method of measurement is used, the results must be recorded as proof that the check took place. The recording of this information can be collected onto a series of measurement forms. These forms need to contain, as a minimum, the following information:

- the critical points to be measured and controlled
- the date of the check
- the name of the checker.

## Figure 7.7: Cooking Procedure

| | |
|---|---|
| <u>PROCEDURE TITLE</u>   Cooking<br><br><u>PROCEDURE NO.</u>     2 | <u>ISSUE NO.</u>   1<br><br><u>AUTHOR</u>    JPE<br><br><u>DATE</u>   14 JULY 1992 |

1. The cooking of all food items will be in accordance with standard recipes and methodologies.

2. A daily production schedule will be prepared to itemise the day's production requirements.

3. Production must be scheduled to ensure that foods are not cooked too far in advance of service requirements. Due care and attention must be paid to time and temperature considerations during the cooking process.

4. The time and temperature of the cooking process should be sufficient to ensure that heat penetration to the centre of the food will destroy all non-sporing pathogens. The core temperature of all foods must reach 75°C by the end of the cooking process. **C**

5. All items to be cooked must be recorded on measurement form QA4.

6. The centre temperature of a random sample of all batches must be taken with a probe thermometer. **C**

7. Where possible, batch cooking should be carried out for such items as vegetables as this maintains the food at the highest quality.

8. Where certain foods are not required for immediate consumption they must be chilled to 0 – 3°C within 90 minutes. The chilling process must be undertaken in line with the chilling procedure No. 21. The details must be recorded on measurement form QA4. **C**

In this way, there is a comprehensive record of the events which took place.

The frequency with which the critical points are measured needs to be established. In some instances it may be every occasion that an activity takes place. In other instances, weekly or monthly checks may be more appropriate. Whatever frequency is decided upon, the collecting of the information must not become meaningless. Time and the amount of paperwork which will be generated must also be taken into consideration.

The member of staff responsible for measuring the critical control points must be identified clearly. A lack of communication will lead to the system breaking down.

Taking the example of the cooking procedures and control points identified in Figure 7.7, an example of a measurement form to record the results of the monitoring process is illustrated in Figure 7.8.

It is important to keep the measurement forms simple and, where possible, avoid excessive writing — a tick and a signature is often all that is required.

Whilst the majority of measurement forms are likely to be based on checklists, other types of monitoring may include surveys, face-to-face interviews, statistical analysis and other management techniques.

## Stage 9 — Implementation Period

Each of the measurement forms must be used on a trial basis before they are finalised. The original forms will undoubtedly be amended two or three times before a real workable document is produced. Changes may well include a reduction in the number of areas to check, the grouping together of areas to check and a change in layout. The final format must be comprehensive, simple and easy to complete. Every effort must be made to assist the catering staff to take a responsible attitude towards this crucial stage of recording the evidence.

Before the measurement system is implemented, all staff who are involved in the process must be trained in the standards and procedures being measured. In addition, the measurement forms must be clearly understood.

The measurement system should be introduced with care. It is a difficult process for members of staff suddenly to start documenting and

**Figure 7.8: Process Monitoring Form**

FOOD PREPARATION AND PRODUCTION                    DATE

| PRODUCT & BATCH NO. | START TIME PREPARATION | START TIME COOKING/ REHEATING | FINISH COOKING/ REHEATING | | HOLDING TIME | SERVICE COUNTER | | CHILL | | | | |
|---|---|---|---|---|---|---|---|---|---|---|---|---|
| | | | REHEATING TIME | TEMP | | TIME | TEMP | START TIME | START TEMP | FINISH TIME | FINISH TEMP | |
| | | | | | | | | | | | | |
| | | | | | | | | | | | | |
| | | | | | | | | | | | | |
| | | | | | | | | | | | | |
| | | | | | | | | | | | | |
| | | | | | | | | | | | | |
| | | | | | | | | | | | | |
| | | | | | | | | | | | | |
| | | | | | | | | | | | | |
| | | | | | | | | | | | | |
| | | | | | | | | | | | | |
| | | | | | | | | | | | | |
| | | | | | | | | | | | | |
| | | | | | | | | | | | | |

measuring their own performance. However, even at this late stage there will be those people who may not be 100% committed to the quality assurance system and may offer some resistance to the completion of the measurement forms. Should this situation arise, a strict approach to ensuring that the critical control points are monitored as and when agreed, must be adopted. If the management and supervision of the system allows a breakdown to occur at this stage, all credibility is lost and the situation is very difficult to retrieve.

Having trial tested the system over a period of two to three months, agreement on the final format of the system must be made. Whilst the system must evolve to keep pace with the business, change for change's sake should be discouraged.

## Stage 10 — Conversion of Data

There must be a mechanism built into every quality assurance system to ensure that the information collected by the measurement system is fed back to the members of the workforce. For example, the information collected *via* a checklist will be raw data. Raw data needs to be analysed, interpreted, summarised and reported back to the various interested parties.

Information can be presented in a number of formats — the written word, in diagrams, verbally and numerically. The way in which raw data is converted into meaningful feedback will depend upon the receiver. Operational staff such as chefs and waiting staff will probably respond well to diagrams and pictorial information — it is easy and quick to read and remember. Management will only require periodic reports summarising the quality information, say monthly.

Selecting the frequency that information is fed back to management and staff is important. Too much information too often is as ineffective as is too little information given infrequently. Where a serious problem is identified at the monitoring stage, it must obviously be dealt with at the time. General information relating to performance must be fed back soon enough for any relevant facts or events not to have been forgotten.

For the purposes of illustrating how raw data can be effectively converted to precise meaningful information, the results of a customer survey will be used as an example.

A typical survey for a staff restaurant is illustrated in Figure 7.9.

## Figure 7.9: Customer Survey

### USERS OF THE CATERING SERVICES – QUESTIONS 1–4

1. Which of the following catering services do you use and how often?

| RESTAURANT SERVICE | NO. OF TIMES PER WEEK | NO. OF TIMES PER MONTH |
|---|---|---|
| Restaurant Breakfast | | |
| Restaurant Lunch | | |
| Beverage Vending | | |
| Snack Vending | | |

2. Please indicate the types of product you buy when you use the facilities.

| TYPE OF PRODUCT | TICK BOX |
|---|---|
| Hot Main Course | |
| Salad | |
| Call Order/Snacks | |
| Sandwich | |
| Hot Pudding | |
| Cold Pudding | |
| Soup & Roll | |
| Other . . . . . . | |

3. How much do you spend per week on food and drink whilst at work?

| FOOD £ | DRINK £ |
|---|---|
| | |

4. What is your opinion of the catering service provided? Please tick the table below.

| ASPECT OF THE SERVICE | VERY GOOD | GOOD | O.K. | POOR |
|---|---|---|---|---|
| Menu Range and Choice | | | | |
| – Hot Main Course | | | | |
| – Vegetables | | | | |
| – Call Order/Snacks | | | | |
| – Salads | | | | |
| – Sandwiches | | | | |
| – Hot Puddings | | | | |
| – Cold Puddings | | | | |
| Quality of Food | | | | |
| Presentation of Food | | | | |
| Attitude of Staff | | | | |
| Portion Sizes | | | | |
| Price Levels | | | | |
| Speed of Service | | | | |
| Overall Value for Money | | | | |
| Quality of Vending Products | | | | |
| Vending Machine Reliability | | | | |
| Other . . . . . . . . . . | | | | |

## NON-USERS OF THE CATERING SERVICES – QUESTIONS 5–8

5.   Why do you not use the service?

COMMENTS

6.   If you purchase food and drink from outside sources, please indicate where from, and how often.

| SOURCE | FREQUENCY OF USE |
|---|---|
| Supermarket | |
| Public House | |
| Fast-Food Outlet | |
| Food from Home | |
| Restaurant | |
| Other . . . . . | |

7.   Please indicate the types of products you buy when you use the facilities indicated in the table above.

COMMENTS

8.   How much do you spend per week on food and drink whilst at work?

| FOOD £ | DRINK £ |
|---|---|
| | |

## USERS AND NON-USERS OF THE CATERING SERVICE – QUESTION 9

9.   What changes to the catering service would you like to see in the future?

After analysing the survey, a series of reports can be produced, for example:

- overall percentage satisfaction score
- average spending per head for food and drink per visit
- overall value for money
- uptake of vending machines
- product popularity analysis.

The above list is by no means exhaustive. It illustrates a small number of reports that can be produced for different departments within the catering operation.

By using simple graphs and bar charts it is often possible to show trends over a period of time and Figure CS 2.7 in Case Study 2 illustrates how this can be achieved for the percentage of acceptable food deliveries over a 12 month period.

In conclusion, the conversion of all the data collected should enable the catering management and staff to assess the success of the quality assurance system, and hence the level of customer satisfaction.

## Stage 11 — On-Going Development

As the business develops, so must the quality assurance system. Standards may change and will need to be included in the operating procedures and the measurement system. Frequencies of monitoring may also change as standards of operation improve.

It is vitally important that the system is not allowed to become mundane and ineffective. Maintaining the system will be as difficult as developing and implementing it. The system must always be meaningful, relevant and up-to-date.

Management have a real responsibility to ensure that the system is relevant — the attitude and commitment of the staff will show whether this is the case or not!

The tailor-made approach will offer many benefits to those caterers who may not be in a position, or indeed not feel it is right, to opt for a more formal structured approach to quality assurance.

The emphasis is certainly on commitment and thorough planning to ensure that this type of system will work well. There is no external assessment and no certificate — it is all down to the internal operators to make it worthwhile.

If the principles of quality assurance form an integral part of the system and the staff are given the tools and techniques to achieve the desired standards, this preventative approach to quality assurance will assist greatly in the delivery of a catering service to meet the needs of the identified customer base.

# Case Study 1

# Enfield Borough Catering Service and BS 5750

In January 1992 Enfield Borough Catering Service achieved certification to BS 5750. The organisation has set a precedent as it is the first multi-site catering operation to be awarded BS 5750 in the UK.

This case study describes the process that the Borough Catering Service undertook to achieve certification and addresses some of the critical success factors and difficulties which they encountered.

## THE SIZE OF THE SERVICE

The Borough Catering Service provides the catering needs for Enfield's schools, social services and the Civic Centre. The table below illustrates the breakdown of schools by type.

| SCHOOL TYPE | NUMBER OF SCHOOLS |
|-------------|-------------------|
| PRIMARY | 57 |
| SECONDARY | 21 |
| SPECIAL | 5 |
| COLLEGES | 2 |

The total number of meals served each day to the schools and social services is approximately 18,000. In addition, up to 1,200 meals are served in the Civic Centre restaurant daily.

There are four social service kitchens which produce all the meals for Meals on Wheels and Day Centres within Enfield.

In excess of 500 staff are employed by the Borough Catering Service — this figure includes all management and supervisory staff as well as full- and part-time employees based at each site.

# THE NEED FOR BS 5750

The provision of catering services for the Borough of Enfield was put out to competitive tender in 1988/89. The in-house catering department became a Direct Service Organisation (DSO) and alongside other contractors, prepared their bid to continue to provide catering services to the Borough.

The tender specification categorically stated that all prospective tenderers should either have or be working towards BS 5750 certification.

Therefore, as part of the tender submission, the DSO prepared and presented a quality assurance manual which set out their approach to the maintenance of quality in the catering service.

In August 1989 the catering contract was awarded to the DSO. It was at this point that the DSO planned formally their approach to meeting the requirement to gain BS 5750 certification. The process is shown in the flow diagram in Figure CS 1.1.

After being awarded the contract, the Borough Catering Service appointed a DSO manager whose sole responsibility was to work towards the achievement of BS 5750.

The organisation was very new and the management team were having to deal with the new contract as well as planning the way forward for quality assurance.

Having produced the quality assurance manual, the organisation had already implemented and documented the way in which they operated the contract. This was a major contribution to satisfying the requirements of the Standard.

However, the detailed requirements of the Standard were new to the management team and it was agreed that external help would be required.

# Figure CS 1.1: Enfield Borough Catering Service BS 5750 Timescale

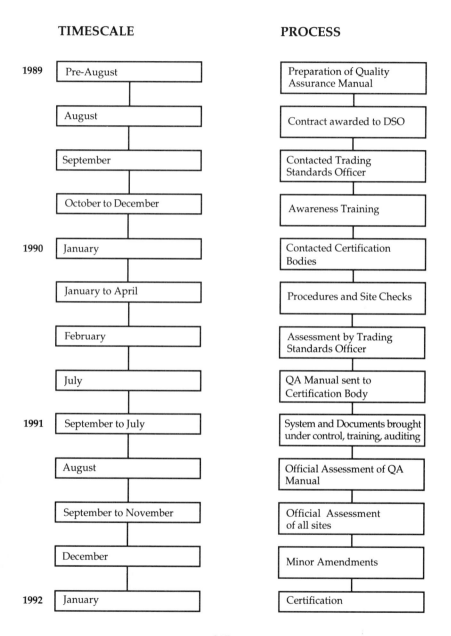

TIMESCALE

PROCESS

| TIMESCALE | PROCESS |
|---|---|
| **1989** Pre-August | Preparation of Quality Assurance Manual |
| August | Contract awarded to DSO |
| September | Contacted Trading Standards Officer |
| October to December | Awareness Training |
| **1990** January | Contacted Certification Bodies |
| January to April | Procedures and Site Checks |
| February | Assessment by Trading Standards Officer |
| July | QA Manual sent to Certification Body |
| **1991** September to July | System and Documents brought under control, training, auditing |
| August | Official Assessment of QA Manual |
| September to November | Official Assessment of all sites |
| December | Minor Amendments |
| **1992** January | Certification |

217

Contact was made with the local Trading Standards Department and it was agreed formally that an officer would be made available to support the Borough Catering Service throughout the period leading up to the final assessment.

The DSO manager and the TSO were the main members of the team and additional support was sought from other catering managers and supervisors as required.

An outline plan of action was drawn up to identify clearly what further work was needed to meet the requirements of the Standard. The plan did not detail a finite time frame within which certification was to be achieved. The organisation was new, complex and providing catering services across 86 sites. It was felt that to impose a tight timescale for achieving certification across such a large multi-site operation would be impossible. Furthermore, it was agreed that to gain real commitment from every member of staff from each site was going to take a considerable period of time. The team, however, wanted to maintain the momentum of striving towards their goal and therefore set a target for certification within a two-year period.

# AWARENESS TRAINING

The first major stage of the plan was to design and implement an awareness training scheme.

A two-day course was designed for managers and supervisors. After completing this course, further training was given to this group of staff to enable them to carry out second party assessments in their role as internal auditors. The awareness training for managers and supervisors was undertaken over a period of two months.

The supervisors then developed a programme to educate all staff at each site. The heads of kitchen received a half day course and all other staff were talked to on a less formal basis over the following months. The cascade approach to training worked well and commitment to the quality programme soon became evident. This was demonstrated in the staff's support for the managers and supervisors as they worked hard towards implementing the quality system at each site.

# SELECTION OF ASSESSMENT BODY

In January 1990, contact was made with a number of certification bodies, and the Borough's proposals were discussed with each organisation. Discussions continued until the summer of 1990 when firm proposals were submitted by the certification bodies.

Yarsley was selected to be the assessment accredited certification body for the Borough Catering Service.

# PROCEDURE WRITING AND QUALITY MANUAL AMENDMENTS

After the majority of the awareness training had been completed, catering managers and supervisors concentrated on undertaking regular site visits and inspections of working practices.

The quality manual and the procedures contained within it were used as the standard against which the catering service was checked. New procedures were written to support existing procedures and amendments were made to the quality manual as appropriate.

At this point in time, the system was not brought under document control. It was important that the systems and procedures were operating well before document control was introduced.

In February 1990, arrangements were made for the Trading Standards Department from a neighbouring local authority to carry out a formal assessment of the quality system in place. This was invaluable as it enabled the management team to make any necessary amendments to procedures and the quality manual before the assessors from Yarsley carried out their formal assessment.

In July 1990, the management team decided that the necessary systems and procedures were working well at each site and that the quality manual should be assessed. The quality manual was sent to Yarsley for a preliminary assessment — not the formal assessment. Comments and suggestions for improving the manual were received back after a month and the necessary amendments to it were made.

# QUALITY SYSTEM UNDER CONTROL

At this point the management team made a decision not to go for immediate assessment of the total system. It was felt that, whilst the system was working well, it would be advantageous to allow the system a period of time to become really established and part of the everyday working life.

In September 1990 all the documents were issued and brought under formal control.

Formal quality assurance visits were undertaken at regular intervals between September 1990 and April 1991. The main emphasis was to ensure that both supervisors and staff were all adhering to the quality manual and that the system was working as documented. This involved further intensive training for staff and supervisors in the use of the quality manual and procedures.

## FORMAL ASSESSMENT

In April 1991, Yarsley was contacted and informed that the Borough Catering Service was ready to be assessed.

The first part of the assessment was undertaken in August 1991. In the first instance the assessors examined thoroughly the quality manual and other documentation over a two-to three-day period. The site visits began in late September. Over a two-month period every operating outlet was visited. Each visit comprised an assessment of the systems and procedures in operation and discussions with members of staff. At the end of the formal visits, Yarsley identified six minor offences and only two major offences. The management team were given a month to rectify these problems before a final accredited certification of the two major offences was undertaken.

In January 1992, the Enfield Borough Catering Service achieved accredited certification to BS 5750.

## CRITICAL SUCCESS FACTORS

In working towards BS 5750, the management team identified a number of critical factors that led to their success. These are outlined below.

## Factor 1 — Commitment

Without full and *real* commitment to BS 5750, it would have been extremely difficult to achieve certification and thereafter to maintain it.

## Factor 2 — Team Effort

A team effort was required to ensure that the momentum was sustained, particularly with a large multi-site operation.

## Factor 3 — Training

Training was a very large contributor to the successful implementation of the catering quality system. If staff are not aware of the need for BS 5750, it is more difficult to gain their commitment. Training in the procedures is vital.

## Factor 4 — Quality Manual

It is important to set realistic requirements for quality — the management and staff had to be able to meet the standards laid down in the quality manual and the procedures.

The manual must be as simple as possible — it is a mammoth task to complete.

## Factor 5 — Cost

Never underestimate the time inputs required and the cost of certification — it is very expensive!

# DIFFICULTIES ENCOUNTERED

Over the two and a half year period a number of difficulties were encountered.

The biggest task faced by the Borough Catering Service was to disseminate information across 86 sites and to 500 members of staff. This was achieved by:

- each site holding its own quality manual
- holding supervisors meetings three times per year to discuss major issues relating to quality assurance
- supervisors updating their staff continually
- catering officers discussing with each supervisor any quality related problems when carrying out their audit reports: supervisors had to sign the corrective action reports highlighting deviations against the quality manual
- sending out regular bulletins and circulars to every kitchen.

Ensuring that all staff adhered to the standards and procedures was also extremely time consuming. The setting of realistic targets was crucial because many of the premises and the catering equipment contained within them was old and obsolete.

The task of pulling the whole system together, particularly the documentation, was similarly time consuming and difficult. The major difficulties arose because of the number of sites which had to be covered and the staff involved at each of the sites. In addition, it was time consuming carrying out the audit checks and compiling all the paperwork such as corrective action reports and follow-up procedures. Ensuring that the documentation was being followed on all 86 sites was not an easy task.

## THE FUTURE

The management have recognised the very real need to maintain the motivation and commitment to BS 5750.

In 1994, the Borough Catering Service need to re-tender for the catering contract — BS 5750 will be a requirement of the specification. The local authority are monitoring the contract and any problems which start to arise will be noted by the monitoring team.

The six-monthly surveillance visits by the certification body and the on-going internal audits will help to ensure that the quality system is being adhered to. In addition, the management team have set up a programme to train all new supervisors and staff on joining the organisation.

The Borough Catering Service achieved an enormous task which they set themselves in 1989. Whilst it took two and a half years to gain accredited certification, the end result is to be commended.

# Case Study 2

# St. Helier NHS Trust

In April 1991, Merton and Sutton Health Authority received Trust status and became known formally as the St. Helier NHS Trust.

Prior to gaining Trust status, the Health Authority had experimented with a number of local quality initiatives, but it became clear that discrete initiatives could never achieve the aim of making quality synonymous with the delivery of health care.

It was recognised that to achieve this aim would involve changing the culture to one in which *everyone*, including medical professionals, administrators and other support staff, would understand and include quality as part of their everyday working practice.

The Trust embarked on a Total Quality Management process as a means of bringing about the cultural change required. The principles of TQM have been addressed in Chapter 6 and the Trust's programme has embraced the total philosophy.

## THE SIZE AND STRUCTURE OF THE ST. HELIER NHS TRUST

The Trust encompasses four hospitals with a total of 949 beds. The Trust is organised into a number of core strategic business units which provide the clinical services for direct patient activities, and one non-core business unit which provides all non-clinical support services.

The non-core business unit was named the Facilities Organisation and all support services came under the control of this unit; 700 staff are employed within the Facilities Organisation and about £11 million of the Trust's money is spent on the services which patients and customers use to measure the quality of caring, as opposed to the quality of clinical care.

The new Facilities Organisation set itself a number of objectives which would meet the overall objectives of the Trust. Of particular relevance to this case study was the objective which stated that the Facilities Organisation would need:

to have clearly defined areas of responsibility and *quality*

The overall intention of the new Facilities Organisation is to be at the forefront of providing value for money and innovative service to support improved quality for patients.

One of the first departments within Facilities to address the issue of quality was the Hotel and Support Services Department. This case study describes the process that the Hotel and Support Services Department went through to introduce quality into the services provided.

# THE HOTEL AND SUPPORT SERVICES DEPARTMENT

Hotel and Support Services is one of the key departments which make up the Facilities Organisation. The main functions which are incorporated within this Department are detailed in Table CS 2.1 and these services are provided across all four sites. The functions include both internal and external contracts.

Approximately 600 staff are employed within the Department across the four hospitals.

Several of the services are provided by external contractors. A site services contract operates at the St. Helier Hospital, the largest of the four hospitals, covering nine of the services shown in Table CS 2.1.

The linen service is provided by a different contractor, but all other services at the hospitals are provided by internal resources.

| Table CS 2.1: Hotel and Support Services |
|---|
| Security * | Stores |
| Grounds and Gardens * | Portering * |
| Car Park Management * | Main Hall Reception |
| Residences * | Linen Services |
| Window Cleaning * | Switchboard/Telephones |
| Pest Control * | Laundry Services |
| Catering * | Maintenance |
| Cleaning/Housekeeping * | |

\* denotes part of site services contract at St. Helier Hospital. These services are provided by internal resources at the other 3 hospitals.

# PRE-TRUST QUALITY INITIATIVES

Prior to the Health Authority receiving rust status, many quality initiatives had been introduced, particularly *via* the competitive tendering process which specified services and agreed requirements. The site services contract resulted from this work.

Checking the quality of the site services contract was probably the first structured approach to quality to be introduced. The approach used is illustrated in Figure CS 2.1.

Whilst at the time this approach was satisfactory, the move towards TQM meant that a new, pro-active quality management system needed to be developed.

# THE DEVELOPMENT OF THE SYSTEM

A senior quality management team, including external consultants, was established to drive the development of the TQM system forward. The decision to use consultants was taken to assist the management team with this high priority development work at a time when major reorganisation

## Figure CS 2.1: Monitoring at St. Helier Hospital — "Pre-Trust"

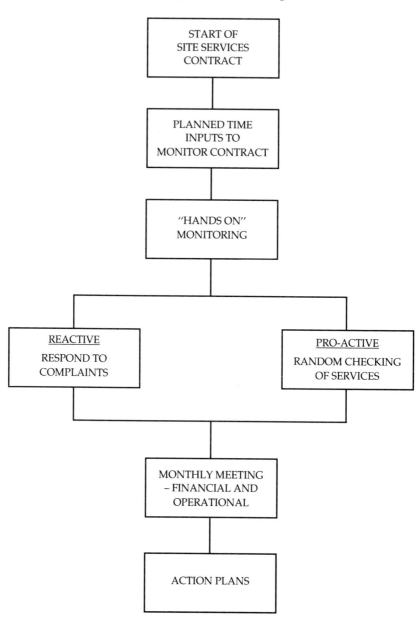

and change was happening as a result of the Health Authority gaining Trust status.

The services which were involved in the development of the system are those shown in Table CS 2.1, with the exception of the linen service, which is provided by an external contractor who is a certified BS 5750 organisation. Whilst representatives of this service were involved in the initial development stages, no changes were made to their current system.

The phased approach to the development of the TQM system is illustrated in Figure CS 2.2. The whole process up to Stage 9 was undertaken over a period of nine months and all 14 services developed their system within this time frame. Each of the key stages are discussed in the case study and it is important to understand that the process was undertaken by each service department, not just once for all service departments.

## Stage 1 — Discussion of Principles and Objectives

Management representatives from each of the 14 services came together to discuss and agree the principles and objectives for the TQM system. The lively and frank debate culminated with an agreement that the system must:

- identify whether customers' (patients, staff and visitors) needs are satisfied
- assess value for money
- measure the quality of the service
- be simple and straightforward to operate
- offer identifiable benefits to the Trust.

Other secondary objectives included the desire for the system to act as a motivator to the staff and as a potential marketing tool to project a high quality image to the Trust's customers.

To achieve these objectives, a number of fundamental principles were addressed, as follows:

- the need for commitment from *all* levels of staff
- the need to provide an error-free service every time
- the need for effective communication between all departments within the Facilities Organisation.

**Figure CS 2.2: The St. Helier NHS Trust Total Quality
Management System — Stages of Development**

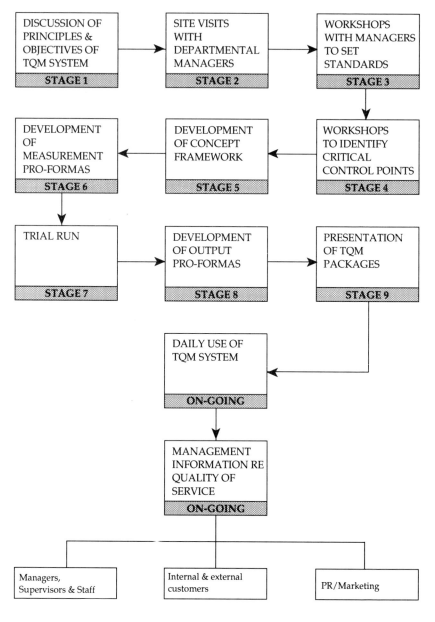

From the outset of Stage 1, the need for positive discussion, forward thinking and the creation of an honest working relationship between the providers and receivers of the service, was stressed to everyone involved with the development process. To reinforce this point and to make sure that the TQM system would work in practice and would be used by the operators, the system was developed hand-in-hand with the managers, supervisors and operators from each service department. It was essential to ensure that the system developed would be owned by everyone within the service department and not be seen as just another management fad — the involvement of staff from all levels was felt to be the best way to achieve this objective.

## Stage 2 — Site Visits

In order for the quality management team to understand fully how each service department functioned, meetings were held at each of the sites with each service manager to discuss the work that they and their staff undertook. This familiarisation process was important in establishing the links between various departments and in understanding operating strengths and weaknesses.

## Stage 3 — Setting Standards

The objective of this stage was to establish what levels and standards of service were required by the customer receiving each particular service.

Workshop sessions were held with a nominated group of representatives for each service. Each service department formulated a flow diagram to illustrate the *key activities and work processes* undertaken on a day-to-day basis. An example of the work process flow chart for the catering department is illustrated in Figure CS 2.3.

The next stage of the process involved the identification of the current standards for each of the key activities. Taking catering as an example, the tender specification was used as the benchmark for current standards.

Other services such as switchboard/telephones which had not been specified as part of a competitive tendering process, had to identify those standards which were being achieved.

# Figure CS 2.3: Catering Work Process

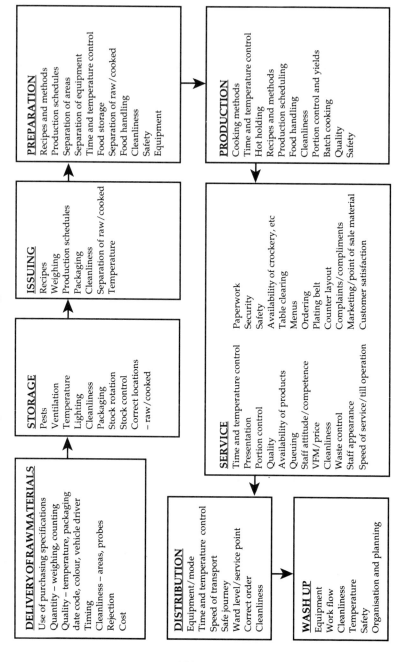

**DELIVERY OF RAW MATERIALS**
Use of purchasing specifications
Quantity – weighing, counting
Quality – temperature, packaging
date code, colour, vehicle driver
Timing
Cleanliness – areas, probes
Rejection
Cost

**STORAGE**
Pests
Ventilation
Temperature
Lighting
Cleanliness
Packaging
Stock rotation
Stock control
Correct locations
– raw/cooked

**PREPARATION**
Recipes and methods
Production schedules
Separation of areas
Separation of equipment
Time and temperature control
Food storage
Separation of raw/cooked
Food handling
Cleanliness
Safety
Equipment

**ISSUING**
Recipes
Weighing
Production schedules
Packaging
Cleanliness
Separation of raw/cooked
Temperature

**PRODUCTION**
Cooking methods
Time and temperature control
Hot holding
Recipes and methods
Production scheduling
Food handling
Cleanliness
Portion control and yields
Batch cooking
Quality
Safety

**SERVICE**
Time and temperature control
Presentation
Portion control
Quality
Availability of products
Queuing
Staff attitude/competence
VFM/price
Cleanliness
Waste control
Staff appearance
Speed of service/till operation
Paperwork
Security
Safety
Availability of crockery, etc
Table clearing
Menus
Ordering
Plating belt
Counter layout
Complaints/compliments
Marketing/point of sale material
Customer satisfaction

**DISTRIBUTION**
Equipment/mode
Time and temperature control
Speed of transport
Safe journey
Ward level/service point
Correct order
Cleanliness

**WASH UP**
Equipment
Work flow
Cleanliness
Temperature
Safety
Organisation and planning

Extensive discussions between the nominated service team members followed, as it was apparent that in some cases, different standards were being achieved at different hospitals and additionally agreed standards were not always visible.

Having established what standards existed, the service teams moved forward to determine what standards would be desirable to satisfy the customer.

At this point it was necessary to set some ground rules to enable the teams to look forward, rather than be restricted by current and past operational constraints. These ground rules were:

- that the issue of resources should not be allowed to affect the level of standard desired
- that the standard of the fabric of the building and working conditions would be upgraded to a standard comparable to a private hospital.

It was difficult for the teams to grasp these ground rules in the first instance, but understanding the need within a TQM organisation to strive for continuous improvement made the situation much clearer. In other words, the service teams understood that it was important to aim for the most desirable standard to meet customer needs, even though in the short term it would be unlikely that the standards would be achievable. This process enabled the separate teams to set their own goals. A sample of the key activities and desired standards agreed for the switchboard operators is illustrated in Figure CS 2.4.

## Stage 4 — Identify Critical Control Points

This stage involved an analysis of the key activities to determine which activities should be measured.

It was agreed that it would be impossible to measure all activities within a service department. Therefore the approach taken was to identify the *critical control points* of the service, at which control must be exercised if customer satisfaction was to be ensured. This use of critical control points facilitated the development of a simple, manageable and meaningful system of measurement. Every effort was made to ensure that the measurement system did not involve mountains of paperwork and loss of focus.

**Figure CS 2.4: Switchboard — Key Activities and Desired Standards**

| JOB | DESIRED STANDARD |
|---|---|
| Answering calls | <u>Number of rings</u><br>External    4 – 6<br>Internal    8 – 10<br><u>Engaged</u><br>Immediate return to caller plus standard phrase<br><u>On hold</u><br>Allow 20 seconds and return to caller<br><u>Attitude</u><br>Always polite and courteous |
| Faults | Report all line and alarm faults immediately<br>Check exchange lines daily |
| Answering phrase | Comply with standard phrase —<br>"St. Helier NHS Trust, how may I help you?" |
| Private calls | Record length of call and bill customer weekly |
| Bleep system | Bleep immediately — if no response, return to caller within one minute and offer to take number<br>Maintain record of bleeps and pagers sent for repair<br>Maintain record of all pager numbers and corresponding ID numbers |
| Fire and cardiac | Immediate response<br>Test cardiac bleeps once daily, including weekends |

The approach of controlling the critical points meant that the service providers could focus on the vital elements of the service. However, it was recognised at this stage that the measurement of critical control points would have to happen *in conjunction* with the full internal control system — they needed to complement, not replace, each other.

Workshop sessions were held with the service teams to identify the critical control points with the emphasis on "what is important to the customer?". The service teams were asked to "step into the customer's shoes" and to think and agree what should be measured. The agreed measurement points formed the critical control points.

## Stage 5 — Development of the Concept Framework

At this point, each service team had established the key operational activities, desired standards and the critical control points.

The next stage involved discussions on how each of the critical control points were to be measured, how often and by whom. Having agreed these issues, all the information was pulled together to form a Service Concept Framework. This document formed the basis whereby each team could move forward to the practical implementation of the system.

The Concept Framework developed by the catering service team is illustrated in Figure CS 2.5.

## Stage 6 — Development of Measurement Pro-formas

Each team moved forward to the detailed development stage of drawing up the charts which would be used to measure the critical control points identified in the workshop sessions. The majority of the charts took the form of checklists and surveys. A series of meetings were held to design the checklists. Thereafter the checklists were changed and redesigned until all team members were happy that the resulting charts were workable, produced useful information and did actually measure the critical control points. Each service team had approximately four drafts of all charts before agreeing on the final version. This stage was extremely time consuming and one which was eventually stopped to avoid excessive changes to the charts being made. It was important to try the checklists in the work situation before further alterations were made.

**Figure CS 2.5: Catering Concept Framework**

| CRITICAL CONTROL POINT | STANDARDS | METHODOLOGY | FREQUENCY | BY WHOM |
|---|---|---|---|---|
| Raw materials delivery | Quality, temperature, quantity, packaging, date | Checklist | Daily – random sample | Storeperson |
| Temperature control – chilled and frozen storage | Chilled – varied by food category<br>Frozen – minus 18°C | Checklist | Daily | Catering staff |
| Temperature control – food preparation | Preparation, cooking and holding time and temperature restrictions | Checklist | Weekly | Head Chef |
| Temperature control – during service | Hot food – above 63°C<br>Cold food – below 8°C | Checklist | Daily | Chef and Restaurant Manager |
| Service – Patients and staff | Various product standards<br>Various service standards | Checklist | 10 per month | Restaurant Manager |
| Customer comments | Not applicable | Survey | Monthly | Catering Manager |
| Temperature control – wash-up | Wash – 65°C<br>Rinse – 85°C | Checklist | Daily | Catering staff |
| Food hygiene | Detailed by area and activity | Checklist | Monthly | Catering Manager |
| Personal appearance | Uniform, ID badge, hair, hands, jewellery, footwear | Observation | Daily | Catering Manager |

Note: Precise standards were detailed in a supporting TQM system manual

234

A problem emerged during this stage. Many teams had changed their members during the development stages and where this occurred during Stage 5, progress was often slowed down. In one particular service, four changes were made to an original checklist and the final checklist was very similar to the original. Several team changes were made during this time and unnecessary time was wasted as the continuity and understanding of the first four stages was missing.

An example of the checklist produced for raw materials deliveries is illustrated in Figure CS 2.6. It was agreed that checklists should be as simple as possible and involve the minimum of writing. This checklist involves a combination of writing and ticks. Staff refresher training in receipt of food products was undertaken in conjunction with the introduction of the form. This ensured that the standards agreed in Stage 3 were communicated accurately to the appropriate staff.

Measurement charts for the catering service were prepared for each of the critical control points shown in Figure CS 2.5.

## Stage 7 — Trial Period

Further changes to the checklists were stopped and the trial period was instigated. The trial period offered each team the opportunity to try out the checklists in the real work situation and to make amendments based on practical experiences.

During the trial period, it was agreed that each service should have a person nominated as co-ordinator. This person had responsibility for the on-going development, implementation and running of the TQM system. By adopting this approach, it ensured that "ownership" of the system and the responsibility for its well-being lay with the service managers, and not the quality management team.

The trial period lasted for three months before the final development stage commenced. This three month period allowed sufficient time for a reasonable data base to be collected.

## Stage 8 — Development of Output Pro-formas

This penultimate stage involved the detailed analysis and conversion of the data generated by the measurement charts. Each service team assessed the information produced from the trial run and determined how best it could be used and presented.

**Figure CS 2.6: Raw Materials Delivery Checklist**

| Item | Supplier | Date | Probes clean? | Quality | | Temper- ature °C | Correct quantity | Pack- aging | Use by date | Checker | Comments |
|------|----------|------|---------------|---------|---|------------------|------------------|-------------|-------------|---------|----------|
| | | | | Acceptable | Unacceptable | | | | | | |
| | | | | | | | | | | | |
| | | | | | | | | | | | |
| | | | | | | | | | | | |
| | | | | | | | | | | | |
| | | | | | | | | | | | |
| | | | | | | | | | | | |
| | | | | | | | | | | | |
| | | | | | | | | | | | |
| | | | | | | | | | | | |
| | | | | | | | | | | | |
| | | | | | | | | | | | |
| | | | | | | | | | | | |
| | | | | | | | | | | | |
| | | | | | | | | | | | |
| | | | | | | | | | | | |
| | | | | | | | | | | | |
| | | | | | | | | | | | |
| | | | | | | | | | | | |
| | | | | | | | | | | | |

Three forms of presentation were considered: using the written word, using diagrams and graphs, and using numbers. It was stated clearly that if any measurement chart produced information that could not be used, the chart would be deleted from the system.

The objective was to produce information that would be useful to a variety of people. It was important to give good, meaningful management information to the staff on how well they have performed, to the existing customers to show how well the service is being delivered, and to potential customers to demonstrate what the service is capable of. It was also important to be able to use the data in a powerful way as a promotional tool to attract external customers.

The service teams were keen to ensure that the outputs from the measurement charts were capable of showing trends in performance over a period of time.

The favoured method of presentation was the use of graphs which show month by month performance. The output pro-forma developed to illustrate the data collected from the raw materials deliveries checklist is illustrated in Figure CS 2.7. This output graph enables the performance of a supplier to be monitored month by month.

Output pro-formas were developed for each of the measurement charts produced to monitor the critical control points illustrated in Figure CS 2.5.

### Stage 9 — Presentation of the Total Quality Management System

The final stage of the development of the TQM system for the Facilities Organisation culminated in a presentation by each service team of their total quality package. This last step was the acknowledgement that the service operators really owned the system.

# THE ON-GOING DEVELOPMENT OF THE TQM SYSTEM

The system has been up and running since December 1991 and is producing useful data which is being converted into "output" information for presentation in a number of ways. One of the key outputs is a monthly report — these are prepared by each service co-ordinator for senior management. The information from the monthly reports which detail any

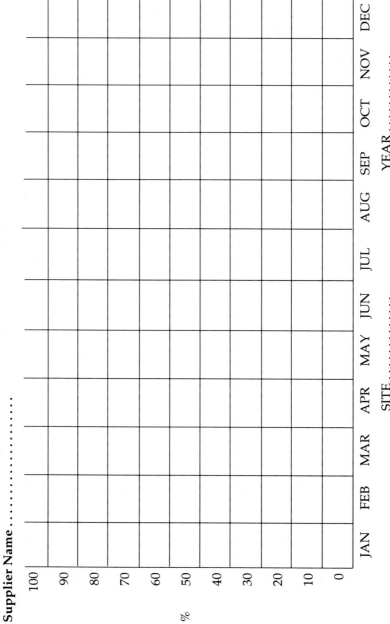

Figure CS 2.7: Catering — % of Acceptable Deliveries

significant change or which require action to be taken, is presented at a quarterly internal Trust Business Review meeting. The reports will also be used to form the backbone of the quality related information for the Facilities Annual Business Plan.

Since the introduction of the system, many services are already making changes. Where significant improvements in quality are being achieved, the frequency of checking has been reduced; similarly, other issues have arisen and new measurement charts have been introduced.

Having developed and implemented the system, the Facilities Organisation is very conscious of the fact that on-going review is essential to keep the system alive and meaningful.

It has been recognised that there will be internal pressures from inside the Trust, for example, changes in personnel, changes in customer demands and changes in requirements, and there will be external pressures such as legislation, competition and maybe even Government intervention. To keep abreast of these pressures, it is certain that the system will change. Figure CS 2.8 illustrates the on-going development process which the Facilities Organisation has put in place.

The review process will check that requirements, procedures, measurement charts and outputs are still appropriate.

Where change is required, it is imperative that change does actually happen. The mechanism for the review and change process will ensure that all changes are communicated to everyone and that all persons involved understand what the changes mean.

The development process does not stop with change. Each service team will need to control, monitor and evaluate the changes to ensure that they meet the requirements of the customer.

It has been recognised that there is a need for the development process to be co-ordinated to keep it going and to maintain motivation and commitment to the system. With this in mind, a Quality Manager was appointed in April 1992 to undertake this role.

# MANAGING THE CHANGE — THE KEY CRITERIA

The development and implementation of the TQM system involved the management of a major change in the way the staff worked and their

**Figure CS 2.8: On-Going Development**

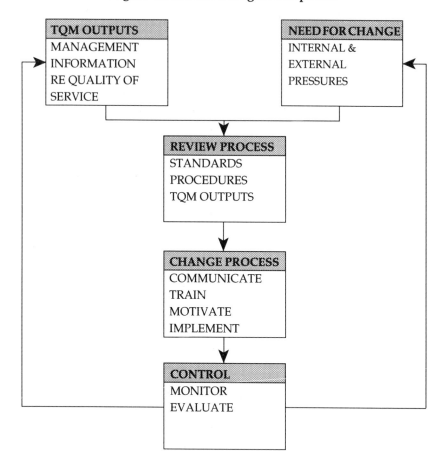

attitude to work. The ultimate aim was to make quality a part of the working day, not an add-on.

Whilst managing this change was, and still is, not an easy process, a number of key criteria were identified to facilitate this process.

In the first instance, *clear objectives* were established. The Facilities Organisation had already decided to introduce a TQM system as part of the Trust-wide approach. As a new organisation, the Facilities management team recognised that there was a need to change and challenge sacred cows and that the mechanism for this change was through the TQM process. Difficulty was experienced in persuading people that breaking customary ways of doing things is desirable — change involves spending more time and effort and learning new ways of doing things.

Second, there was a need to *create an awareness* of the need for change by exposing staff to the facts of the situation. It was necessary to ensure that all supervisors and staff were aware of and understood the reasons for developing a TQM system and what was going to be required of each member of staff. Awareness was driven from the top of the organisation with the purpose and requirements clearly defined. The key message was that "Quality is everyone's business".

Third, the appointment of an appropriate *leader or facilitator* in the process was vital to success. The important qualification for appointment to a service co-ordinator was a total commitment to the principles of TQM. The service co-ordinators' role was to plan and organise the workshops and other activities, exercise control of the groups, admit and dismiss group members and facilitate group working. It was important for the service co-ordinators to be respected by the other team members and accepted as a credible source of information. Throughout the development process, tough times were experienced and the role of the co-ordinator was vital in keeping the momentum going and maintaining the service groups as cohesive units.

*Responsibility and ownership* must eventually lie with the managers, supervisors and operators within each service department. The hand-over to the lower levels of staff was a difficult period. Staff had to be encouraged to take ownership and not just to do the job because that's what is expected of them. Those at the sharp end of the operation had to adopt the final system because without their commitment the system would fail. In some services, it became clear that certain supervisors and staff found it difficult to make decisions and set standards — they did not want the responsibility. Many staff had never been encouraged to make decisions and to think and express themselves; this situation is still in evidence and a huge culture change is taking place within the lower levels of the Facilities Organisation. Senior management have projected that whilst some change has taken place, there is still a very long way to go.

It was necessary to equip the staff with the tools and knowledge to bring about change and the cost of doing so must be recognised at an early stage.

Finally, good *communication* is essential to the TQM process.

# THE REALITIES OF IMPLEMENTING A TQM

Over 60 people from 14 different service departments were involved in developing and implementing the system.

Throughout the nine months taken to introduce the system, there was a remarkable change in the managers and supervisors from a negative "I'll do it because I have to" attitude, to "I'm doing this because it helps me to do my job". There is no doubt that there was a definite change in the way the service departments worked.

Throughout the work there were high and low points and a selection of comments and words expressed at each of the nine stages is shown in Figure CS 2.9.

The Facilities Organisation has invested considerable time, effort and resources in establishing the TQM system. To keep the system functioning, the senior management team have committed resources for training and key quality improvement schemes. These resources are only a part of the way forward and the need to keep abreast of the customer's needs and the need to review continually the quality system will contribute towards the effectiveness of the change process.

The Facilities Organisation is planning to extend the TQM system across the other service departments over the next two years.

## Figure CS 2.9: The Realities of Implementing a TQM System — The People Issues

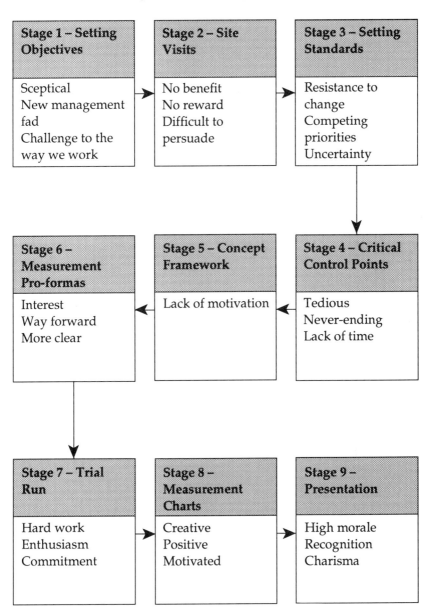

# Case Study 3

# Hospital Catering Service

The catering department in this case study has not been named but is a typical traditional hospital catering establishment, catering for 500-600 patients, staff and visitors daily.

The catering service is operated on traditional lines with food being cooked and served on the same day wherever possible.

The catering management has taken a pro-active approach to food hygiene and the implications of the Food Safety Act 1990 by sending key managers and staff on external food hygiene training courses.

It was during an advanced hygiene course that the issue of quality assurance and control was raised and the HACCP system discussed. The hospital catering management decided that its application in the catering department may be appropriate to overcome some of the current food safety issues which were becoming apparent.

## THE INTRODUCTION OF HACCP

It was agreed that HACCP should be introduced into the department, as it would provide an opportunity to re-examine the operational methods in use and to consider the hazards within the operation. The overall aim was to introduce a quality assurance system and take a preventative approach to ensuring that all food produced was safe to eat.

Prior to introducing the HACCP concept, it was considered essential

245

that all management, supervisors and staff received appropriate training in food hygiene to raise the general awareness and importance of the subject.

All staff attended a basic food hygiene course which was highly participative and gave plenty of opportunity to discuss current operational difficulties. As a result of the course and subsequent discussions, some changes to procedures and working practices were made immediately before the HACCP process commenced.

## HACCP Training

Having gained a greater understanding of food hygiene in general, external consultants were appointed to assist in the introduction of HACCP.

In the first instance, the catering manager attended a one day external HACCP course, to gain a greater understanding of the subject prior to its introduction into the catering department.

## The HACCP Process

The HACCP process was introduced by the external consultants who held two internal workshops. The first workshop was run with the catering manager and higher grades of staff and the second with the lower grades of staff.

The workshops covered the following topics:

- charting the steps in the work processes
- identifying the hazards at each step
- assessing hazards as either high or low risk
- the action needed to control identified hazards
- the information needed to check that the necessary control had been exercised.

The workshop groups discussed their current operation and considered which products and processes presented the highest risk, based on their experience of food safety.

Four processes were agreed as being priorities to resolve; namely

Process 1 – hot food supplied, stored and served to visitors and staff in the café

Process 2 – sandwich preparation

Process 3 – defrosting, cooking and serving roast meats

Process 4 – the delivery and storage of all raw materials and ingredients.

During the workshops, the steps in the current processes for each of the above activities and the hazards identified were discussed and documented. The information was collected on the simple table illustrated in Figure CS 3.1.

A separate team from the workshop groups was assigned to each of the four areas under discussion. The team had to collect further information about the process and observe the activities which took place. It was important that the team was made up of at least one member of staff who actually carried out the process as part of their working day.

After a set period of time, a full group meeting was held and each team reported back on their key findings. All the processes were discussed at length and suggestions put forward to eliminate the hazards identified.

Critical control points for the processes were set up and the information collated on the table in Figure CS 3.2.

The outcome of the review process was the production of an action plan which detailed the following:

– the implementation of CCPs
– work instructions to be documented
– training to be undertaken.

Examples of two of the tasks which were considered a priority are outlined below.

## Example 1 — Hot Food Supplied to, Stored and Sold in the Café

The steps in the process were:

– food requisitioned by the café
– food cooked in main kitchen, transferred into gastronorm containers and covered

Figure CS 3.1: HACCP Product Process Flow

PRODUCT . . . . . . . . . . . . . . . . .     DATE . . . . . . . . . . .     NAME . . . . . . . . . . . . . . . . .

| PROCESS FLOW | HAZARDS IDENTIFIED | NOTES |
|---|---|---|
| | | |

# Figure CS 3.2: CCP Record Sheet

HACCP MODEL

DEPARTMENT................    DATE................

PRODUCT................    PART IN PROCESS................    COMPILED BY................

| STEPS IN THE PROCESS | CRITICAL CONTROL POINT | HOW TO CONTROL AND MONITOR |
|---|---|---|
| | | |

- food delivered to café in unheated trolley
- food transferred to hot storage cabinet or hot display unit
- hot holding and sale to customers.

Time and temperature information was collected and it was discovered that the food temperature on arrival at the café was unacceptably low.

A heated trolley was subsequently purchased. The resultant HACCP Model is illustrated in Figure CS 3.3.

Further work was then required to:

- implement temperature monitoring record sheets
- train the staff in the use of probe thermometers
- documentation of new working procedures
- development of appropriate training programmes.

## Example 2 — Defrosting and Cooking Roast Meat

Many hazards were identified, including poor time and temperature controls and the risk of cross-contamination from food handlers working with raw and cooked foods.

The cross-contamination issue was considered first and the following remedies were discussed:

- complete changing of overalls after handling raw meats
- allocating one person to raw meat preparation all the time
- providing plastic aprons and gloves for use with raw meat only.

The latter option was selected as being the most practical and the new procedure was introduced.

Defrosting of the meat was also considered a critical operation. The current operation did not include monitoring defrosting times or probing the meat at the end of defrosting to check the temperature and ensure that defrosting had been completed successfully.

Thorough checks were made on the operation of the thawing cabinets, the capacities and the defrosting programme. Subsequently a comprehensive defrosting programme for all frozen products was introduced.

## Figure CS 3.3: HACCP Model

**HACCP MODEL**
**DEPARTMENT** . . . . Kitchen & Café . .  **DATE** . . . . . . 10/8/92 . . . . . .
**PRODUCT** . . Food to Café . . . . . . . .  **PART IN PROCESS** . . . . . . . . . . . . . . . . . . . .  **COMPILED BY** . . E.X. Pert . . . . . . . . .

| STEPS IN THE PROCESS | CRITICAL CONTROL POINT | HOW TO CONTROL AND MONITOR |
|---|---|---|
| 1. Food requisitioned from café | 1. None | 1. None |
| 2. Food cooked in main kitchen | 2. Food to achieve 70°C for 2 minutes | 2. Temperature probing and recording |
| 3. Delivery to café in hot trolley | 3. Maintain temperature above 63°C | 3. Switch trolley on 1 hour before required<br>Test temperature before food placed inside<br>Deliver to café within 5 minutes |
| 4. Transfer to hot cupboard or bain cupboard | 4. Maintain temperature above 63°C | 4. Immediate transfer to storage or bain marie<br>Temperature checking of food during service |

251

Cooking, cooling and reheating of the roast meat was the final area of concern. The major problems were associated with inadequate cooling, slicing the meat at temperatures in the danger zone and inadequate reheating practices.

The hazards identified were of a serious nature and the options for radically improving the current difficulties included:

- deleting roast meats from the menu
- buying in cooked joints and slicing them cold
- slicing the roast meat hot above 63°C
- cooking the joints, chilling down in chilled storage, slicing cold and reheating
- cooking the joints, blast chilling to 3°C, slicing cold and reheating.

The first option was not considered viable because of customer dissatisfaction. The second option would involve a considerable increase in the cost per portion. The third option was tried and tested but was unsuccessful because of the disastrous effect on portion control. The fourth option was similarly tried, but the meat took 14 hours to chill down and therefore it was in the danger zone longer than the current method of operation. Option five required capital investment in a blast chiller.

It was agreed that the most favoured option was the purchase of a blast chiller which could be utilised for other products, not just for roast meats.

In conclusion, the catering department has completed HACCP models for the first four priority processes identified. Work is continuing to complete HACCP models for all products, complete with new operating procedures and training programmes.

# Appendix 1

# Sources of Advice and Useful Addresses

1.  The Institute of Quality Assurance
    8–10 Grosvenor Gardens
    London SW1 W0DQ
    Tel: 071–730 7154

2.  The British Quality Association
    10 Grosvenor Gardens
    London SW1 W0DQ
    Tel: 071–823 5608

3.  Department of Trade and Industry
    General Enquiries re TQM
    Room 320
    Kings Gate House
    66–74 Victoria Street
    London SW1 E6SW
    Tel: 071–215 8142

4.  British Standards Institute
    Enquiry Section
    BSI
    Lindford Wood
    Milton Keynes
    MK14 6LE
    Tel: 0908 221166

5. Hotel Catering and Institutional Management Association
   191 Trinity Road
   London SW17
   Tel: 081–672 4251

6. HMSO Publication Centre
   Mail and Telephone Orders
   PO Box 276
   London SW8 5DT
   Orders: 071–873 9090
   General Enquiries: 071–873 0011

7. Leatherhead Food R.A.
   Randalls Road
   Leatherhead
   Surrey
   Tel: 0372 376761

8. Ministry of Agriculture Fisheries and Food
   Nobel House
   17 Smith Square
   London SW1 P3JR
   Tel: 071–238 6550

9. Health Publications Unit
   No. 2 Site
   Heywood Stores
   Manchester Road
   Heywood
   Lancashire OL10 2PZ

10. Department of Health
    Eileen House
    80–94 Newington Causeway
    London SE1 6EF
    Tel: 071–972 2000

11. Consumers' Association
    2 Marylebone Road
    London NW1 4OX
    Tel: 071–486 5544

12. National Consumers' Council
    20 Grosvenor Gardens
    London SW1W 0PH
    Tel: 071–730 3469

13. Institute of Trading Standards Administration
    4–5 Hadleigh Business Centre
    351 London Road
    Hadleigh
    Essex SS7 2BT
    Tel: 0702 559922

14. Retail Consortium
    Bedford House
    69–79 Fulham High Street
    London SW6 3JW
    Tel: 071–371 5185

# Appendix 2

# List of Useful Publications

1. Practical Food Safety for Business – MAFF (free)
2. FoodSense, Best Before and Use By – MAFF (free)
3. FoodSense, Understanding Food Labels – MAFF (free)
4. FoodSense, Food Facts not Fads – MAFF (free)
5. FoodSense, Food Safety – MAFF (free)
6. The Food Safety Act and You
   – A guide for caterers and their employees – MAFF (free)
   – A guide for farmers and growers – MAFF (free)
   – A guide for the food industry – MAFF (free)
7. Guidelines on the Food Hygiene (Amendment) Regulations 1990, SI 1990 No. 1431 – HMSO

# Appendix 3

# Accredited Certification Bodies

| Certification Body | Date of Accreditation | Registration No. |
|---|---|---|
| Associated Offices Quality Certification Ltd<br>Longridge House<br>Longridge Place<br>Manchester M60 4DT | May 1990 | 14 |
| Tel: 061–833 2285    Fax: 061–833 9965 | | |
| ASTA Certification Services<br>Prudential Chambers<br>23/24 Market Place<br>Rugby CV21 3DU | June 1989 | 10 |
| Tel: 0788 578435    Fax: 0788 573605 | | |
| BMT Quality Assessors Ltd<br>Scottish Metropolitan<br>Alpha Centre<br>Stirling University Innovation Park<br>Stirling FK9 4NF | September 1992 | 24 |
| Tel: 0786 50891    Fax: 0786 51087 | | |
| BSI Quality Assurance<br>PO Box 375<br>Milton Keynes MK14 6LL | January 1987 | 3 |
| Tel: 0908 220908    Fax: 0908 220671 | | |
| British Approvals Service for Electric Cables<br>Silbury Court<br>360 Silbury Boulevard<br>Milton Keynes MK9 2AF | April 1987 | 4 |
| Tel: 0908 691121    Fax: 0908 692722 | | |

| | | |
|---|---|---|
| Bureau Veritas Quality International Ltd<br>3rd Floor<br>70 Borough High Street<br>London SE1 1XF | November 1988 | 8 |
| Tel: 071–378 8113    Fax: 071–378 8014 | | |
| Central Certification Service Ltd<br>Victoria House<br>123 Midland Road<br>Wellingborough<br>Northants NN8 1LU | June 1991 | 18 |
| Tel: 0933 441796    Fax: 0933 440247 | | |
| Ceramic Industry Certification Scheme Ltd<br>Queens Road<br>Penkhull<br>Stoke-on-Trent ST4 7LQ | July 1987 | 6 |
| Tel: 0782 411008    Fax: 0782 412331 | | |
| Construction Quality Assurance Ltd<br>Arcade Chambers<br>The Arcade, Market Place<br>Newark<br>Notts NG24 1UD | July 1989 | 12 |
| Tel: 0636 708700    Fax: 0636 708766 | | |
| Det norske Veritas Quality Assurance Ltd<br>Veritas House<br>112 Station Road<br>Sidcup<br>Kent DA15 7BU | July 1989 | 13 |
| Tel: 081–309 7477    Fax: 081–309 5907 | | |
| Electrical Equipment Certification Service<br>Health and Safety Executive<br>Harpur Hill<br>Buxton<br>Derbyshire SK17 9JN | April 1992 | 20 |
| Tel: 0298 26211    Fax: 0298 79514 | | |
| Electricity Association Quality Assurance Ltd<br>30 Millbank<br>London SW1P 4RD | July 1992 | 22 |
| Tel: 071–834 2333    Fax: 071–931 0356 | | |

| | | |
|---|---|---|
| Engineering Inspection Authorities Board<br>c/o Institution of Mechanical Engineers<br>1 Birdcage Walk<br>London SW1H 9JJ | June 1991 | 17 |
| Tel: 071–973 1271      Fax: 071– 222 4557 | | |
| Lloyd's Register Quality Assurance Ltd<br>Norfolk House<br>Wellesley Road<br>Croydon CR9 2DT | **February 1986** | 1 |
| Tel: 081–688 6882/3      Fax: 081–681 8146 | | |
| National Approval Council for Security Systems<br>Queensgate House<br>14 Cookham Road<br>Maidenhead<br>Berkshire SL6 8AJ | February 1992 | 19 |
| Tel: 0628 37512      Fax: 0628 773367 | | |
| National Inspection Council Quality Assurance Ltd<br>5 Cotswold Business Park<br>Millfield Lane<br>Caddington<br>Beds LU1 4AR | July 1990 | 15 |
| Tel: 0582 841144      Fax: 0582 841288 | | |
| SIRA Certification Service<br>Saighton Lane<br>Saighton<br>Chester CH3 6EG | June 1989 | 11 |
| Tel: 0244 332200      Fax 0244 332112 | | |
| SGS Yarsley Quality Assured Firms Ltd<br>Trowers Way<br>Redhill<br>Surrey RH1 2JN | April 1987 | 5 |
| Tel: 0737 768445      Fax: 0737 761229 | | |
| Steel Construction QA Scheme Ltd<br>4 Whitehall Court<br>Westminster<br>London SW1A 2ES | May 1992 | 21 |
| Tel: 071–839 8566      Fax: 071–976 1634 | | |

The Loss Prevention Certification Board Ltd     October 1988     7
Melrose Avenue
Boreham Wood
Hertfordshire WD6 2BJ

Tel: 081–207 2345     Fax: 081–207 6305

The Quality Scheme for Ready Mixed Concrete     December 1988     9
3 High Street
Hampton
Middlesex TW12 2SQ

Tel: 081–941 0273     Fax: 081–979 4558

TRADA QA Services Ltd     February 1991     16
Stoking Lane
Hughenden Valley
High Wycombe
Bucks HP14 4NR

Tel: 0494 565484     Fax: 0494 565487

TWI Qualification Services     September 1992     25
Abington Hall
Abington
Cambridge CB1 6AL

Tel: 0223 891162     Fax: 0223 894219

UK Certificating Authority for Reinforcing Steels     October 1986     2
Oak House
Tubs Hill
Sevenoaks
Kent TN13 1BL

Tel: 0732 450000     Fax: 0732 455917

Water Industry Certification Scheme     July 1992     23
c/o WRC Swindon
PO Box 85
Frankland Road
Blagrove
Swindon
Wilts SN5 8YR

Tel: 0793 410005     Fax: 0793 511712

# Bibliography

Adams, C.E., Applying HACCP to sous-vide products, *Food Technology*, April 1991, pp. 148–51

Allen, P., European Community policy on food safety and quality, a Trading Standards Officer's view, *Environmental Health* February 1990, pp. 43–5

Anderson, K.G., The Official Control of Foodstuffs Directive 89/397/EEC — Article 13: a food industry view, *Food Science and Technology Today*, Vol. 5 (2), June 1991, pp. 79–82

Archer, D.L., The need for flexibility in HACCP, *Food Technology*, May 1990, pp. 174–78

Ashwell, M., The role of expert committees in regulating food safety, *Food Science and Technology Today*, Vol. 4 (4), 1990, pp. 234–41

Audit Commission, *Safer Food: Local Authorities and the Food Safety Act, Occasional Paper No. 15*, December 1990

Audit Commission, *Environmental Health Survey of Food Premises, Information Papers No. 2*, June 1990

Bauman, H.E., The HACCP concept and microbiological hazard categories, *Food Technology*, September 1974, pp. 30–74

Bauman, H.E., HACCP: concept development and application, *Food Technology*, May 1990, pp. 156–58

Berry, L.L., Parasuramen, A. and Zeithaml, J.A., *Delivering Quality Service — Balancing Customer Perceptions and Expectations*, The Free Press, New York, 1990

Bigalke, D.L. and Busta, F.F., Quality management systems for the food industry, HACCP approach to increased profits, *Food Technology in Australia*, Vol. 34 (11), November 1982, pp. 515–17.

British Quality Association, General Information Pack, London, 1992

British Standards Institute, *Quality Systems*, London BSI, 1987; British Standard 5750: Part 2

British Standards Institute, *Annual Report and Accounts*, 1990–1991

BSI Quality Assurance, *Quality System for Food and Drink Industries: Guidelines for the use of BS 5750 Part 2 1987 in the manufacture of food and drink*, BSI, October 1989

BSI Quality Assurance, *Guidance Notes for the Application of ISO 9002/ EN 29002/ BS 5750: Part 2 to the Hotel and Catering Industry*, BSI, QGN/66/392: Issue 1, 1991

Brown, D., The industry's concept of quality, *Food Science and Technology Today*, Vol. 1 (2), 1991

Bryan, F.L., Application of HAACP to ready-to-eat chilled foods, *Food Technology*, July 1990, pp. 70–7

Bryan, F.L., Hazard analysis of food service operations, *Food Technology*, February 1981, pp. 78–87

Bryan, F.L., HACCP concept, *Dairy, Food and Environment Sanitation*, July 1990, pp. 416–17

Bryan, F.L., and Lyon, J.B., Critical control points of hospital foodservice operations, *Journal of Food Protection*, Vol. 47, No. 12, December 1984, pp. 950–63

Campden Food Preservation Research Association, *Guidelines to the Establishment of HACCP*, Technical Manual No. 19, 1987

Canadian Restaurant and Foodservices Association, *HACCP: Safe Handling Techniques*, 1990

Carson, J., The keys to quality, *Managing Service Quality*, November 1990, pp. 19–21

Clarke, D.A., Chilled foods — the caterer's viewpoint, *Food Science and Technology Today*, Vol. 4 (4), 1990, pp. 227–31

Cleaning and Support Services Association, *BS 5750 Information Pack*, London

Cockbill, C., Food law by the year 2000, *Food Science and Technology Today*, Vol. 4 (2), 1990, pp. 109–11

Cockbill, C., UK food law: the influence of Europe, *Food Science and Technology Today*, Vol. 5 (2), 1991, pp. 90–2

Comen, T., Making quality assurance work for you, *The Cornell H.R.A. Quarterly*, November 1989, pp. 23–9

Commission of the European Communities, *European Community Food Legislation*, Background Report, February 1991, ISEC/B2/91

Cook, D. and Baxter, T., Maintaining momentum, *The TQM Magazine*, June 1991, pp. 149–51.

Corrlet, D.A., Regulatory verification of industrial HACCP systems, *Food Technology*, April 1991, pp. 144–46

Cowley, P., The need for quality products, *Food Science and Technology Today*, Vol. 5 (2), pp. 97–102

Craddock, N., Food law: the industry's viewpoint, *Food Science and Technology Today*, Vol. 5 (3), 1991, pp. 149–55

Crew, S., Quality assurance — a taste of the future, *Environmental Health*, February 1990, pp. 38–40

*Croner's Practical Food Hygiene*, Croner Publications Ltd, 1991

Cullen, J.M., Conditions for success, *The TQM Magazine*, June 1991, pp. 153–56

Davis, P. What does the future hold?, *The TQM Magazine*, June 1991, pp. 141–43

Dean, K.H., HACCP and food safety in Canada, *Food Technology*, May 1990, pp. 172 and 178

Dennis, C., Processing to provide consistent quality for the consumer, *Food Science and Technology Today*, Vol. 4, (1), March 1990, pp. 28–32

Department of Trade and Industry, *BS 5750/ ISO 9000: 1987, A Positive Contribution to Better Business*, DTI, 1992

Department of Trade and Industry, *Getting to Grips with Quality*, HMSO, 1989

Department of Trade and Industry, *Managing into the '90s, The Route Ahead*, DTI, 1992

Department of Employment, *The Management of Quality: BS 5750 and Beyond*, Employment Department Group, 1990

Department of Health, *Guidelines on the Food Hygiene (Amendment) Regulations 1990 (SI 1990 No. 1431)*, HMSO, 1990

Department of Health, *HACCP, Practical Food Safety For Business*, HMSO, 1991

Express Foodservice, *The Caterer's Guide to BS 5750*, Internal document

Fallows, S., European food law: trends and actions, *Food Science and Technology Today*, Vol. 5 (2), 1991, pp. 85–8

Flores, A., Professional ethics and food safety, *Food Technology*, May 1991, pp. 124–29

*Food Safety Act 1990*, HMSO, 1990

*Food Hygiene (Amendment) Regulations 1990*, HMSO, 1990

*Food Hygiene (Amendment) Regulations 1991*, HMSO, 1991

*Food Safety — Protecting the Consumer, The White Paper*, HMSO, 1989

Fulks, F.T., Total Quality Management, *Food Technology*, June 1991, pp. 96–119

Grikitis, K., Proper protection, *Food Processing*, May 1991, pp. 23–9

Haldane, T., *Meeting Quality Standards, A Practical Guide to BS 5750: Part 1: 1987*, Pergamon Press, 1st. edn., 1989

Hayman, K.G., Quality assurance route to corporate survival, should we be concerned as it is sure to cost money? *Home Economist — The Journal of the Institute of Home Economics,* Vol. 10 (4), August 1991

HCIMA, *BS 5750 — Quality System Guidelines*, Technical Brief, Sheet No. 20, 1991

HCIMA, *Food Hygiene (Amendment) Regulations 1990 and 1991*, Technical Brief, Sheet No. 21, 1992

HCIMA, *Hazard Analysis and Critical Control Point, The Effective Approach to Food Hygiene and Safety*, Technical Brief, Sheet No. 5, 1991

HM Government, The Food Safety Act 1990 and You,
  – *A Guide for the Food Industry*, HMSO, 1991
  – *A Guide for Farmers and Growers*, HMSO, 1991
  – *A Guide for Caterers and their Employees*, HMSO, 1991

Horovitz, Jacques H., Putting service quality into gear, *Service Industries Journal*, Vol. 10, 1990, pp. 249–65

Hotel and Catering Training Board, *New Employment Forecasts 1988–1993*, HCTB

Hutt, G., Understanding the perception, *The TQM Magazine*, June 1991, pp. 161–65

Institute of Food Science and Technology, *Good Catering Practice: A Guide to its Responsible Management*, IFST, 1991

Institute of Quality Assurance, *Quality Forum, the Journal of the IQA*, Vol. 17 (4), December 1991

Institute of Quality Assurance, *Quality News, The Magazine of the IQA*, Vol. 17 (12), December 1991

Institute of Quality Assurance, *Training for Quality*, IQA, 1991

Jones, P., The restaurant — a place for quality control and product maintenance?, *International Journal of Hospitality Management*, Vol. 2, pp. 93–100

Landsman, S., A public analyst's perspective of the Food (Safety) Act 1990, *Food Science and Technology Today*, Vol. 5 (3), 1991, pp. 129–32.

Light, N. and Walker, A., *Cook-Chill Catering: Technology and Management*, Elsevier Science Publishers Ltd, 1990

Lloyd's Register Quality Assurance Ltd, *Assessment of Quality Management Systems*

Lloyd's Register Quality Assurance Ltd, *Food Industry Guidelines*, 1991

Lloyd's Register Quality Assurance Ltd, Guidance document to quality systems for use in the food processing and allied industries, *Quality Systems Supplement*, QSS 4100, 1988

MAFF, *Food Hygiene — Report on a Consumer Survey*, HMSO, 1988

MAFF, *A Guide from the Food Safety Directorate, Food Safety*, No. 1 Foodsense, MAFF, 1991

MAFF, *A Guide from the Food Safety Directorate, Understanding Food Labels*, No. 3 Foodsense, MAFF, 1991

MAFF, *A Guide from the Food Safety Directorate, Food Facts Not Fads*, Foodsense, MAFF, 1991

MAFF, *Scientific Research and Development, The Composition, Quality and Safety of Food*, MAFF, 1990

Manley, R., Due diligence, *Food Law Monthly*, January 1992

Marketpower and Berkeley Scott Group, *The Hotel Catering and Leisure Business Review*, 1991

Martin, W.B., Measuring and improving your service quality, *The Cornell H.R.A. Quarterly*, May 1986, pp. 80–7

Mayes, T. and Kilsby, D.C., The use of HAZOP hazard analysis to identify critical control points for the microbiological safety of food, *Food Quality and Preference*, Vol. 1 (2), 1989, pp. 53–7.

Mossel, D.A.A. and Drake, D.M., Processing food for safety and reassuring the consumer, *Food Technology*, December 1990, pp. 63–7

Munce, B.A., Hazard analysis critical control points and the food service industry, *Food Technology in Australia*, Vol. 36 (5), May 1984, pp. 214–22

Nightingale, M., The hospitality industry: defining quality for a quality assurance programme, a study of perceptions, *The Service Industries Journal*, Vol. 5 (1), 1985, pp. 9–22

Oberoi, U. and Hales, C., Assessing the quality of the conference hotel service product: towards an empirically based model, *The Service Industries Journal*, Vol. 10 (4), 1990, pp. 700–21

Pallett, A.J.M., *A Guide to BS 5750 and Food Safety*, SLG Consultancy Services

Pearson, R., *Catering for Quality BS 5750*, Food Dialog, 1990

Peters, R., Implications of the Food Safety Act, *HCIMA Reference Book 1991/ 92*, Sterling Publications Ltd, 1991, pp. 215–17

Peters, R., Registration of food premises, *Hospitality*, April 1992, p. 10

Pettipher, G., HACCP audit lauded, *Food Processing*, May 1991, pp. 31–2

Phillips, D., The new food safety legislation, *Frozen and Chilled Foods*, September 1991, pp. 29–30

Price, R. and Gaskill, G., TQM in research, *Managing Service Quality*, November 1990, pp. 51–6

The Retail Consortium, *Food Safety Act 1990, Guidelines on the Statutory Defence of Due Diligence*, 1991

Richmond Report, *The Microbiological Safety of Food, Parts 1 and 2 — Report of the Committee on the Microbiological Safety of Food*, HMSO, 1990 and 1991

Sasser, W.E., Olsen, R.P. and Wychoff, D.D., *Management of Service Operations*, Allyn and Bacon, 1978

Shapton, D. and Shapton, N., *Principles and Practices for the Safe Processing of Foods*, Butterworth Heinemann Publications, 1991

Sheard, M., The hazard analysis and critical control point concept, in *Hygiene for Management* by Richard A. Sprenger, Highfield Publications, pp. 207–12

Sheppard, J., Kipps M. and Thomson, J., Hygiene and hazard analysis in food service, in Cooper, C.P. (ed), *Progress in Tourism, Recreation and Hospitality Management*, Vol. 20, Belhaven Press, 1990

Snyder, O.P., Food safety 2000: applying HACCP for food safety assurance in the 21st century, *Dairy, Food and Environmental Sanitation*, Vol. 10 (4), April 1990, pp. 197–204

Society of Food Hygiene Technology, *The HACCP Concept and Q.A. in Food Manufacture and Catering*, Proceedings of Yorkshire and Humberside Branch Meeting, November 1985

Solberg, M., Buckalew, J.J., Chen, C.M., et al, Microbiological safety assurance system for foodservice facilities, *Food Technology*, December 1990, pp. 68–73

Stevenson, K.E., Implementing HACCP in the food industry, *Food Technology*, May 1990, pp. 179–80

*The UK Catering Market*, Key Note Publications Ltd, 1991

*Total Quality Management and BS 5750: The Links Explained*, The Employment Department Group Training Agency

Waite-Wright, M., Chilled foods — the manufacturer's responsibility, *Food Science and Technology Today*, Vol. 4 (4), 1990, pp. 223–27

Walker, J.R. and Salameh, T.T., The Q.A. payoff, *The Cornell H.R.A. Quarterly*, February 1990, pp. 54–9

Wilburn, W., Quality assurance audits and hotel management, *The Service Industries Journal*, Vol. 6 (3), 1986, pp. 293–308

# Index

Note: abbreviations used: BS = British Standard; FSA = Food Safety Act;
HACCP = Hazard Analysis Critical Control Point; QA = quality assurance;
TQM = Total Quality Management